THE
BOOK OF JOEL

JOEL CARROLL

Edited by Krystal Berry

Fulton Books, Inc.
Meadville, PA

Published by Fulton Books 2021

ISBN 978-1-63710-586-3 (paperback)
ISBN 978-1-63710-625-9 (hardcover)
ISBN 978-1-63710-587-0 (digital)

Printed in the United States of America

IN LOVING MEMORY OF

BERNICE MARY WEATHERFORD

August 23, 1935–November 12, 2018

"But seek ye first the kingdom of God, and His righteousness; and all these things shall be added unto you." MATTHEW 6:33 (KJV)

DEDICATION

To everyone who has inspired me and shared
your testimonies with me…

To every single addict and individual who suffers from mental
illness around the globe—please know you are not alone…

To the Salvation Army—you opened your
doors to me, and I found God…

To my sons, my parents, my grandparents, my sister, my daughter's
mother, and every person I've harmed, throughout my life—I
am truly sorry for who I was and for the things I have done…

To my wife—without your patience none of this would
have been possible. You are a strong, amazing woman who
has inspired me with your tolerance and work ethic…

To my daughter—though I am a changed man, there are
no excuses for my actions. I aspire to be the best man
and father who God created me to be. I love you with all
of my heart and please forgive me for who I *was*…

Thank you.

CONTENTS

INTRODUCTION

A captivating and true story of the ups and downs, joys and sorrows that one man has experienced in the past four decades. A member of a violent street gang and struggling to know myself, substance abuse became the great coping mechanism. Visited by spirits that tormented my days and nights, I faced each day not knowing if I would see the next. This book will take you on a miraculous journey that is a testament to God's healing power and is an advocate to those who seem to have lost their way in life. You can make it. It is with great transparency that I share this story with you knowing God kept me alive to do just that. From the darkest of nights to the brightest and most beautiful days, I will share experience, strength and hope to prove recovery from addiction and mental illness is 100% possible and that real-life miracles do in fact happen.

With all sincerity, I believe I am still alive to share this story with you

CHAPTER 1

In Sixteen Hours

It was difficult as a young child to fathom life's lessons or the meanings of each experience when I was barely learning to ride my first bicycle. I'd witnessed dark spirits creeping toward our home from an old graveyard in Belgium and was encountered by a demonic entity just hours before my best friend passed away. The two of us were just seven years old when he lost his life.

I later questioned if life was warning me that death was near or if death was forewarning me that it was about to take the life of someone dear to me. Was the fact that I was born on Friday the 13th, an 'unlucky' day to many cultures, a reason behind the traumatizing events that took place in my life for the better half of four decades? Or was life just life, and lessons, karma, and bad omens the results of the choices I'd made along my journey? Were my individual connections with people and situations mere coincidences, or was the impeccable timing controlled by a higher power that strategically placed certain persons in my path to tear me down, or on the contrary, save me from the inevitable? And were only specific individuals blessed and or cursed based on our insight of having the ability to see and feel the manifestation of situations unraveling as they developed in real time?

The divine battle within was nothing short of brutal, as I was confronted with countless shortcomings, and though it took multiple near-death experiences for me to acknowledge the signs for what they were, life had its way of prophesying the outcome in order for me to understand who I truly was in the end.

An infant of grandparents whose ancestors were from all over the world, I was born with blood of the Crow Indian, Czechoslovakian, English, French, German, Irish, Mexican, Polish, Scottish and Swedish. The last name O' Carroll or Carroll, are derived from my father's side, and many of my Irish ancestors migrated to America settling on the east coast. The coordinates 111W49'19" 33N25'20" represent the exact location of my birth in Mesa, Arizona, on Friday, October 13th, 1978. The weekend also hosted a full moon. It was a military hospital at Williams Air Force Base just outside of Phoenix, where my father was stationed until October of 1980. My father and my mother were high school sweethearts at Mesa High and had already begun raising my three-year-old sister.

With my father being in the military, at the age of two, we moved to Hampton, Virginia where he was stationed at Langley Air Force Base until 1983. At the age of four, we flew across the Atlantic Ocean, where he was then stationed at USAG Benelux, in Brussels, the capital of Belgium. The Eighties were dangerous times in Europe as terror threats were made, and attacks were carried out against their political foes. Terrorists attacked the offices of the Turkish Airlines in Brussels on February 2nd, 1983, and on May 24th, in Brussels, bombs were detonated in front of the Turkish Embassy's Culture and Information offices. This was followed by an assassination of the Administrative Attaché at the Turkish Embassy. Sadly, as a young boy, I would get used to the threats as they were made continuously throughout the foreign place, we, at that time, called home.

When our family was settled, my sister and I were immediately enrolled into a school named 'AFCENT'—an international school that followed the curriculum requirements of four nations: Canada, Germany, the United Kingdom, and the United States. My mother found employment at the American Express Bank in the Foreign Exchange, as well as the Base Exchange credit department. My father was a computer programmer, a lead singer and guitarist of an American Country-Rock band and played fast pitch softball on the Air Force team after he went 13-1 as a young boxer in the Armed Forces.

The house we moved into was the tallest I'd ever seen. The neighborhood was 'Q' shaped and consisted of many duplexes made of red brick that stood four stories high. While staring out of my third-story bedroom window for the first time, I noticed an enormous grassy hill that had 124 concrete steps that later led us to our school's bus-stop. Regardless of how tired we were each morning, every child had to climb those steps in order to catch the school bus.

At the bottom of the hill and at the entrance to the steps, was a graveyard that seemed to have been there for many years. It had close to twenty tombstones and was enclosed by an old chain-linked fence with weeds growing over it. I'd never seen a graveyard before, and the thought of dead people scared me. Even creepier than that, those dead people were buried in an area where the neighborhood children played.

While curiously walking around the neighborhood one afternoon, I strolled along a dirt path behind our house, and to my amazement, it led to a little tiny Dutch village with little shops and a petting zoo. I could smell the manure in the air as I walked past the animals and saw the native Dutch people tossing hay into the small stables. That same afternoon, my mother had given me a guilder: a Dutch coin with some strange lady on it. I didn't care to learn about the European woman on the coin; I just knew I wanted to purchase sweets with it.

I entered a little shop to see what kind of treats they had, and when I came across sweets I'd never tried before, I handed a kind lady my coin and exited the shop as the little bell on the door jingled. I wandered across the dirt path to visit with the animals, and after enjoying my first experience at the hidden place, I began making my way toward the exit. Before I departed, I came across a family of Guinea pigs and picked two of the little furry critters up.

As I was observing the strange and foreign animals, I noticed an old whiskey barrel full of water next to their home. I figured they were thirsty, so I walked over to the water and dunked their tiny heads, but they began to struggle. I immediately pulled them from the water, but they went ballistic and tried to bite me. I was both nervous and frightened when I was unable to calm the two down and one of the rodents got loose while the other began hissing and continued to be aggressive toward me.

Something came over me as it began biting at my hand, and instead of dropping it, I stepped toward the barrel and began to submerge the restless creature. An old Dutch man saw me from behind and began screaming at the top of his lungs "Hey! What are you doing to my animals?" I panicked. My little heart was beating so fast and within a split-second, I dropped the little animal back into the water and ran for my young life. I ran as fast as a tiny boy could and sprinted down the dirt path, through the trees and back to my house. Luckily for me, I ran fast enough and had gotten away without consequence, but I wasn't pleased with what I'd done. We had a dog named Cowboy and I loved animals, but it seemed as if something was controlling me when I became uncomfortable.

It was bad. Why did I lose control like that? Now I'll never be able to go back to the village. I hope mommy doesn't find out.

I had many questions, but didn't have the answers, because I was unwilling to tell my parents what I'd done.

Months passed and I eventually found new friends in the neighborhood to play with. When I'd adjusted to my new school, I became best friends with a boy in my class named Matthew.

Matthew and I were always together and sat next to one another on the bus to and from school. His father was stationed at Benelux and played fast pitch softball with my father, and both of our mothers were part of the 'military wives' that hung out together while supporting their husbands. I enjoyed going to school and hanging out with my friends. I noticed, early on, that I was attracted to girls despite all of the obnoxious kids calling each other mean names and saying that boys and girls had "*cooties.*" The girls were pretty, and I just figured the other boys were afraid and didn't have the courage to say otherwise.

Making friends in school was great, but at times, school was scary. We were often escorted from the premises due to the bomb threats. At first, I was excited about leaving class, joking around with my friends, but as time passed, I realized we were leaving under serious circumstances. There were thousands of people in our school and the terrorists threatened us constantly. Unfortunately, it became part of our routine as we continued to go to school in hopes that the threats remained threats and nobody died.

Outside of school, my parents enrolled me in soccer (which I was really great at), I joined karate, became a Cub Scout, and somehow my parents were able to get my sister and I into separate commercials. While continuing to excel on the soccer field, where I was the lone American kid on the team, I became the littlest big man on the European football field. I was so small in stature, that the other boys thought I was on the wrong field. It was intimidating to say the least, but I stepped up to the challenge and learned to utilize what advantages I had as a smaller and faster opponent. In fact, I scored so many goals, that to be fair to the other teams, my coach placed me in as goalie, but that didn't make a difference either, as I shut down our opponents from scoring. And as my family cheered me on and encouraged me from the sidelines, I quickly realized that playing sports was my favorite thing to do.

I continued playing with my friends in the neighborhood but if they weren't home; I would venture off by myself to find other things to do to occupy my time. Before I went outside, on one particular evening, I saw a lighter in our kitchen and I was curious as to how it worked. I put it in my pocket, went outside, and began to flick it. Walking around behind the houses, I finally figured out how to light it without the flame going out. I got excited but didn't want to get into trouble from my mother, so I walked past the graveyard, toward the cul-de-sac, and something inside me told me to light a big pile of dry leaves that were under an elderly woman's carport. I'd met the woman before and she was very kind, but at that moment, something took over me. I walked toward the large mound of dead leaves. I looked around to see if anyone was looking, reached down, picked up a handful of the crispy leaves, and I lit them. I was shocked! And though I was scared and simultaneously full of amazement, I didn't attempt to put the burning leaves out.

The flame burned my thumb and drove the pain straight to my bone, causing me to drop the fiery leaves, igniting the entire pile. I panicked as it grew out of control and didn't even look to see if there was anyone watching me. I got up and ran like the fire was in my pants. I ran so fast to my house, opened the door, and flew up two flights of stairs straight to my bedroom. I closed my door and jumped on to the windowsill to see if the fire was spreading. Being both frightened and curious, I peeked my head out of the window and saw the smoke coming from the elderly woman's carport. I quickly and very quietly walked down the stairs to place the lighter back on the counter, as I heard a fire truck entering the neighborhood. I was scared of getting caught, and never wanted the kind lady's house to burn down. Fortunately, the fire only caused minor damages to the carport.

I didn't understand at such a young age that being alone with nothing productive to do would put me in a bad place mentally. All I could think about for days was how lucky I was to not have gotten caught in both situations that left me sprinting back to our house.

One summer, while I was playing with two young brothers that moved to the neighborhood, we decided to walk down the road to another Dutch candy shop. My mother had given me a few guilders to purchase more sweets, and as we entered the door, I smelled gummy cherries, gummy colas and an abundance of assorted chocolates. We were the happiest kids in the universe, as we cheerfully walked each isle licking our chops before picking out our favorite sweets. The three of us handed the nice lady our coins, and she graciously weighed it on a little scale, before we were on our way stuffing our faces with the sugary delights.

We continued to visit the shop faithfully, but on one particular day, I didn't have any Guilders after my mother searched in her purse for me. I felt left out because I wasn't able to purchase sweets and watched as the brothers picked out their favorite candies. After the two of them exchanged the coins for the goodies, and anticipating that we were leaving, the old Dutch lady slowly strolled into her home in the back of the shop. The brothers were walking out the door when I got a sudden urge to get some sweets for myself. It was an overwhelming feeling that raced throughout my entire body. Without hesitation, I crept down toward the row of sweets; put my hands in multiple jars, grabbed as many candies as my little hands would hold, and darted out the door.

"What did you do!?" The oldest brother screamed while running away from the shop. "I didn't have any Guilders!" I replied full of adrenaline. "I can't believe you did that Joel! I can't believe you stole something! We ran as fast as we could until we made it back to our neighborhood where we stuffed our faces as we always did. I had gotten away without consequence once again, but the brothers would never look at me the same after that day.

I couldn't understand the urges I was having at such a young age, and the initial feelings they gave me were terrifying. Each incident was overwhelming. I was learning, as I walked through life, but as I was getting away without consequences. The adrenaline rush of each experience confused me on why I was feeling the way I was after doing bad things. I never went back to the candy shop with the boys and was too afraid to go back to the little Dutch village behind our house. I seemed to have had limited places to go in the neighborhood and it wasn't a good feeling when the other kids ventured to those places without me.

As the new school year began, and while my neighborhood friends were off having fun, I would stay home playing video games after my homework was completed. One night, after playing a game called 'Frogger' on the 'Atari' and as I was getting sleepy, I walked upstairs and told my mother goodnight before going to bed. Sometime during the middle of that night, I was awakened by a feeling of someone looking over my bed. I wasn't frightened at first because there shouldn't be anything to be afraid of, so I slowly rolled over anticipating my mother or sister standing there. But before I could move another inch, I instantly locked eyes with a dark being that stood two feet from my motionless body.

Without creating any sudden movement, from under my blanket, I slowly pinched my thigh thinking it was a nightmare, but the thing was still standing in my dark room. I was so terrified that I couldn't breathe. I didn't know what to do and I didn't want it to take me, so I held my breath and kept my eyes slightly opened.

As my tears began to slowly drop to my pillow, its eyes stared deeply into my soul. Its bloody head swayed in slow motion—back and forth like an animal observing its prey before devouring it. I had to breathe or else I would've fainted, and I just knew in my little heart that it would've taken me if I didn't stay conscious. I exhaled as slow as humanly possible without moving the slightest, and it continued looking over me. The flesh on the demonic creature was bloody and seemed to have been burned. It stood like an animal, but its head resembled that of a human who may have been killed in a fire. The eyes had a dim glow like an animal in the dark woods. I imagined it was going to devour me right in my bed or slowly drag me back to the graveyard a few hundred yards away.

At the time, my father was away travelling for TDY (Temporary Duty Travel), and my mother, sister and our dog "Cowboy" were scattered throughout the house sleeping peacefully; no one would've even known if I was dead or gone for hours. I thought of screaming out for help but was overpowered by the fear of the creature shutting me up. Still crying, I finally blinked, and the tears continued to fall soaking my pajamas. The strong stench of urine rose from beneath my blanket and I didn't even realize that I'd wet myself. That thing was holding me hostage with its evil stare, and I had no understanding of why. It stood there bleeding from its burned-like corpse, and never once blinked or moved its hoofs. I knew that I had to get out of the room before it did.

I took another deep breath, and while shaking profusely, I removed my blanket and slid off of the bed passed the demon. Its eyes stayed locked onto mine and turned its head as I slid toward my door. I was able to reach the knob and swing the door open before running into the hallway in a panicked state. I attempted to scream but began vomiting everywhere instead. I was banging on the walls trying to wake my mother up and Cowboy began barking from downstairs. I continued pounding away but was still unable to scream because I was crying as the vomit continued to force itself out of me and onto the hallway floor.

I was finally able to open my mother's door as Cowboy ran to my rescue, but I was hysterical and couldn't speak. I grabbed my mother and held her tightly as she jumped up out of fright, and I never wanted to let go of her again.

When she fully woke up and realized I was panicking, I pointed toward my room and tried to explain what I'd seen but pleaded for her not to go in there. When she entered the hallway passed the vomit, she looked at me and said, "What in God's name? What happened? Your door is opened and there's nothing in there J.R." The demon was gone, but I was afraid it was still in the house. Luckily, our dog Cowboy stayed in the room with me and I pleaded that my mother stay in the room.

So many thoughts came to mind: *Is it still in the house and will it come back for me? Why was the scary monster here and what did it want with me? Was it because I'm being a bad boy? Was its body burned because I lit a fire? Was it going to steal me because I stole the sweets? Is the house haunted, or did it come from the grave site that gave me creepy feelings every time I walked past it?*

I questioned myself to sleep that night in my mother's bed, but by the time I was able to rest, it was time for us to get up to go to school. I was afraid to go back into my room to change my clothes before school, so I took Cowboy everywhere I went. I could smell the vomit even after my mother cleaned my mess, and the urine smell lingered throughout the third floor. I was terrified to open my wardrobe to grab my clothes, but I had no choice, so I opened it slowly, and there were no signs of the demon. I took a shower but kept the curtain open because I was afraid it was still lurking. Cowboy sat loyally by the tub until I was dried off and ready to go.

I went to school but couldn't get the image of its bloody face out of my mind—the way it turned its head, like a curious animal. The way it stood on all fours with no clothing, and its glowing eyes never blinking. *I couldn't speak of this*, of course, because I felt nobody would believe me, and didn't want to get teased for it.

On the bus ride home that afternoon, my best friend Matthew and I were talking as we always did. I kept looking out of the window waiting to see if the demonic creature was following me, and Matthew questioned what I was looking for, but I was hesitant to tell him. He was my closest friend in the whole world, but I was afraid that he would brush it off and say, "It was just a nightmare Joel." And before I could build up the courage to tell him, the bus came to halt and he walked off toward the sidewalk. I attempted to shout out of the window to get his attention, but it was too late. *I felt suffocated.* I wanted to tell him what I saw because it was driving me mad. As I felt a jerk, from the large bus slowly driving away, I slid the large window down, and as he was fading away, he turned and gave me a huge smile while waving goodbye…for the very last time.

I walked off the bus and headed toward the steps with the neighborhood kids. As soon as I reached the top step, I stopped, and looked all the way down toward the graveyard. It gave me the most uncomfortable feeling as if something were watching me and waiting for me to walk down. While all the other kids were laughing, joking and just being excited to be home from school for the day, I heard silence. I looked away from the graveyard as I walked down, but something kept drawing me back to the tombs in the chain linked fence. As we reached the bottom of the hill, I got an overwhelming feeling that something was certainly watching me. I couldn't see anything, but I felt it inside. No more than a second later, I saw the black burn marks in the elderly woman's carport where I had lit the fire. My young spirit was in turmoil and the thought of moving back to America immediately crossed my mind.

As I was finishing my homework that evening and preparing to watch television, my mother approached me in the living room. She sat down next to me and said that something happened to Matthew. "JR? Matthew was playing in his yard after school and something terrible happened. He was outside playing with his toys and he took a drink out of his juice and swallowed a bee. Matthew was allergic to bees…and when he swallowed it, his throat swelled, and he was unable to breathe." The room closed in around me and I couldn't understand what she was saying. And then I heard the most hurtful words, "Matthew passed away JR…he died. I'm so sorry son", she said with tears in her eyes.

My mother held me tightly as she did earlier that morning, and all I could hear was, *Matthew passed away, Matthew died, Matthew passed away, Matthew died.* I couldn't comprehend what was going on or what it meant. It was too much for me to grasp. The only moment of clarity I had from thinking about the demon was the news that my best friend had just died from drinking juice with a bumble bee in it. My young mind couldn't take all the trauma that suddenly erupted in sixteen hours. I just couldn't understand. I pictured the old creepy graveyard across the neighborhood and knew my best friend didn't belong there. I was going to tell him about what I saw the night before, and then poof—*he was gone.*

I heard of God and Jesus Christ and how their love for us was everlasting and thought, *why did you take my friend? He was only seven. And why would you allow a scary monster-demon in my bedroom before my best friend died?* Those thoughts just got deeper, and the answers weren't immediately available to me like many other curious thoughts I had. As sad as I was, I couldn't have imagined how Matthew's family felt. Death was an extremely difficult concept to grasp for me because I never knew anyone that died before Matthew. To have understanding on how a boy that was so innocent and young would've been taken from his parents.

The fact that life just kept moving right along was an extremely horrifying thing to accept as a seven-year-old child. And with the thought of his death still lingering, my parents decided to take us skiing in Austria for the 1986 New Year's celebration. I was excited for the trip, and though I was sad, I felt my lost friend was with me in spirit.

When we arrived, after the near ten-hour drive, we settled in the lodge, and the four of us went outside and I learned to ski in the snowy Alps. My father showed me the way, and for some odd reason, I wasn't comfortable using ski poles, so I didn't use them while going downhill. While on the hills, I skied as if I was one with the land—gliding without a care in the world. Everyone there seemed happy and I desperately needed to be there because it showed me that life still had its fun moments.

On New Year's Eve, I participated in a young people's competition on the "Bunny Slopes." People, from all around, were watching me ski without poles and I grew confident as the cheers grew louder. I was awarded the bronze medal and had the time of my life. It was the same feelings I'd felt when I was on the soccer field or in the Dojo in karate: out of my head and enjoying my time.

After our trip, my father told us that we were going back to Arizona for his next assignment. I had a lot of thoughts going through my mind concerning the experiences I'd had in Europe, both good and bad. I'd sit on my windowsill and look out into the night while trying to find some sense of what the world was all about. I imagined how Arizona looked and what my relatives were like. My mother's youngest sister came to visit us for a while, but I couldn't remember anybody else from our family. I thought to myself, *how are the people there? Do my relatives like Hip-Hop and can they breakdance? Do people in the United States play soccer or do they just play American football? Will I ever find new friends? Will I fit in there? Will I…?*

And at that moment while in deep thought, something caught my attention outside. I slid over to the left of the windowsill so I could see what was moving, but I couldn't focus my eyes on it. I hopped down and looked again. I looked closely but it didn't make sense. I closed my eyes and looked again like an eagle searching for its prey. Creeping out from behind the houses and out of the graveyard, were a group of black masses moving in a straight line toward our side of the neighborhood. I was frozen and thought to myself as I counted them nervously, *what are those things and why are they coming this way?* There were close to twenty of them—as many as the headstones in the chain-linked fence. They appeared to be adults wearing black sheets, but as they crept closer, it was evident that they were not sheets at all, and they certainly weren't people.

I crept down two flights of stairs as fast as I could. I left the light off and slowly moved toward the long, thin window that was adjacent to our front door. Trembling with fear, I closed my eyes and took a deep breath as I peeked my head around the door. It was the strangest thing: there were toads coming from everywhere. It was as if every toad in the forest behind our house was on our doorstep. The thought of toads gathering in my yard didn't frighten me; but the whole situation gave me an overwhelming sense of gloom and wondered if the two were connected in any way. I'd only seen two toads at one time before that moment, but that night, they seemed to be multiplying by the second.

I looked intensely with my eyes squinted and searched for the dark figures out in the background, but they all seemed to have vanished from the dimly lit road. I was afraid that whatever they were, they could still be around our house, or even in it, but I was still curious and wanted to be certain that my family and I were safe. I was concerned and baffled by the events and walked back to my room to look out of my window, and there was nothing. Not a soul. The toads had disappeared from the front of our house and there was no movement from the graveyard all the way down to the main road. I couldn't grasp why these occurrences were presenting themselves to me and it left me questioning if I were somehow doomed from the start. *Am I a cursed child, I thought…* or was I just unlucky from birth?

I went to bed that night and crossed my little hands and prayed to God and His son Jesus. I didn't hear a loud voice in return and no big light shined down on my bed, but I continued to pray that the demon and shadows would stay away from me and that my family would be safe from evil. And it may have been those cries for protection, that night, that saved my lost soul almost thirty years later.

CHAPTER 2

A RAGE WITHIN

We landed at Sky Harbor Airport, in Phoenix, Arizona in June of 1987. As we exited the airplane, I immediately noticed the air was different than anything I'd ever experienced. It was dry and though we'd arrived at night, the temperature was above one-hundred degrees. I couldn't grasp the aroma the desert offered, but the smell of fresh cut grass was non-existent, and it was as if the humidity were extracted from the atmosphere.

Anxiously waiting for us at the airport were my grandparents, who lived in Chandler, on the outskirts of Phoenix. My grandfather and biological grandmother divorced years prior, and he remarried a woman who we all loved and respected. To my generation, she was 'Grandma' as well, and my family and I stayed with the two of them until my parents found us a new place to call home.

I learned that Arizona was almost unbearable during the summer. The heat was like that of an oven, no humidity—just hot. We spent many hours outside in the community swimming pool while staying with my grandparents, but without the pool, I didn't see how anyone could even go outside. It was close to ninety degrees by the time we woke up each morning and reached nearly 120 degrees by the evening hours.

Not long after our arrival to the states, my parents found us a home near Luke Air Force base where my father was stationed, and my sister and I were immediately enrolled in school. I was quickly befriended by a group of kids that I would hang out with for the next three years. Again, I was the smallest kid in the group everywhere we went, and even smaller than the girls I knew.

During my third year at the school, a new student named Jacob was enrolled, and he and I were identical in stature. I most certainly thought that I would've been ecstatic about not being the puniest boy in our grade anymore, but that wasn't the case at all. From the moment he enrolled into our class, he had it out for me. He thrived from being the smallest kid in our grade and didn't like the fact that he had to share the 'little man' title with me.

I felt quite the opposite and didn't understand why he was making such a fuss about the situation, so I ignored his dislike of me. Though he was new, he quickly gained friendships with many of the other students, but my friends began to notice, and it became obvious to everyone in our grade as weeks past. *Is being the smallest boy around **that** unique, that some other kid wants to hurt me? Should I be happy to be the smallest 3rd grader? Have I been looking at it the wrong way the entire time? Do I want to share this title with another boy that is as cocky as a rooster?* I was confused while questioning my size but continued to ignore the kid and the group of boys he befriended.

Still trying to come to terms with the 'little man' problem, rumors began to spread like fire that Jacob was going to fight me after school by an ice cream truck the students gathered around. The community was surrounded by a golf course and the ice cream truck was always parked next to a tee, for a hole, around the corner from the elementary school.

My friends caught wind of the rumor and as soon as the classrooms emptied, "Joel! Joel! He's going to fight you by ice cream truck! What are you going to do? Are you going to fight him? Are you going to fight Jacob?" I'd never been in a fight before, and though I was in karate, I became extremely anxious as the situation began to manifest. I'd watched Sugar Ray Leonard fight Roberto Duran, and Marvin Hagler fight Tommy Hearns, but I'd never boxed before, and those fighters were warriors in the ring. I also witnessed Mike Tyson knocking out Marvis Frazier in thirty seconds, and my father was upset because he spent a lot of money on a Pay Per View event that ended before he was able to open his first beer. But I'd never put my fists to someone else's head and wasn't looking forward to someone else knocking me out in thirty seconds.

Before my friends could shout out another word, I opened my mouth, and without hesitation said, "What do you mean am I going to fight him? Of course, I'm going to fight him. What do you think I am...a chicken? I'm not afraid of Jacob." The truth was I was in an unknown territory, full of fear, and my little heart was beating out of my chest. It was like I was the most famous kid on the planet. Students were gathering from everywhere and hyping up the situation like tiny savages. "There's going to be a fight! There's going to be a fight at the ice cream truck!" It was pure mayhem.

Instead of me going home or getting an ice cream before going to my friends' house, I was on my way to fight a kid that I'd never spoken a single word to.

On our way to meet Jacob and his friends, one of my friends began rubbing my shoulders, predicting that I was going to win the fight. My other friends were mimicking everything he was saying, but I felt their confidence in me was more about their egos than the sureness of me winning the fight. I was going to puke in my mouth, poop in my pants, and was extremely nauseous but was determined not to show any fear.

When our group of girlfriends caught up to us, midway through our stroll, it was said, "We heard about the fight Joel...are you really going to fight Jacob? What if you get in trouble?"... "Hey! Joel isn't scared...huh Joel? He's going to punch that puny kid's head off!" My confident friends smashed everyone's concerns as if they'd seen me fight before.

I played all the scenarios in my mind while my friends' voices seemed to fade away in the background. But again, without hesitation, I said, "Of course, I'm gonna fight him. What do you think I'm a chicken?" My friend replied, "No, I don't think you're a chicken, Joel. I just hope the police don't show up and you get in trouble... or get suspended from school." It was evident that my female friends had more sense than my buddies did, and by the time I'd realized they were still bickering back and forth, we'd arrived.

My mind was in a daze and I shook my head as if I'd just gotten knocked down in the last seconds of a twelve-round boxing match.

I looked around and the only adult in sight was the hefty Mexican man selling ice cream out of his truck. There were students, of all ages, forming a large circle around the tee-off green, and standing in the middle of the crowd was Jacob, jumping up and down. His demeanor and confidence made it seem like it was his thirtieth fight in the Junior Olympics. He was cocky, unafraid, and his conduct was like that of New York City street brawler.

Among the growing crowd were his friends, and they were all egging him on as he stood there soaking it all in. Turning his neck back and forth *like the demon was in my room on that dark night in Europe.* I had so many thoughts running through my mind, and my friends were all hollering disrespectful words toward his friends that were already in the circle.

As our group walked up to the green, I looked around to get a feeling for the environment, and before I was able to take it all in, someone yelled, "Let's do this Joel! Get in there!" My friend rubbed my shoulders so hard it hurt my chest, and then he pushed me through the crowd into the human ring. There were so many voices that I couldn't hear who was on my side. I figured that most of them were just there to watch somebody bleed, so they could talk about it at school the next day. "Hit him!" "Yeah…hit him in the face!" "Kick his butt!" "Hit him!" Everyone's voice seemed to turn into one giant evil being.

I looked up at Jacob and our eyes locked. I wanted to ask him what his problem was, but I knew that time had passed.

Reality set in, and before I knew it, I lifted both arms above my head and slowly lifted my left knee. *What the heck are you doing Joel!?*

I'd watched "The Karate Kid" at least one-hundred times, and when Daniel Larusso did the *crane kick* at the end of the movie, to beat Johnny Lawrence, I went bananas.

I loved that movie. I emulated his every move, plus I'd practiced the kick on my father's punching bag a thousand times.

I felt that day would've been my "Karate Kid" moment, but the truth was I was terrified inside. I stood there on one shaky leg focusing on Jacob's face. I visualized kicking him once in the head and that would've been the end of the whole circus. Everyone was going to hold me up in the air and my kick was going to be remembered for decades to come.

The sweat was beginning to pour down my face as the temperature rose to one-hundred and fifteen degrees. I blinked as the crowd was yelling at Jacob to run at me. He took a deep breath and charged at me like he was stealing for home plate in the ninth inning of a World Series game. I was shaking like a frail homeless boy who had gone without food for a week, but I was hyper-focused and had tunnel vision on his chin. As he ran closer, I could feel the ground vibrate from the roar of the students. *This is it Joel. You can do it. Right in the chin. You got this. This is your moment…this is your moment…this is your moment.* I was nervously growing confident as I was convincing myself that it was my time to stop being scared once and for all.

As he came raging at me like a bull, the sweat dropped into my eyes. He made it across the short grass, and I let it go. I kicked. I kicked so hard that I would've broken his jaw, but I didn't. I missed and I fell on my back. "Hahaha! He fell! Hahaha…" "Get up, loser" Jacob said with confidence as I laid on my back. I could hear in the crowd, "That's hilarious! Joel thinks he's the karate kid! Hahaha!"

Students were laughing at me and I was embarrassed.

I was ashamed of myself. I looked over and saw my female friends looking at everyone laughing at me. *"Get up Joel!* I heard my friends hollering at me through the laughs.

As the salty sweat was flowing from my face, I realized that it wasn't just sweat, I was crying. I was crying and my body was trembling. My mind, my body and my spirit were reacting in a way that was unfamiliar to me. I was slipping into a different dimension mentally. Someone yelled, "Aww… Joel's crying!

Hahaha! He's crying everyone!" The insults magnified as the tears continued to drip. It felt like something was growing inside of me as the voices were penetrating my ear drums. Someone else yelled, "Why are you crying loser? Get up and fight. Is that it? Are we done here Karate Kid? What a loser… I can't believe you're crying." I was being disrespected and bullied in front of dozens of students, and I didn't know how to react.

Between Jacob's voice irritating me and the students in the crowd making fun of me, the combination of the two was fueling whatever it was that was inside of me. I placed the palms of my hands on the green grass and began to push up off the ground as everyone's voice began to fade but Jacob's, and his was fading fast. I noticed the amount of sweat and tears on the back of my hands as I was getting up and everything I'd ever known was gone. It was complete silence and the color of day was disappearing. All of my fears along with every emotion that I'd ever had in the past was deleted.

By the time I reached my feet, the rage within me had complete control. *Run! Run, Joel!* Everyone was scattering in every direction possible. Students were sprinting past the ice cream truck toward anywhere but where the fight was. My friends were trying to give me instructions on what to do, but I felt like I had just woken up from a deep sleep. I looked up and noticed a small group of students with their hands covering their mouths, standing over a body on the ground.

I wiped the burning sweat from my eyes to get a better look. *Run Joel...let's go! Now!* One of my friends shouted as he grabbed my backpack and pulled me toward the golf course. We ran through the fairway so fast that it reminded me of when I stole for the first time. We cut through the neighborhood and ran until we couldn't run anymore. We were panting like dying dogs, and then suddenly everyone agreed to split up to go our separate ways.

I had no clue as to why we separated and no recollection of what happened, after I attempted to kick Jacob in the face. My friends wanted to split up for some reason, and that was very unusual for our group. I wondered why everyone left the scene at sonic speed and wanted answers to why a small group of students stayed behind looking down at one person. I tried hard to play the tape back in my mind, but my head was hurting, and my memory seemed to have hit a stand still after getting off the ground and the students were making fun of me. There was so much adrenaline and too many thoughts. I looked over my body in the mirror and didn't notice anything unusual. No bruises, no black eyes, nothing. I couldn't comprehend what was going on and I was confused about why I couldn't remember.

The next day when I arrived at the school, I noticed two police cars parked outside of the main office. My stomach was flipping, and in knots, like it was right before the fight. I walked to my classroom and as soon as I walked through the door, everything felt odd. The entire classroom of students turned their heads toward me, and nobody made a sound, until an adult said, "Joel, will you please come with me to the front office? There is someone who would like to speak with you." "Uh…yes, ma'am" I replied, as if I had no clue that the police were there.

The walk to the office paralleled what it would've felt like to be an adult walking down death row. The teacher didn't say one word to me, and I surely wasn't going to open my mouth about what had happened the day before. "Okay, Joel; there's your mother" she said to me. As soon as I walked in the main office, it felt like I was going to die. I was surely about to get executed and my mother's face almost did me in the moment we locked eyes.

The principal looked toward me and said, "Joel, will you come into my office please? This police officer would like to speak with you about an incident that happened yesterday after school." As I entered the principal's office and sat down next to my mother, I could feel her stress. My father was on TDY again, so she was the one that had to deal with most of my wrong doings while he was away providing for our family.

I glanced over to my right where there were other offices adjacent to the one that we were sitting in and noticed one of my friends speaking to another officer. I couldn't hear what they were saying and though I could hear my mother's voice vaguely in the background, I was more interested in what they were talking about next door. *Wait…what? Why is he pointing at me through the window? What the…*

My thoughts were politely interrupted. "Excuse me Joel." "Huh… What? Oh…yes sir," I replied. I was so lost in the fact that they were over in the next office talking about me. As the office began to fill with adults, and questions were beginning to turn my direction, I knew something bad had happened. I could feel it.

Then the police officer said, "Joel, will you walk us through what happened yesterday after school?"

"Yes, sir. I...I was told by many students that this new boy Jacob wanted to fight me. I didn't want to fight him because I'd never fought before, but I also didn't want to be known for being a chicken, so I met him at the golf course by the ice cream truck. I never hit him, and he never hit me, so...," I replied.

The officer asked, "Are you being honest, Joel? Because we have many students saying you were the one who assaulted that student with a painted boulder from the golf course. Is this true?"

Collecting my thoughts, I said, "Uh...I'm...I'm sorry, sir I don't remember doing anything like that."

Doubting me, the police officer said, "You don't remember?" "I don't. I..." I replied.

"Well, even your friends over there are saying that you did. And Jacob is in the hospital recovering from some serious injuries. He may be in the hospital for quite some time," the officer replied.

I couldn't believe what they were saying to me, and my mother was in shock. I truly couldn't remember what I'd done to Jacob, and the fact that everyone, including my friends were saying that I did that to him was mind boggling. The fact that nobody believed that I couldn't remember was even more concerning. I didn't know how to explain that I blacked out. I didn't even know what the term 'blacking out' meant until that day, and I didn't understand at that time that, being disrespected, humiliated, or embarrassed, would trigger my rage.

I was immediately placed on In-School Suspension. After my mother and the officers left that morning, I had to do all my schoolwork in a tiny cubical away from all the other students and it would prove to be the most boring experience of my life. On top of that, I had orders to go straight home from school and was on restriction until my father was to come back from TDY.

When school ended that day, the bell finally rang, and I was able to leave my quiet and lonely dungeon in the main office. I walked outside and was waiting for my friends, when suddenly I heard, "Hey weirdo! Our friend is in the hospital because of you! What, you can't fight without a weapon you loser? You're a crazy person." I wasn't outside two minutes before Jacob's friends were bullying me. I turned to walk away but they kept at it. Another one said, "We'll beat you up loser! You don't have anything to use now! What are you going to do if we tackle you right now? Do you hear me, you stupid freak?" I was most certainly trying to keep my cool and was still exhausted from the whole ordeal—one I never even asked for, but their threats kept coming and I began to feel uncomfortable again.

It wasn't but twenty-four hours since I blacked out and their friend ended up in the hospital, but my body was cringing, and I didn't have time to think things through. "What are you going to do now freak? You don't have a big rock now do y..." And before they could finish hollering at me, I charged. I charged at them with so much adrenaline I must have caught them off guard, and instead of them jumping on me, they took off running.

The rage was already triggered and there was no pulling it back. The boys took off past where the police cars were parked earlier that morning and sprinted off the school grounds. I was chasing them without even realizing I was running and had so much adrenalin that I couldn't feel the hot sun burning my forehead. When they realized I was catching up to them, they crossed the street into a cul-de-sac and toward a house. Two houses down, on the left, was a vacant house and the boys cut through the front yard, and for some odd reason the door was opened. As soon as I reached out to grab the slower boy's backpack, they slammed the front door on my fingers. My fingers were smashed, and the door opened and slammed again.

The physical pain was so bad that my brain hurt, and I was shaking profusely, but the pain subsided as I hyper focused on retaliation. I heard the door lock and it was like a switch in my soul.

I stood upright and turned toward the naked bay window to look at the disrespectful boys faces. One of them yelled, "What are you crying again you cry baby? Waaah... Cry you loser! What did you break your little fingers? Come on karate kid...what are you going to do now?" I was crying, but it wasn't from the physical pain and the hatred in me was growing by the second. The boys continued to taunt me as I cracked my neck saying, "What are you going to do now? Run and cry home to your mommy?" The negative energy that filled my body was warm, and I began grinding my teeth. Then I heard, "Joel! What are doing!?" I looked over toward the school and it was one of my friends sprinting down toward the cul-de-sac. "Don't do it, Joel! Don't do it," he pleaded. I slowly turned my head toward the boys again. Then one of them yelled again, "Come on cry baby, go and run home to your mo…"

And everything went silent.

I looked at the boys through the window and their mouths were moving, but I heard nothing. I felt my jaw clenching down so hard my teeth could've shattered out of my mouth. With so much adrenaline flowing, I glanced at my friend, right into his eyes, but before he could reach the front yard, I turned my head, and threw my fist through the window breaking the glass everywhere. I grabbed one of the boys by his shirt and pulled him out. It happened so quickly, and the crashing of the large window was extremely loud. The overwhelming feeling inside me was like twenty trombones playing in my bloodstream and the symphony wasn't done playing yet.

There was blood all over my shirt and the scared boys tried to run, but I wheeled a piece of glass in my hand and was trying to put it through one of the boys head. My buddy grabbed me from behind and turned my body in the opposite direction. The boy's friend ran out of the house and began dragging his friend across the yard until he got him on his feet, and they took off running. I attempted to chase the boys, but my larger friend grabbed me and asked, "Are you okay Joel? Calm down…it's okay." Still a little disoriented, I replied, "What? Get off of me…Get…off…of…me. I'm okay." The front yard was shining from the sun reflecting off thousands of shards of glass. Every step we took there was a cracking sound beneath us. There were still large pieces falling from the frame and my eyes were burning from the sweat. I dropped the piece of glass and was fortunate that it didn't destroy my hand.

My friend was breathing harder than I was and yelled, "Dude! You're bleeding! You're bleeding from somewhere!" I looked over my hands again and there weren't any large cuts on my palms, but when I turned them over, we both saw a piece of glass sticking out of my wrist. "Aw dude you're bleeding," he said. My friend was freaking out more than I was, and when I attempted to pull it out, it broke off inside. I took my shirt off, wrapped my wrist, and the two of us walked away before the police or school staff heard about the incident. After I tossed my bloody shirt and put a bandage on my wound, I heard someone knocking at our front door. My mother had just gotten home from work and when I peeked around the corner, I saw her standing in the doorway speaking to a police officer.

I was confused on how I was getting into so much trouble and wasn't the one bullying other kids. Besides me stealing, drowning the Guinea pig, and almost burning down the old lady's house, which my mother knew nothing about, all of my life altering experiences were out of my control and came without warning. I didn't create the chaos that had the police questioning my mother twice in one day, but when I added everything up that I'd been through in my ten years of life, I was definitely concerned. I didn't ask for the evil spirits, entities, or shadows to come after me, and I never asked for my best friend to die.

It seemed that my mother got the dirty end of the stick during my troubles. She was, in fact, home when the demon tormented me, she had to explain to me that my best friend Matthew passed away just hours after I was with him, and then she was lost for words on why I was in trouble at school and being questioned by law-enforcement twice in one day. My mother was always there to help her family—even when we didn't show our appreciation. She loved us no matter what we did. She even opened our doors to my Aunt and little cousin when they had no safe place to rest their heads. She may have questioned our choices, but she always looked past the disappointments and did what she felt was right. When my father would return home, she would be the one to explain all the things that our family was going through whenever he was gone.

When he returned home, after my two confrontations, he looked at my wrist and drove me to Urgent Care to have medical staff remove the glass. I knew it couldn't have been easy for him to leave his family to provide for us, only to return to hear the news that I was in trouble with the law. On top of hearing that concerning news, I got into trouble a few months later for throwing rocks through windows because older kids simply dared me to.

For some reason, I wanted to prove to the other kids that I wasn't afraid of any challenge, when really, my actions were based on fear or I was acting out of fear. I would continue to hang out with the same group of kids, but never forgot the memory of my friend who pointed me out to the police in the principal's office that day. It was a feeling of betrayal, and unfortunately for me, it wouldn't be the only time, on my life's journey, that it would happen to me.

During the remainder of our time in Arizona, I was able to keep out of trouble from the law but would continue to steal from stores. I began collecting baseball, basketball, and football cards, and if I didn't have enough money to support my hobby, I would steal due to my lack of patience. A few of my friends began smoking cigarettes and chewing tobacco; but I was afraid to lose my mother and father from cancer due to their tobacco habits, so I chose the latter. There were many times when I would throw my mother's cigarettes away, in an attempt to spare her from the cancerous addiction, but my strategy was short lived when they found an unopened carton in the trash and I was punished.

As a family, when my father was home, we would drive south to Tucson on the weekends to visit our relatives. As the older folks would party and drink, my cousins and I were given $20.00 each to stay out of the adult's way. We often ate at a place called New York Pizza behind their house and walked a mile or so down the road and spent the rest of our money in an arcade. Other times, we travelled to Mexico. My cousins' grandparents were a wealthy couple, and their grandfather had many connections with the Mexican people, so they too had a beautiful home built near the ocean, where we spent a lot of time during our vacations. My grandmother and her sisters owned a small house in Kino Bay, and it sat no more than fifty yards from that same ocean.

The cultures, between each country I'd been in, were all so different. From Europe to the United States to Mexico—the lifestyles were nothing alike. The natives of each land had different means of surviving and the history of each land had its own way of showing. From the savory to the sweets, the food was tremendously different from one country to the next, and I enjoyed the different ingredients that each region utilized and added to their cuisine. I didn't know then, but the experiences of taste testing many different foods, would benefit me decades later, in what I'd thought was going to be the most successful career of my life.

After eating dinner, at our family's favorite seaside Mexican restaurant, the adults continued to drink the nights away, in a going away event for my family, since we'd learned that my father was being stationed back to Virginia later that month. I'd sit outside away from the noise and was taken back on how enormous and intimidating the ocean was. I felt so miniscule in the grand scheme of what life was trying to teach me and knew that there was much more to life than just going to school, or as the adults did, working, and partying as an adult during the weekends.

Such an amazing and powerful force the ocean was. So serene to witness at night, and then to see the tide so far back in the distance when I awoke each morning. I would stand with my feet in the water and listen to the sound of the waves forcing themselves on to my toes and felt the sense that the ocean was alive as one giant organism, understanding precisely what it was created to do. It was calming to my spirit standing there alone appreciating its presence, hearing no human voices, hollering, bickering, or belligerence.

There were no kids around bullying and being mean to other kids; it was just me and a system of nature that was minding its own business.

At times, I was able to recognize specific moments for what they were and acknowledged the blessings or curses of each. Gazing into the distance at where the water met the sky, was one of those moments where I felt something greater than myself, and it blessed me with a moment of peace.

Before leaving Mexico that week, we spent the night out at sea on my relatives' two large boats. The moon and stars reflected off the dark water while millions of sea creatures swam beneath us, possibly wondering why we humans were there. I was able to appreciate the night sky without light pollution and was mindful about how intriguing the Earth really is to experience. I laid down on the deck that night, as the boat slowly swayed back and forth, and thought about my life as I did in the windowsill in Europe years prior. I was upset because my father was being stationed to different places around the world and saddened to leave my life behind once again.

As I examined the stars and the constellations, I wondered if Heaven was a real place and if my best friend Matthew was in the night sky looking down on me with God. I wondered if all the kind people that died were up there living in harmony without bullies and terrorists. Because I was stealing, I wondered if I would have been banished from Heaven, because I stole things from others instead of patiently waiting. I also continued to question why humans caused so much harm and chaos to one another, instead of helping each other and spreading love and joy. I thought about the confrontations I had at the school and anxiously speculated on whether or not I was going to have rage for the rest of my life whenever I felt disrespected or embarrassed.

Nevertheless, I still had no answers to any of those questions but floating in the middle of the ocean that night may have been the most peaceful night of my entire life. I relished the moment and didn't want it to end, because the reality was, I was moving to another unfamiliar place, and my fear of the unknown was terrifying to examine. There were no clues on what life was going to be like for me on the east coast, or what type of young man I would become as I was learning from my experiences in the early stages of my adolescence. Only time would tell how I would be able to handle each situation as they arose, and whether or not my choices would benefit me or lead me down a path of destruction.

CHAPTER 3

BECAUSE THEY WERE GANGSTERS

My family and I packed up our belongings and headed back across the country to Virginia. It wasn't ever easy saying goodbye to my friends and having to leave everything I knew, but I had no voice in the matter. Though we'd moved three times before, it remained difficult to deal with, and my heart weighed heavy as we drove onto the highway and headed east on I-10.

When we arrived, I was surprised about how gratifying it was to see the trees, grass, lakes and the rivers. It seemed to have rained more in the first week than it did in an entire year back in Arizona, and I enjoyed cloudy and rainy days.

We moved to Northern Virginia to Prince William County, which was located south of Washington DC, where my father had received his orders to work at the Pentagon. My mother quickly found employment at a bank in town, where her most famously known customer would eventually be a woman by the name of Lorena Bobbitt. The woman was recognized globally for cutting off her husband's penis while he slept. It was a funny story for us youngsters, but my mother's perspective was that the young woman was a kind person, who was tired of being abused and literally took measures into her own hands.

As soon as we moved into our new home, I immediately turned to sports to help with my anxiety and depression and continued collecting trading cards while following the best players and their stats. I could talk statistics with any sports fan regardless of their age. Of course, with my luck, with us moving away, Arizona finally decided to own an NFL franchise in 1988, with the Cardinals moving from St. Louis to Phoenix. Though I was excited to have a home team, by the time the Cardinals team moved to the desert, I was already a diehard San Francisco 49ers fan and Jerry Rice was my favorite NFL player. I eventually became a diehard Cardinals fan.

At the time, Arizona didn't own a Major League baseball team, so I followed the Atlanta Braves and began following the Baltimore Orioles and Cal Ripken Jr. because Virginia didn't own any major sports franchises either. The only team that I followed faithfully from Arizona was the Phoenix Suns. My father and I would go to the Arizona Veterans Memorial Coliseum to watch my favorite team play, and thus, my passion for basketball was much greater than every other sport. I also played little league baseball after joining the AAU (Amateur Athletic Union) and Boys and Girls Club basketball leagues, but my focus was centered on the court and utilizing my dribbling and passing skills because I was ambidextrous.

On the basketball court, I emulated Suns point guard Kevin Johnson, but since I wasn't an African American kid, boys on the court called me 'little John Stockton' from the Utah Jazz. I despised the Jazz, and though John Stockton was one of the greatest to ever play the game, I quickly reminded everyone who my favorite player was before beginning each pick-up game.

As time went by, I was befriended by the neighborhood boys, as I was by a group of students at Lake Ridge Middle-School. One boy in particular named John, loved playing basketball just as much as I did. If the two of us weren't playing in a league, we were faithfully at the recreation center playing against other boys. John and his mother lived only a half a mile away and I spent the night at his house almost every weekend. And he, like the majority of boys I knew, was a Chicago Bulls fan, emulating his game after the great Michael Jordan. We were two young 'white boys' in Northern Virginia, amongst a large population of African Americans, and both of us idolized great black athletes. But John and I didn't have a racist bone in our body, and coming from homes that didn't discriminate against others, it was never an issue for the two of us, though it was for many kids I met.

Meanwhile, the depression subsided and eventually, like the other times I was forced to move, I forgot about ever being depressed in the first place. My life was good again after settling in, and I was more focused than ever on being the best tiny athlete in the neighborhood.

One evening, after playing basketball, a few of the neighborhood boys decided that breaking into the elementary school would be a great idea. I immediately had a bad feeling in my gut and told the two boys that they were on their own, and that I wanted no parts of their foolishness. As they climbed to the top of a classroom, I stood back on the basketball court, and no more than two minutes later, I noticed a flashlight coming from the other side of the building and someone yelled, "Hey! What in the hell are you doing up there?" I knew it, and my spirit was precise in knowing that something was going to happen before it happened.

I yelled up at the two dupes, "Get down guys!

Security! Security's coming!" They climbed down as the man was gaining ground on them and we all ran through the trees back toward the houses. Somehow their mothers found out about the incident and blamed me for their sons' being on top of the school. I couldn't believe it. They made it seem as if I threw both of their boys onto the building, and told them to break in. Again, something happened, and the other boys told on me. Their mothers must have been in denial and wouldn't accept the fact that their sons were growing up and making poor choices.

After that evening, whenever I walked to their houses and asked if the boys were home, I would hear the mothers calling me names and making hurtful statements like, "The rat boy is here..." or, "I don't want the little beaver boy getting you into trouble again sweetheart." It did hurt my feelings, and people called me names for years because of my size and buck teeth, but I just dealt with it as it came.

During another evening, not too long afterward, we were at the same elementary school playing a three-on-three pick-up game of basketball. There were a few older teenagers playing with us and one of the boys kept fouling me throughout the game. Even when I didn't have the ball, he kept pushing me around, and I ended up feeling an elbow to my head. I kept asking him respectfully to stop fouling me, but it continued, and then he mocked me.

The boy outweighed me by eighty pounds, and easily had six inches on me, but the more I felt disrespected, the more my mind, body and spirit were changing again. I did everything in my power to show him that he wasn't getting into my head, but he became irritated when I continued to out play him.

I caught a pass and shot a three pointer in his face. The next possession, I dribbled around my back, between my legs, and made him fall to the ground with a nice crossover move and scored. The next play, I went around my back with the ball and passed it over my head to one of my teammates and we scored again. It got to a point that everyone else on the court was telling him to stop fouling me, but for some reason he wouldn't, *and then I just snapped.* I punched him in the face and broke his nose. It all happened so fast, and the anger that I was trying to tame, got the best of me once again. There was no fight, no retaliation; afterwards, I walked away to calm myself down and everyone else went home.

No longer than ten minutes after I got home to clean up before dinner, the doorbell rang. I knew it was his parents, and I was scared to death. I didn't want to answer the door while the thoughts of my father being upset with me were pouring in. When my father opened the door, the boy was standing on our front porch holding his nose with his mother by his side, "Did your son tell you that he assaulted my son while playing basketball?" My father replied, "Uh, no he didn't mention that." "Well he did…now look at his nose" the boy's mother insisted. I just knew that I was in trouble, even though I was standing up for myself while the bigger boy was bullying me on the court.

My father had me apologize to the much larger kid and assured the boy's mother that I would be punished for my actions. After he closed the door, he turned and looked at me and said, "Good job! That was a big boy!" and he walked past me, up the stairs, to eat dinner.

At school, and as I grew older, I always found myself being sent to the back of the classroom for talking too much. I couldn't stay quiet and didn't understand how other students would sit in a classroom for eight hours a day without saying a word. When I was placed in a large room full of people, I wasn't able to focus on the task at hand, and since my last name was Carroll, I'd begin the morning in the front of class, but would eventually be sitting in the back row by the end of each day.

One morning, while being moved to the back of the class, an extremely quiet girl that I didn't even know was in the class, looked over to me and said, "You haven't changed one-bit Joel...do you ever shut up?" She reached down into her backpack and pulled out a book, opened it to a specific page, and handed it to me. It was a yearbook, and on that specific page was a picture of the two of us sitting next to one another in a classroom in Europe six years prior. She and I were on the opposite sides of life's spectrum. On her journey through life, she was focused, quiet, extremely intelligent, disciplined, and not at all worried about how many friends she had or if anyone at school knew about her at all. She knew exactly where she wanted to go and was working diligently to get there.

On my journey through life, I was a puny, cute kid, that didn't know how to handle situations that irritated me. I was a shy kid until I wasn't. I went from a quiet kid to becoming extremely loud very quickly. I was polite and respectful, until I felt uncomfortable or irritable, and then I lost control. When someone pushed me, I showed discipline until I didn't, and wouldn't quite comprehend why I wasn't able to fully hold it together like other kids my age who showed obedience.

At that moment, after she handed me the yearbook, I realized how small Earth really was. I went back to that place in my mind where I was looking up at the stars while atop the ocean's surface. How insignificant we were, and how infinite the Universe was.

After expressing her displeasure in my lack of maturity, I thought to myself, *how could two young people that sat next to one another six years ago because of my lack of discipline during school, share this exact scenario, 3,944 miles from one another?* I doubted that she thought about the situation in depth like I did, or maybe she did, but those same circumstances presented themselves for a reason and it had me thinking about what the meaning of the connection was.

Though she and I seemed to be polar opposites, my life's journey had given me enough experience to understand that there was something mysterious happening on this planet. Was it coincidence, timing, or life testing us continuously at specific times for specific reasons?

During the next summer, while my sister and I were out of school, my parents decided to purchase a different house two miles south of where we were living. The house sat on two acres and my parents were excited about having a more private place to call home. The discouraging thing for me was that the house wasn't in a neighborhood with other houses right next door, and that meant, there were none of my friends nearby. I'd just graduated the eighth grade and though I was depressed about moving into another home, I was looking forward to attending Woodbridge High School with all of my friends at summer's end.

Woodbridge was also the high school that my older sister attended, but unfortunately for me, another one of life's curveballs was pitched to me, when Prince William County decided to change the school zoning plans that summer. The new layout on the zoning map was a small dirt road two-hundred feet from our new house, and that borderline negated me from attending Woodbridge with my friends. Instead, I was sent to another high school called Garfield.

All the friends that I spent three years with while in middle school, were going to high school without me. My parents did everything in their power to convince the district to allow me to attend Woodbridge with my sister, but the only students that were able to attend that lived outside of the zoning, were the ones that attended Woodbridge high school the year prior.

I was heading into uncharted territories again and my mind was in shambles. I was extremely anxious and became depressed all over again. I despised the fact that I would build a little life for myself, and in the drop of someone else's decisions, I would be forced to leave it all without a say. I continued playing basketball with a few of my friends throughout that summer, and though it was my greatest coping skill, the thoughts continued to race through mind that I was going to Garfield, and it became more of a reality as the school year was set to begin.

When that dreadful morning arrived, I walked over to the dirt road and waited for the school bus to come. I hadn't ridden on a bus in seven years and was full of anxiety and fear. I ended up being the only kid waiting until it arrived, and when I walked through the door and up the steps, the bus was full of students that I'd never met before. When I walked toward the back to find an empty seat, I noticed another boy from Lake Ridge Middle School sitting by himself. He was a soccer player at our old school and looked as nervous as I felt.

When the two of us walked off the bus and into the school, I was terrified. Garfield had more than three thousand students and was absolutely nothing like my other schools. It was a madhouse. There were so many students walking past me and I had no clue as to what to do or where to go. There were different groups already solidified and segregating themselves in certain areas of the hallways. I felt non-existent as if I had been surrounded by the ocean, but this school was everything but tranquil and serene. I stood in the crowded hallway at five feet tall and eighty-nine pounds. Some of the students looked like adults, and the girls had bodies like women in the dirty magazines I'd snuck from my father's closet. I was truly intimated.

As the first few weeks unfolded, I ate lunch with the soccer player from Lake Ridge Middle, and the two of us shared our experiences and how life at Garfield was treating us. I remained quiet and observed my surroundings, and as time passed, began to open up to the students in each of my classes. I continued to play sports that year, but when tryouts began for the schools' team, I was ousted by the greater talent. The other athletes were freaks of nature: big, super-fast, and had talents exceeding anything I'd ever competed against. Boys my age were dunking the basketball, pitching eighty mile-an-hour fastballs on the baseball diamond, and hitting like grown men on the football field. I was simply outclassed, and my self-esteem was crushed, sending me into another depressive state.

Every moment I was away from school, I practiced basketball at the Chinn Aquatics and Fitness Center down the road from our house. Many of the boys from Garfield would play ball there during the winter months because of the snow, and of course, they continued to call me John Stockton and it irritated me. Still, I created new relationships on that court, and boys from Garfield were beginning to acknowledge me.

On one side of the gym, we ran three on three games on two baskets. On the other side of the gym, is where the really good players played five on five. There was something about the young men that caught my attention and drew me to watch them. They were really good on the court, and I noticed quickly that they were both respected and feared, because they were gangsters. Whenever I wanted a break from playing, I'd walk over and sit on the bleachers to study their ways. They had an immense swag about them, and their confidence was limitless as individuals, but even greater as a unit. I witnessed beautiful girls walking into the gym to deliver them food. Other young men would arrive to show their allegiance and respect—it was something I'd only witnessed in movies. I'd sit there imagining that I was on the court with them and what the possibilities were of people showing me recognition like that.

One evening, after leaving the gym, I dribbled my basketball up the road toward our house, and noticed an unknown car parked in our driveway. I walked in the front door and while I was removing my shoes, I glanced over toward our living room, and there, sitting with my family on the couch, were two of the young men that I'd been watching at the gym. I was nervous and confused. One of the gang members looked over to me and acknowledged my presence saying, "What's up little man?" I walked over to our living room, with so many scenarios going through my mind, and my parents looked at me and told me to introduce myself to my sister's new boyfriend.

I couldn't believe that my older sister was dating a gangster. He greeted me, "Hey little fella, my name's Dre. We've noticed you playing ball at the Chin Center. That's good; keep practicing and maybe, one day, you'll be playing with us." I was already envisioning myself on the court with the men before I'd even met them, then here they were in my house telling me that it was a possibility if I didn't give up.

My sister's boyfriend, Dre, respected my father because my father was a military man and worked in the Pentagon. He also showed kindness toward my mother because my mother was kind toward him. My parents are an outgoing couple who work hard, love their children, and didn't discriminate against others because of the color of their skin. They didn't judge people's character until they had reason to, and that showed true since Dre and the other gang members were African American, and two of them were sitting on our couch holding a respectful conversation.

From that evening forward, Dre took care of me as if I was his younger brother. I rode with him around the Metropolitan area while he was doing whatever it was that he did, and he made it very clear at the beginning that I was not to follow in his footsteps and become gang affiliated. He took me to Georgetown University, and I was blessed to witness Allen Iverson while he played for the Hoyas, and my father and I would continue to go to games whenever the Phoenix Suns played the Washington Bullets across the bridge.

My life was good again.

As my sophomore year arrived, I continued to practice for the upcoming tryouts for the school team. I was feeling confident as ever while playing against greater talent, but my life was thrown in a tilt after I lost my virginity to the girl that lived in the house closest to ours; *I had no idea what had hit me.* She was definitely more experienced even though she was a year younger than I was, and I had no clue then how much sex would change my mindset. From the moment I had intercourse with that beautiful girl, I gained a new perspective on life because I loved how she made me feel, and I became addicted immediately. While still having sex with my neighbor, I began dating another beautiful girl at Garfield named Nora. She was from West Philadelphia and rumors began to spread that we were married because the two of us shared the same last name. Our relationship quickly manifested into something greater than I'd anticipated, and my neighbor and I stopped seeing each other soon after.

The gang-members, in our school, got wind that I was connected to Dre, and because I knew who they were through playing basketball, I felt like I was getting closer to my mission of becoming affiliated. But as time passed, I realized that it was Dre's name that they respected and not my own. Many of them, including rival gangs, thought Dre and I were biological brothers. Though he was African American, he also came from a family of many cultures and was considered "light skinned." Anytime someone had an issue with me in school, other students quickly mentioned his name and his affiliation, and the assailants resentfully walked in the other direction. My life was definitely different than it was a year prior. I stopped talking to the quiet soccer player from Lake Ridge, I was sexually active and had a beautiful girlfriend, people knew me as the little brother of a known gang member, and I didn't care about playing for the school team anymore.

I loved playing basketball more than anything else, and without being able to fulfill that dream, I began looking at different ways to cope with life. I was still, in many ways, quiet and shy, but the more people I met, the more I was able to open up and witnessed other teenagers using tobacco products, drinking alcohol, and smoking marijuana. I'd also witnessed throughout the years how my parents were having such a great time when they were drinking with their friends and our family. I contemplated on why people that drank alcohol, continued to drink at great lengths, and by the age of fifteen, I became curious enough that I wanted to experience those things for myself.

CHAPTER 4

OMEN

I *took a shower, threw my clothes on, and waited for my mother to leave for work. As soon as I saw her car exit the gravel driveway, I walked into the kitchen and grabbed a small thermos. I anxiously reached into the cabinet where my parents stored their favorite liquor and pulled down a large bottle. I opened it, smelled it, gagged a little bit, and carefully poured it into the thermos. I then grabbed a small sandwich bag and walked to my mother's ash tray sitting next to her favorite chair in the living room. She always smoked half of her cigarettes while drinking and the ashtray was full by morning. I grabbed a handful of half smoked cigarettes, placed them in the small bag, and headed out the door.*

I walked to the bus stop early that morning so I could partake in my new activities before the bus arrived. I lit up my first cigarette and coughed while another boy looked at me as if I'd lost my mind. I opened the lid to the thermos, took a deep breath, and poured the liquor down my throat. It was so powerful that it burned my little body internally and I couldn't fathom how folks were drinking gallons of the nasty stuff only to crave more. It was disgusting, but within seconds after that first guzzle, my body was warm, and I felt good...*really good.*

I sat down on the bus and took another drink. The girl I sat next to must've caught a whiff because she too shook her head and looked at me like I'd lost my mind, but I didn't care, I just kept drinking. It felt like I was drinking happiness, a magic potion, and at that moment, I understood why my parents had consumed it for decades.

So, my morning routine was set; after everyone departed, I stocked up and happily headed out for the day. I felt confident while consuming the new drink heading to school and was becoming increasingly closer to the students that were affiliated with the gang, and the long-standing relationships I'd had in Lake Ridge were all but gone.

One of the young men I grew close to also played basketball and lived around the corner from Nora in Dale City. His name was Marley, and he had a confidence about him on and off the court and I admired that about him. He lived with his mother in a part of Dale City where most of the gang members lived, and the closer our relationship became, the more I stayed away from home after school.

Midway through my sophomore year, while I was creating connections with many new people; a different group of teenagers were picking me up before school and I was no longer riding the school bus. I began smoking marijuana daily and combined that with the alcohol before I walked into school each day. Many of the boys that I knew were getting initiated into different gangs across the county, including my close friend, as he became affiliated with the gang I was striving to join. I immediately noticed the changes in each of their demeanor as they transformed, individually, overnight. They no longer spoke about certain things around me, and I was fully aware that it was because they were part of a new family and had to carry themselves a certain way. Unfortunately, I was thought of as an outcast and considered an "off-brand," or someone that wasn't affiliated with that gang.

I would often pass the gang in the neighborhood when Nora and I were walking to the store, and on many occasions, they wouldn't even acknowledge me. The ones that didn't know me were disrespectful because I was a puny kid that wasn't from the area and was dating a beautiful female from their neighborhood. The few that did know me still acknowledged me, and though word spread outside of Garfield that my older sister was dating Dre, I was still far from respected. On several different occasions, I was approached while walking to Nora's house, and guns were pulled on me, in an attempt to scare me away from their neighborhood.

One incident stemmed from when I was with a kid named Samuel during the end of our Summer break. We were hanging out having a good time at his grandparent's house when two older and feared gang members asked Samuel if he and I wanted to ride over the bridge to DC to purchase and smoke marijuana or weed. Samuel's older sister was dating one of the gang members who just so happened to be in the gang that Samuel and I wanted to join, so he and I accepted the invitation. We got in the car with the two men and drove across the bridge to pick up the sack of weed. On our way back into Virginia we were pulled over by multiple Virginia State Troopers on Interstate 95. I had no clue that the tags were stolen, and moments before they pulled us over, we started smoking formaldehyde, otherwise known as "Embalming Fluid, PCP, Wet, Dippers, Eely Mo, Buck Naked, Love Boat, or Water."

I personally didn't even know the gang members that were in the front seat. I'd heard of them, and I knew they were considered dangerous by other gang members in the area, and I knew that regardless of the situation, I was going to keep my mouth shut and continued to mind my own business. By the time we knew it, we were all handcuffed and forced to lay face down on the side of the busy interstate until the men were subsequently arrested and placed in the patrol cars. An uneasy feeling came over me as they were driven away. They both turned their heads through the windows and looked directly in my eyes as if I had something to do with them being arrested. Samuel and I were picked up by my father at Springfield Mall a few hours later, and I had a hunch that my supposed friend Samuel was the one that gave the police information.

A rumor quickly spread that I'd told on, or 'snitched' on the gang members to keep myself out of trouble, but there was no trouble for me to get out of. I had no clue what was going on because I didn't ask questions and was not for one second going to tell on anyone else for multiple reasons. One reason was that I'd been "told on" multiple times in the past and *despised everyone who told on me*. Another reason was that I was close to Dre and a lot of other gang members in Prince William County that were affiliated with the two men that got arrested. Lastly, I wanted nothing more than to be affiliated with that specific gang and was simply not going to tell on another man that had been in that gang for years. It just didn't make sense for me to say anything when I had nothing to say in the first place.

I'd known in my heart that Samuel either said something to the state troopers or began a rumor that I did, so he would look good for the gang since he was attempting to become affiliated like I was. At the forefront, it seemed to have been a good plan for him because his sister was dating one of the gang members. He must've thought he was going to get away with it while turning their attention toward me. There was no way that I was going to sit back and accept someone lying on my name, so I contacted Dre and other higher ups that didn't necessarily know I even existed. I explained the situation in its entirety, and because a lot of their younger brothers went to school with me, it was necessary that I got to the bottom of the situation before something bad happened to me or my family.

I figured the arrested gang members didn't get the memo, because when they saw me standing on a corner with a group of my friend's by Marley's house, one of them put a pistol to my head and told me to watch my back, before getting into a truck and driving away. During another incident, Nora and I were walking back to her house after going to the store, and the same SUV drove up to another gang member's girlfriend's house as we were walking past. I knew it was them and Nora encouraged me to keep walking, but I stopped and turned around when they said something to me. One of the men jumped out of the SUV and headed in my direction.

I was carrying a juice in a large glass bottle and hid it behind my back. "Come here, little man," he commanded. "Joel, don't go," Nora pleaded. I wasn't one to run away most of the time, though I knew the gang member could've killed me in a second. But I was determined not to show fear because I felt destined to become affiliated with his gang and wanted to prove that I wasn't afraid of being in their neighborhood. Nora tugged at my hoodie and attempted to drag me away, but I wasn't moving. "What do you have behind your back, little man?" he asked. He pulled out his gun and approached me until his face was touching mine. Malcom, one of the well-respected gang members from my school, ran out of his girlfriend's house and confronted the older gang member.

Malcom stood between us and explained to him that I was connected to Dre and that they truly believed that I wasn't the one who told them. That I may have been an escape goat for Samuel that used his older sister's relationship as a means to blame me. God looked out for me that day, because the two gang members were feared for a reason. They were known for handling business and without Malcom seeing the situation unfolding on the street, I may have been shot dead in front of Nora.

Another gun was pulled on me on the same street by different gang members a few months later. I'd just walked Nora's Rottweiler to her house and was heading in the opposite direction to meet with Marley, when a red car passed me and suddenly stopped in the middle of the street. A gang member with a ski-mask on walked toward me with a gun and demanded my backpack. I looked over toward the car and noticed three other gang members sitting in it, and knew I had no chance. I took off running, hopping over fences and cutting through backyards until I reached Marley's house. It ended up being four young men that were affiliated with the gang and didn't respect me, and though Marley knew who it was, he held that information from me out of loyalty to his gang.

I continued getting tested by that gang, and besides the few gang members that I was welcomed around, I knew a lot of people in the county that weren't affiliated with any crew. And because I was known as the little brother of Dre, the young men that wanted to become affiliated, understood that I had the connection they desired. One by one I was introducing thorough young men to meet the gang. As they were chosen, I continued to search for more within the smaller gangs in Woodbridge and Dale City. The new recruits continued to acknowledge me, but I understood when it was time for them to work for the gang, I wasn't to be involved. Dre acknowledged the work I was putting in, and because of that, he gave me a street name, an alias, and that name was *Omen*.

My life changed that day and I was intrigued by Dre's choice because I was born on Friday the 13th, on the weekend of a full moon,

I'd literally seen demons, and my best friend Matthew died the same day. When people pushed me to my limit, though I was extremely small, I raged, and bad things happened. I was a Libra, the scales of balance between good and evil, and it became *Omen versus Joel*, as the alias began to tilt the scale in my life.

I quickly read the definition for Omen and it stated, *prophetic significance. Events regarded as a portent of good and evil.* I read that definition without knowledge of what it meant. Everything that I thought I knew of the meaning was exactly the way it fit into my life. It was an omen that Dre named me *Omen*. There couldn't have been a more precise alias for what my existence had already gone through.

After Dre gave me the name, he had someone make me a shirt that read *Go Hard or Go Home* across the front, and *Lil Omen* on the back. I wore that shirt to school with pride, and a necklace he gave me that had the gang's emblem on it. The gang members in the school were angry because I wasn't ever initiated. I never did what it took to gain respect or to wear the symbol, but everyone else around thought that I was part of the gang already.

One night while I was walking through Dale City with another kid that I met in the neighborhood; he told me that one of the well-known gang members on 'K' street had some weed and that he was going to knock on his window so we could get high. After he knocked on the window, the kid came jogging back and said Joker was going to take a shower, but for us to return twenty minutes later. We began walking up a dark hill to see if anyone else was outside when not even two minutes later, gunshots rang out. It echoed throughout the entire neighborhood and we heard tires screeching from behind us; when we turned around, we witnessed a white car leaving Joker's house.

We ran down the hill and through the smoke from the screeching tires; the stench of burned rubber was overwhelming. I stood back, looking around as concerned neighbors began walking outside. I ran to the corner house where two of my friends lived, the Gomez brothers, and used their phone to call Dre. Within minutes, gang members gathered in the street and the block was filling fast. Police officers were pleading with older gang members not to retaliate, but vehicles began driving off as soon as word spread of the description of the car that was used to get away.

Joker was shot three times by a rival gang member, and though it was a close call, he survived. It was also a close call for the kid and me. If Joker had chosen to smoke with us before taking a shower, or had he just gotten out of the shower, we would've been standing in his front yard getting high and they may have shot us all dead. That night marked the fourth time that life allowed me to escape, unharmed, in that same neighborhood. Though I could've taken those situations as warnings, or signs to walk away and return home to my family, I continued to show my presence and more people were noticing.

During that summer, between school years, I took it upon myself to catch a ride to an undisclosed location where I'd heard they were going to be initiating new gangsters. I was nervous when I arrived, but my determination outweighed any fear I had about how they were going to react when I approached them. One by one, young men from the neighborhood were called and eventually faded in the distance as they walked by themselves into the unknown. When it was time for me to meet my fate, I began the walk up the ominous steps until I reached the top. There were dozens of gang members spread out at the beginning of the tree covered path, and the man on the last step looked at me and said, "What are you gonna bring to the table?" As soon as I opened my mouth to reply, I was punched flush in my temple by another gang member. "Get the fuck out of here! You can't handle this shit," he yelled, and I went tumbling down the steps.

It took me a while to gather my senses, and when I was able to get up and open my eyes, I was both dazed and extremely confused. I was red-green color blind and that hit to the head must've flicked a switch because I was fully aware that in one eye, I saw nothing but orange, and out of the other eye nothing but purple. I'd never been hit like that before and it saddened me because I wanted nothing more than to show my allegiance toward these people that rejected me and had me eating through a straw for days. I was embarrassed and full of shame, and the only thing I knew to do was to drink alcohol, smoke weed with formaldehyde to alleviate the pain in my head and face.

Not long after, I was walking out of a huge party at the Chinn Aquatics and Fitness Center by my house with a group of teenagers, and a young man punched me in my collarbone, fracturing it. He was from a rival gang and because I was wearing the emblem on my necklace that Dre had given me, he thought I was in the gang and knocked me to the ground. And though I was in pain for many weeks and had been humiliated again in front of a crowd, I was far from broken and not willing to resign from the task at hand.

During that same year, many of the 'off brands' across different neighborhoods created small gangs, and the more I felt certain young men were worthy, I introduced them to Dre where they would be acknowledged. That became the norm for me, and the young men that I surrounded myself with continued abandoning the smaller gangs and became aligned with the more dangerous and solidified street gangs.

My friend Marley ended up being in most of my classes the next school year. We went everywhere together. After each class, he and I strolled the hallways to meet our girlfriends and everyone else knew if they disrespected one, they disrespected both. One morning, during class, a student who was sitting to my right, was having words with Marley who was sitting to my left. The three of us were all high as kites, and I did my best to be a peacekeeper, hoping their words wouldn't erupt into violence, but it was to no avail.

The student told me that he didn't have any problems with me, but I continued to warn him about disrespecting Marley and that I wouldn't take that disrespect lightly. Just seconds before class ended, one of the well-known girls walked out of our room and told her sister in the next room that a fight was about to ensue. The students began to gossip as students did best, and before I could create a strategy to save the student, the bell rang. The hallway filled quickly, and the only students that exited the area, ran to alert the staff. The rest of the students stood quietly and knew something was about to happen as you could feel the tension in the atmosphere. I looked over toward the student and suggested that he walk down the stairs and keep his mouth closed, but he continued to shrug off my warnings and made direct eye contact with Marley instead of walking away.

I was becoming aggravated within myself for the lack of respect that I'd felt the student was showing me, when I was in fact trying to help him. Marley hit the student three times and he stumbled across the hallway and fell into a corner. I looked over toward the stunned student and suggested again that he kept his mouth shut, but he looked at me and said something disrespectful to me. I dropped my bag and slowly jogged through the crowd, and as he attempted to get up, I kicked his head into the bricks with the heel of my boot. With the crowd of students frozen in shock, Marley and I nonchalantly walked away into the crowd of thousands of students and walked to our next class

I couldn't control myself even though I was trying to assist the victim, and all it took was him disrespecting me with one foul word and *I lost it.* Unfortunately, his injuries were so severe, an ambulance transported him to the hospital, and I was escorted to the police station in our school.

For years, my parents hadn't spoken to law-enforcement or administration at any school about my conduct, but those years were clearly over. I stayed in trouble. My addiction to alcohol, weed, and formaldehyde were ruining the relationships I had with my family and with Nora. In school, I noticed her wearing another student's coat and I snapped. Within a blink of an eye, I grabbed her by her hand and broke her thumb without meaning to. Another morning while she and I were walking and I was pleading for her to forgive me, a teacher attempted to snatch my hoodie and headphones from my head, and I turned around and smashed the teacher's head against a brick wall and she dropped to the ground.

I was changing as a person and felt extremely remorseful for hurting the girl I loved, assaulting and injuring the teacher, and even felt bad for the student that I could've given brain damage to. I had no control over my emotions and nothing I did seemed to stop me from violently attacking anyone that made me feel uncomfortable. I'd acknowledged that mentally healthy individuals would've walked away after the first gun was pointed at them, or would've given up when they'd received a concussion while not being welcomed into a gang, but I had underlying issues that hadn't been addressed, and the more I used drugs and drank alcohol, the more I lost control of my impulses.

The events that occurred since attending Garfield High School transformed me. I went from an anxious and scared boy standing in the middle of the school, surrounded by thousands of strangers, to a young man that became an addict to many vices and was making a name for himself. I wanted everyone that was affiliated in the county to acknowledge the name Omen, and the more I grew closer to my mission of becoming gang related, I realized that I was becoming addicted to the lifestyle itself.

CHAPTER 5

DRAMA CITY

At five feet tall and one-hundred pounds, my body took a pounding as dozens of gang members assaulted me while I was on my own personal quest. As one of the only non-African American men in the gang, I knew I was going to be tested by both my gang and rival gangs, but I could never see the consequences of what I'd signed up for. When the gang assisted me to my feet, after being initiated, I wiped the blood from my mouth and one of them handed me a bottle of liquor and a blunt of weed. Every one of my new brothers, at the undisclosed location, showed me love like I'd never felt from anyone outside my family, and four of us got into a car and we drove away.

As I sat in the back seat, the physical pain that I endured was outweighed by a sense of relief. For the first time, I felt I hadn't been rejected. I was welcomed as a part of something much bigger than anything I'd ever experienced. The physical and mental stress that I endured wasn't for a lost cause, and though I was exhausted from the journey getting to that day, I was humbled and proud to be in that car with my new brothers.

I quickly learned that there were rules, and that it was structured and organized. If you tried too hard to show off in the public eye, you were dealt with accordingly. If you thought you were above the rest, unfortunate situations occurred. Within the gang, there were smaller cliques, individuals that were always around one another, but everything we did, we did it together. We knew when rival gangs were plotting, so we always stuck together. When we went to parties, we went in large numbers. My brothers always went home at night, but for some reason I always found myself wanting to stay away from home. I had a nice home, a loving family, good food on the table, a fire in the fireplace, a warm bed, security from people like us that were outside at night, but something was tugging at me from another direction.

It may have been that I wasn't able to drink alcohol at home at a young age—or the fact that I wanted to smoke cigarettes and do drugs while my parents wanted a better life for my sister and me. Though I knew my mother began to worry, the addiction to the substances and being able to have sex everywhere but home, unfortunately overpowered the love that I received from my family.

One of new places that I began to hang out, after I was initiated, was at Kane's house—the gangster who took me under his wing, or volunteered to look over me and pass down knowledge of what it meant to be a soldier in the gang. He lived with his mother and his younger sister, and we set up shop in his garage, and whenever we were done doing our rounds in streets, we'd return to the garage to discuss our affairs while drinking and smoking weed.

Often, since I was so small, we would take a drive at night while smoking formaldehyde and go to an undisclosed location where we would be out of sight and out of mind. We would pull into an empty cul-de-sac and just sit in the car while we drank and smoked. I would look out of the window and stare at miles of empty fields under the bright moon thinking about how I became *Omen* and what it meant for me to be respected by my peers. When we were done smoking, we'd all get out of the car and they would fight me until I couldn't take anymore. They wanted to toughen me up. Make sure that I could handle the punishment when we fought with rival gangs, and though my scrawny body continued to take a beating, I continued to show up.

I was still attending Garfield while this was going on but not putting forth the effort to learn and complete the curriculum. It was more of a meeting place for some of us and the perfect place for us to network and talk to girls. My sister and Dre were about to have a baby as well, and many times while Dre was busy handling his affairs for the gang, he would have his right hand in the gang to assist my sister and I whenever we needed anything. Conor was an Irish brother that collected money and debts for the gang, and if I had basketball practice, a game, needed money, or just needed a ride somewhere, Conor was always there for me.

He was always welcomed into our home by our parents, but my mother always said that he was unwise because he followed orders and never spoke up for himself. But regardless of her wise opinion, he was my brother, and because he wasn't an African American brother in our gang, I could relate due to the fact that there were only a few of us that were welcomed and acknowledged with that affiliation.

During that same year, the relationship between Nora and I was all but demolished. She gained a lot of interest from other young men, especially when they noticed we weren't on good terms. She was a beautiful girl, and the more I pushed her away with my antics, the closer they moved in. One of the young men that caught her eye was in a gang that we didn't get along with and that caused violence to ensue in and outside of the school. I was still much smaller than every other gang member in the county, but that didn't mean anything to me. They wanted to cause me harm, and I was willing to do whatever it took to cause them harm.

It became such an issue in Garfield that the administration called for a mediation between me and the rival gang member. But all that did was give us a platform to threaten one another and let the school know that our intentions were far worse than they could've ever imagined. Another student that wasn't affiliated with any gang, had feelings for Nora and thought it would be funny to call and threaten to blow up my parents' house. Instead of being himself, he disguised his voice and acted like he was the gang member that I was at war with.

He likely planned it out to where both of us gang members would kill each other off or be sent to jail, so he could live happily ever after with Nora without either of us in the picture. Unfortunately for him, one of Nora's sisters told me who it was, and I created a plot to take his life. Fortunately for him, there were too many real threats in my life to remember that I was going to burn his parents' house down with him in it.

While the chaos was just getting started, I met a student named Hayes that moved to Virginia from a southern state. Hayes was one cool cat. He dressed nice, spoke quietly, and drove a beautiful older model Cadillac. He didn't speak much and stayed to himself, but he and I became increasingly close throughout the remainder of the school year. The gang knew that Hayes and I were close, and one evening while we were talking some things over in Kane's garage, they saw an opportunity and presented it to the table. They requested that I'd speak to Hayes about doing business with his connections down south. They wanted to make the trip when school let out for the summer to pick up a large quantity of marijuana, while possibly creating a new connection in the southern state.

I spoke to Hayes about the proposition the next day after school, and a few days later, he said his connections gave us the green light. When school was to let out for the summer, my brothers and I were to travel south, with Hayes, to introduce ourselves to the marijuana supplier, but two days later, my father told me that my family was going to Tucson for my Aunt and Uncle's wedding renewal. By that time, my sister had her beautiful baby girl and my family wanted to get away from Virginia, the Pentagon, my mother's job, and spend some much-needed time in Mexico relaxing on the beach with our relatives. The kicker was, I was to go with them, and I was beside myself. There was no way that I'd be able to back out of the plan that my brothers presented to me. I was the one who was closest to Hayes and felt it would be disrespectful to back out.

The next day, I decided I was going to tell my father that I wouldn't be travelling to Tucson with my family. That it wasn't a good time for me and that I was going to stay in Virginia, but that plan backfired and didn't go over so well for me. I ended up going to Kane's garage and telling the gang that I was going home with my family, and that I wouldn't be going on the trip down south. They gave me the okay and told me that their trip was moving forward as planned. A few days later when school let out for summer break,

Hayes and I showed our respect for one another and we both went our separate ways.

My trip to the southwest was exactly what I needed without acknowledging it at real time speed. It was serene to stand with my feet in the ocean as I did as a young boy and I was taken back by a sense of peace that I hadn't felt since I was in Mexico years prior. My relatives were the same as they were when we moved away, just older, and it was a blessing to see everyone in one place enjoying each other's company.

But reality came back quickly. No more soft sand between my toes or waves crashing onto the shore. I was back in Dale City and anxious to see how the trip down south went with my brothers. I immediately called my 'off brand' buddies to pick me up because they were the guys that helped me make money. I wasn't selling to my own gang of course, so I had a large group of people that I kept close that loved to party. They were stocking up on alcohol, LSD, formaldehyde, cocaine, weed, and most importantly, they were calling every female they knew. They were planning for a big night of partying and I was their connection for the weed, and they were happy that I was back in town.

When they arrived at my parents' house, they were already high on LSD and laughing hysterically when I got in the car. I knew right then that it was going to be a long day. We drove to Dre's house and I told the "dazed and confused" to stay in the car while I went in to pick up the package. While I was loading the marijuana into a small duffle bag, I asked Dre how it went down south and where Conor was, but he must not have heard me because he didn't answer. I asked him again as I raised my voice, thinking he may have left the room, but there was still no response.

I stood up with the bag over my shoulder and headed for the front door. As I headed toward the stairs, I stopped and admired a large painting of a Jesus that hung above the staircase. I paused for a moment as it felt like the image was staring into my soul. I began to feel that something was happening in the house, so I took a deep breath, shrugged it off, and began walking down the steps. Dre was standing at the bottom next to the door and our eyes locked like the painting of Jesus did that was now hanging above me. He looked up at me and shook his head in a 'no' motion as tears began to fall from his eyes. My spirit was uneasy and immediately knew something happened to Conor when he avoided my questions moments prior.

I looked down, exhaled, and without a word, I walked past him out of the door and continued to the car full of high partygoers. It wasn't an easy ordeal to get past while going through each day wondering what happened to Conor, but I never asked questions. We all knew, going into the lifestyle, that at any given moment, it could've been any one of us. We could've been hit by a bullet, stabbed, beaten to death, or by any other means the darkness deemed fit. It was our choice to become affiliated and that side of life was violent, wicked and disturbing. I knew I had to humble myself and follow what was written before us or unfortunate consequences would follow.

I could hear my mother's voice calling Conor an unwise young man for following the demands from the men that he looked up to, and it was hard to believe that a brother that was always there for me and my sister was now gone. While law-enforcement investigated his death and learned who he was affiliated with, the garage where only a select few of us hung out in, was raided. We all knew his disappearance would bring questions, and though I had an alibi because I was in Arizona and Mexico during that time, I was mindful of doing anything that may potentially bring unnecessary heat to the gang and me.

When the investigation was complete in the missing persons case, the news stated that his decomposed body was discovered next to a highway in a southern state. Kane, along with another brother that I was always with, Einstein, were arrested for murdering our twenty-two-year-old brother Conor execution style and abandoning his body. After our gang was exposed, I spent most of my time with the 'off brands' laying low. Many people asked questions about Conor's death, but instead of talking about it, I continued to drink and get high, avoiding those questions, because I felt it wasn't anyone else's business.

Conor was dead, Kane and Einstein were incarcerated for his murder, and I learned that Marley was fooling around with Nora behind my back before I was initiated into the gang. I was hurt and full of resentments but continued to stay away from home even though my parents loved me more than anyone in the streets ever would. I'd already rested my head in at least six different houses while still in high school, but the freedom my parents granted me was pushing me closer to the edge of darkness, and no one could foresee the trouble that was about to be unleashed in my life.

That year, all hell broke loose in Northern Virginia. Homes were burnt to the ground, cars were set on fire, and the gangs from Alexandria, Dumfries, Manassas, Woodbridge and Dale City were in an all-out war. Every weekend there was violence at high school football games, basketball games, in restaurant parking lots, house parties, and in the clubs in and around D.C. In Northern Virginia, Washington D.C., and certain areas in Maryland, there was a regional music called Go-go. It originated in Washington D.C. in the mid-sixties to early seventies, and its origin came from the Funk-Soul era. By the nineties, there were dozens of new bands from different neighborhoods, streets, or sides of the city in which they resided. The bands had all the components of a regular band, but as time passed, Hip-Hop became more influential in the Go-go scene, and a new era was taking over.

Some of the members of the gang, along with other young men that were well known in Northern Virginia, put together a Go-go band in Dale City. They practiced at the Gomez brothers house that let me use their phone, years prior, when Joker was shot through his window. Their home became a place where I eventually rested my head at night.

And the corner stayed busy. There was always alcohol, marijuana, Pit Bulls, Go-go music and girls. It became a hotspot in the neighborhood, and though the Gomez brothers themselves weren't ever affiliated, I loved and trusted them more than I did most. It became more evident, as time went by, that the new era of Go-go had become more violent than previous years. The recipe for violence came when different gangs and neighborhoods attended the shows and would show force through large numbers. People were constantly getting assaulted at the shows and more times than not, the victims were right in the thick of things throwing up gang signs before being hospitalized.

I witnessed a young man get beaten to death within a massive crowd that had erupted, and the fight eventually spilled out into the neighborhood where even more people were vulnerable. The wars were a violent game of Chess in the streets, but when we were crammed into large public venues, these situations became all-out riots with only one exit to escape.

One night, we mobbed into a number of vehicles and drove across the bridge to the "Ice Box," a Go-go venue where the local band, "The Northeast Groovers," were performing. On the way there, we smoked formaldehyde and passed several bottles around, so we were all tipsy enough to enjoy ourselves while listening to the live band. When we arrived, the band was performing, and beautiful girls were already dancing to the Go-go beat. The room was dark, and I was so high that I just stood in the back of the hall, out of sight and out of mind. My brothers, along with some other young men that rode with us from Dale City, were already in the middle of the crowd throwing up gang signs, while others wandered off to talk with girls.

A few moments later the song they were playing ended and the entire venue became silent. Folks were sweating and trying to catch their breath, when suddenly the band started their next tune. The lead singer opened his mouth, "Play truth or dare! Play truth or dare!" I knew immediately what song it was, and I knew all hell was going to be unleashed in the club. I felt the tension from within the walls, and every thugs' demeanor in the building changed instantly. Everyone knew what was coming next, and I literally felt evil taking over the dark room.

I scoped the entire venue to prepare myself from what was manifesting within the crowd, and to see where my brothers were. Though the band was performing, and the man on the microphone's voice was slowly rising, I couldn't hear a thing.

I noticed a large group of men walking in from the entrance, as another group from inside began walking toward them. The two groups merged and entered the crowd as one. I could feel their energy and knew that they resided in the neighborhood by the way everyone was acknowledging them. Many of the smaller groups backed away from the crowd, but my brothers didn't move an inch. They weren't intimidated by anyone, regardless of how low our numbers were compared to some of the other gangs in front of the stage.

I began walking toward my brothers to alert them that something didn't feel right, when suddenly, *someone yelled*, "Play truth or dare! Play truth or dare… FIGHT!" As soon as he yelled "fight," punches were being thrown and bodies were flying. "FIGHT," the lead singer continued, and I couldn't reach the middle of the crowd as bodies were knocking me to the ground. I attempted to force my way through but to no avail. The gang from D.C. and my gang, along with our 'off brand' counterparts from Dale City, were in front of the stage throwing haymakers. The band stopped playing but the fighting didn't stop. People were scattering, trying to stay away from the violence, and after a few minutes, everyone from Northern Virginia began walking toward the exit. When I walked outside, I felt more evil manifesting amongst the large crowd, and I knew in my heart that the fighting wasn't over.

I got separated from my gang as we walked toward the parking lot, then I noticed Joker walking toward me yelling, "Run, Omen! Behind you!" I turned my head to see what he was hollering about, and…*BOOM!* I got hit in the side of my face. Another man ran up from behind and hit me in the back of the head. I looked up and saw Joker running, in the opposite direction. He was the same brother that got shot years prior through his window and I ran toward the gun shots. I then ran to the Gomez brothers' house to call Dre to alert the gang about his well-being when I wasn't even affiliated yet.

I was trying to come to terms about why he would run away while I was getting man handled, but those thoughts were immediately being knocked out of my mind. Blow after blow, I was taking punishment by the D.C. gang. I glanced up for a second and noticed two D.C. Police officers smoking cigarettes, watching as the neighborhood gang handed me the worst beating that I'd ever taken. Another blow connected to my mouth. I was fighting for my life and knew they were going to kill me if I didn't continue to fight back. I could hear more of them jumping a chain link fence and running toward me, and every single one of them got their punches in.

I saw five or six men running up to the growing crowd, and for a split second I had hope that they were there to help me, until one of them punched me directly in the forehead. At that point I saw light. I swung and prayed and swung and prayed as they continued to punish me. Two of the men grabbed the Timberland boots off my feet, another tore the shirt from my chest, when another hit me in the stomach knocking the wind out of me. One…two…three…four…five…six more blows to the head until I couldn't find the strength to swing anymore. Another blow landed to the side of my face as I was crouched down praying for them to stop.

I didn't want to look up anymore because I truly felt one more blow to my head would kill me. As the blood poured from my face, I heard doors closing and vehicles driving away as innocent bystanders outside the club began to ask if I was alright. I knew from experience that if a neighborhood gang was involved in any acts of violence, innocent bystanders were not to get involved. They were always afraid of retaliation, even if they were to have watched me die that night, they would have said nothing.

As for Joker leaving me to find the rest of our gang, I made a conscious decision that I wouldn't put myself in a situation where I could be in danger around him. Within the gang, we all had different strengths.

As they were strengths to some, they were weaknesses to others. Some had the business mentality and could sell ice to an Eskimo; thus, they were hustlers. Some of us weren't successful in that area because we used the product before we could make the profit. There were pimps. Again, some of us weren't productive at that because we would sleep with the girls instead of focusing on the profit. Then there were those that put in work. Had no respect for life and bulldozed their way through every relationship they ever had. If someone tested their manhood, wicked things happened.

There would be no logical reason, after that night, for me to surround myself with certain individuals that would run from another brother that was in distress. I did learn a lesson that night. *Another lesson.* Trusting people was going to be a difficult thing to do. Always contemplating if this brother or that brother would tell on me, leave me for dead, sneak around with my girlfriend, or overlook the loyalty they promised to represent. It wasn't an easy issue to bring to the table when you didn't trust certain individuals. Putting their character in the spotlight, in front of many other gang members that were in fact trustworthy, was dangerous. I knew that everyone played a position in this life, but unfortunately for some, they never found theirs before they lost their lives.

Mentally, it was an everyday battle, how to go about handling situations that I couldn't wrap my head around. I questioned others honor and separated myself from many of my brothers and continued to drink myself comatose. I met every morning with a drink and a blunt of weed. I dressed in fatigues, laced up my boots, grabbed my ski-mask and walked out of whoever's door I was laying my head at for that night.

I often stopped by my parents' house to see how they were doing even though they were upset and disappointed at my actions. One evening, while I was high on formaldehyde, I entered their house but forgot to put on a long-sleeved shirt that always covered my gang-tattoo; that was my way of showing respect in my parents' home. My mother and I greeted one another in the living room, and as I moved in to give her a hug, she instantly noticed my tattoo. She slapped me across my chest and face continuously as I was attempting to justify how the gang wasn't filled with bad people. She screamed at me. "Liar! You liar! You guys killed Conor! How can you say you're not bad people? Your gang murdered him!" As she continued, I put my hands up and attempted to gently sit her down on the large sofa behind her, but her foot stubbed the coffee table and she fell back onto the soft couch.

She wasn't in any way injured, but my father must have heard the commotion from upstairs, and when he witnessed my mother falling on to the sofa, he immediately assumed that I was being aggressive. He walked into the living room, grabbed me by my throat, and carried me into the hallway by their front door. He then slammed me on my back, began choking me, and cocked his right arm up above his head.

My father was a very strong man. He lifted weights and exercised constantly since I could remember. And though I was extremely high on PCP, I knew his patience for my lack of respect had worn thin. "You listen to me, you little punk. I will fucking kill you if you ever put your hands on my wife again. I have two kids, and only one wife. It will be you if one has to go," my father said. He swung down as I awaited the brutal blow to my face, but he spared me and chose to hit the ground instead. He wrapped my undershirt into his fists, snatched me up, opened the front door, and threw me through the screen door onto the porch. As I attempted to reach my feet, he grabbed the broken screen door and bent the aluminum frame around my neck until I couldn't breathe. My mother ran outside and begged him to let go, but his adrenaline was at its core and he continued as I was losing consciousness.

My mother was finally able to reach him with her pleading cries and he miraculously let go. As I stumbled into the grass and grasped for air, I turned around and threatened to kill him. He openly invited me and everyone I knew to come to his house to test him, promising that he would shoot every single one of us if we returned to his property.

High and coming to terms with what happened, I walked through the small, wooded area in front of their house and stumbled onto the dark road, continuing to walk until I reached a small gas station a mile away. As I was searching for change in my pocket to make a phone call, a dark sedan pulled up from behind me. I immediately thought, with my luck, it was another gang that was finally catching up to me, and they were going to finish what my father started. Then a voice yelled, "Damn, Omen; what the hell happened to you?" I turned around and was a bit relieved when I saw that it was a friend of mine named Pete from the 'K' streets in Dale City.

Pete and his girlfriend gave me a ride to my brother Remy's apartment, and in the morning after I was able to sleep off my high, I came to my senses and wanted to apologize to my parents. I walked in my parents' home, like I'd done one hundred times, to say sorry for something I did. I knew at that point that my words meant nothing. I was a liar, I was a thief, and I was becoming everything they wished their children wouldn't become. I entered the opening of the kitchen and my father was cooking, as he did faithfully and well after a long day's work at the Pentagon. Before I was able to open my mouth, he began speaking to me without ever looking at me, "Did you hear about your buddy Pete? He was murdered today. Shot in the back of the head." I didn't believe him. It couldn't have been true. "It's not possible," I replied in disbelief. I continued, "He...he and his girlfriend found me at a gas station last night after I walked off. He was going to Florida; they were leaving. How did you hear that?" "It's all over the news. Another one of your friends is dead and you need to figure something out before you're all over the news," my father demanded.

Pete's death was a result of hatred. Though he was a young white man, he had many friends from all walks of life. And the day after he dropped me off, he along with three young men, that we all knew from Dale City, drove into a cul-de-sac in search of a dead deer that one of them had seen earlier. When they exited the vehicle, to find the carcass so they could remove it, two white men chopping wood spotted them and began yelling racial slurs at two of the young men that weren't white. When all four young men, that we all knew, attempted to enter the vehicle to leave without incident, a thirty-one-year-old white man pointed his gun at the scrambling group, shooting Pete dead.

In the streets, there were unwritten rules. They were guidelines of sorts that we all needed to follow in order to stay alive. For those of us that chose that lifestyle, we signed up for whatever happened to us the day we stepped over the so-called line. And if we crossed that line, without having absolute knowledge of what we were walking into, we wouldn't have been able to watch our own backs throughout the chaos. People owing money, talking too much and not humbling themselves, being incarcerated and testifying on their so-called brothers or sisters, disregarding what higher ups laid out as far as what not to do, turning away from loyalty and honor, were all reasons why we were losing people close to us.

But Pete's tragedy held no logical reasoning. He was a funny young man that was loved by all that knew him. He respected those of us in the gang, and because he chose to live differently, we all respected him even more so because he never crossed that line of becoming affiliated. The men that killed Pete hated the skin color of two young men that were with him that day. I was very close to both young black men, before I was initiated, and they were great friends of mine before I crossed the line into the gang life. They weren't criminals and had no intentions of harming anyone. Unfortunately, racism toward humans with a different skin tone, left all three of his close friends remembering that moment, and a loving father childless, without ever being able to hold his son again.

It wasn't long after that tragedy that one of the most violent nights I ever experienced happened. It was chaos in the streets. A back-and-forth bloody mess. On this specific night, my brother Otto and I were on a mission. For hours, we travelled through different neighborhoods retaliating on other gangs without letting our rivals know who we were. While we crept into hostile territory later that night, a rival gang member unloaded an entire clip of bullets at me, and my life was spared by mere inches, maybe even centimeters. At the end of our violent and adrenaline filled night, I told Otto and two other brothers to drop me off at my parents' house, after a vision came to me while I was sitting in the back seat of the car. I'd already been told on numerous times in the past, and if one of my brothers started talking, I didn't want to be around in case one of them were taken down by law-enforcement.

When I walked in the front door of my parents' house, I saw them sitting in their favorite spots in the living room by the fireplace. With all the thoughts going through my mind, I headed straight for the stairs attempting to flee any conversation. As I reached the first step, my father asked to speak with me in the living room. As I sat down, they expressed their concerns for my well-being and told me that I was dropping out of high school, because I wasn't putting forth the effort to pass my classes, and that my young life had become unmanageable. Then they went on to say that I was being flown out of the state.

At first thought, I was upset because of my loyalty to the gang, and I didn't want to leave Nora even though our relationship was long over. I resented my parents' decision, but as I sat there listening to them voice their concerns, I began to contemplate the situation at hand. I'd just been involved in multiple acts of violence, folks were being 'told on' left and right, and my spirit was telling me to hear my parents out.

My father expressed his disappointments about my lack of effort in life, and how my mother was truly afraid of all the violence surrounding me since my brothers in the gang were dying or going to prison. They had no clue about the things I'd done outside of school, but they knew I was gang affiliated, they saw things my gang and I had a hand in while watching the news, they saw many of the injuries I endured on multiple occasions, and they were working closely with the school after I committed multiple acts of violence.

My loving parents were at a loss as everything in my life went full tilt and realized they couldn't handle me anymore. My mother then looked at me and told me that I was going to Apache Junction, Arizona to live with my grandparents for a while. I was torn at the thought of leaving what I'd created since being at Garfield, but if there was ever a time that I needed a change of scenery, it was at that exact moment, and I hoped that this change of scenery would bring peace into my life and I would change my negative ways.

CHAPTER 6

SELF WILL RUN WILD

Though I was away from the environment in Virginia and the people who I associated myself with, I was still a thief and a liar. It was an all-out battle within myself, in my own mind, and there wasn't anything anyone could do but sit back and watch as I made a fool out of myself time and time again.

My loving grandparents gave me an opportunity to find myself as a young man and they were willing to open their doors to assist me with whatever I needed to succeed. I worked with my grandfather in their mobile home community, maintaining the large swimming pool every morning, and landscaping residents' yards for those that were unable to keep up due to their age and or physical disabilities. I had a wonderful time with my grandparents, but it was necessary that I moved closer to Phoenix, where I could find a job and study for my GED. While the plan had been set for me to go to my mother's cousin's house in Scottsdale, my great-grandmother passed away and my grandparents needed to travel out of state to attend her service.

I loved my grandparents. I appreciated them for taking the time to assist me, but it didn't matter how kind people were to me, or how much they sacrificed to help me, I had serious issues. At the end of the day, I was the way I was, and it was as if I was allergic to making righteous decisions. I was to stay only one night in their home alone and my cousin Royce would be picking me up the next day. I expressed my gratitude and hugged my grandparents before they drove away into the night. As soon as they were gone, I went through their nice home looking for anything valuable to steal. I came across two guns in a dresser drawer and put both guns in my bag. I quickly thought it over and put one of the guns back because I wanted to leave my grandfather at least one to protect themselves if need be.

I also stole a nice flask that my grandfather owned for years. I justified my actions internally due to the fact that I was an alcoholic and felt that I needed the flask more than my grandfather did. I also justified myself taking one of his guns because I was paranoid after everything I'd been through, and in my mind, it was a good gesture by not stealing both.

The next day, my cousin Royce picked me up in his low-rider truck that had hydraulics and took me to their home ten miles Northwest of Phoenix. This was a cool family. My mother's aunt, Pearl, lived in the home for years and when my great uncle passed away, her son Miguel and his family moved in to be closer to her. The father Miguel, who was my second cousin, had just returned home from the war in the Middle East and was a disciplined man. His wife Sandy was a sweet woman who loved her family and you could tell by the way the family appreciated each other's company. Royce and his sister Alexia were my age and I spent the majority of my time with my cousin Royce before finding a new job.

They opened their home to me, and again, I was appreciative of their kindness. I was able to obtain my GED and got my first job at a pizza place around the corner. As time passed, Royce introduced me to a few of his friends and while I wasn't working, I began spending time with them because they drank and smoked weed. They would take me to parties when I wanted to get out of the house, but whenever young men thought they were tough and started mouthing off, I quickly pulled my grandfather's gun. I had no self-control. No regard for human life. And though people spoke about fighting with fists, and how people were weak that used guns, I was much smaller than everyone else, and didn't want to get caught by someone else who may have had a gun themselves.

If you added alcohol and any other substances to an environment, where there were dozens of people, anyone could be shot for being disrespectful. Because I'd committed some serious violent acts against others and was a gang-member, I also knew when people were soft as tissue; I knew that most of the young men that instigated confrontations, were weak, bogus, and wanted to be gangsters.

After a while, I was spending a good amount of time with Royce's friends, regardless if he was around or not. Royce didn't use drugs or engage in illegal activities, and it was strange to me that he even associated with the young men. He was a clean cut, good looking young man that was great at playing baseball. His buddies were quite the opposite. They had no jobs, loved getting high, and were exactly what I needed for the time being.

One day, while we were sitting around one of the young men's swimming pool, a young female brought out a plastic bag and a can of spray paint. She handed it to one of the young men, he sprayed it into the bag, and began huffing it. I had no idea what was going on and I questioned what they were doing, but they respectfully asked me to stay quiet while he huffed the chemicals. They told me if we spoke loudly, or made too much noise, that it would affect the process while he was huffing. I sat back in the lawn chair thinking to myself, *I've partaken in a lot of stupid things in my life, but huffing spray paint out of a grocery bag is way out there. No way am I stooping to that level just to get high.* Moments later, the group asked me if I wanted to try it, but I respectfully declined. Royce's friend explained that he was huffing quietly one day looking off into the sky, when an airplane took off from Sky Harbor Airport. He went on to say, as soon as the plane flew into the background, he ended up on the airplane's wing, flying through the clouds while swinging his legs and drinking a soda pop. Me being the weak-willed addict that I was, I liked how that sounded.

The young female then handed me a plastic bag and the can of spray paint. I glanced at everyone and looked down at the bag. I sprayed the paint into the bag, cupped the top of the bag in my hand, and began to huff slowly. I was staring off into the swimming pool and the slower and longer I huffed, the deeper I transcended out of reality.

A friend of theirs walked through the house and into the backyard yelling and hollering to his friends. Everyone was cursing at the young man and telling him to be quiet, but the damage had already been done. My brain was in shock. I was stuck. My head was vibrating, and it felt and sounded like a gas generator was running inside of me. It took me a few moments to come out of the sudden and brutal interruption by their friend, and the group apologized and suggested that I tried it in a quiet place away from people. That way I would be able to enjoy it like they had in previous experiences.

The next evening while my relatives were gone, and Royce was sleeping, I walked into their backyard and into their shed. It didn't take long before I found a can of spray paint and it was the exact type I needed to get high. It read, "DO NOT INHALE." I entered the house, grabbed a plastic bag, and walked outside and sat by their swimming pool. I took a deep breath, sprayed the paint into the bag, and cupped it as I made a closed fist. I began huffing slowly and stared off into the evening sky. As I felt the chemicals taking over, I noticed an airplane flying low through the palm trees. I thought to myself, *this is my chance to experience what they experienced*. As soon as I attempted to focus on the plane, the streetlights on the main road behind their house flickered on, and I was stuck.

I immediately beamed into the streetlamp. The electricity was running through my body at the speed of light and I couldn't escape it. I transported into a different dimension and at the bottom of the electrified tunnel it showed two options. "Negative or Positive." It was all happening so fast and I felt that if I chose the incorrect option, something terrifying would occur. Without difficulty, I quickly chose positive. It may have been the wrong choice and I would never know. As I made my decision, electricity bolted through my body and exited out of my throat. I literally felt my skin melting and blood shot out into the swimming pool. I could smell my skin sizzling. I panicked. I dropped the can of spray paint along with the bag and ran into the house.

I made it through the hallway and jumped onto Royce who was sound asleep. He immediately jumped in panic and threw me into the bathroom. I felt I was dying and believed I was having a heart attack as he turned on the lights. I quickly but nervously glanced at the mirror expecting my throat to be disintegrated, but it wasn't. I seemed to have been physically well at first glance. I closed my eyes, bowed my head, and took a deep breath. I slowly looked up to the mirror and there was in fact no burning skin or blood anywhere on my body. I turned to Royce and apologized for causing such a ruckus. He looked at me, shook his head, and went back to his room.

I stared at myself in the mirror for quite a while. I couldn't believe what just happened. My throat which was sizzling from being electrocuted just before was intact. There were no physical injuries to my exterior, and I will never know if I was having a heart attack at such a young age. It did take a while for me to recover from what happened that day, and though I never got to experience a good high like the other addicts did, I never huffed paint again.

I continued to work at the pizza place and got comfortable with just smoking weed and playing video games on my down time. One evening, while I was walking home from work to do just that, I noticed my relatives were in the driveway talking with my grandfather. I was excited and looking forward to seeing him since we hadn't spent much time after I'd left Apache Junction a few months prior. As I approached the house to greet everyone, I looked around and the mood was somber, and I noticed that my grandfather was upset. "What's going on, Grandpa? What happened?" I asked with concern. But my grandfather responded, "How could you steal from me after everything your grandmother and I did for you? How dare you act like you care!" I was busted and caught off guard, but replied, "I...I...I'm sorry, Grandpa, I w...," but he wasn't willing to hear my lies, as he immediately turned his back and walked away.

While my great-aunt Pearl was folding my clothes and placing them in my suitcase, she found the gun and the flask inside a large pocket, before calling my grandparents. I was exposed, and Miguel knew that I'd been stealing from his family ever since I arrived in Scottsdale and requested that I take a ride with him to Casa Grande to where his National Guard Battalion was located. As we drove through the desert, he began explaining that his brother was an unreliable, dishonest, alcoholic that abandoned his wife and daughters. And how if we were to have seen his brother walking in the scorching desert heat or stranded along the desolate road, he would have continued passing without slowing down, leaving my untrustworthy second cousin for dead.

I knew in my heart what he was insinuating, but instead of him leaving me in the desert after disrespecting him and his family, he drove me through the desert to speak to me about life and to plant a seed about me possibly joining the military before I wasted my life like his brother did. After we returned that evening, the items that I'd taken were nonchalantly tossed back into their rooms, and within days, I was passed along to another family in Corona De Tucson.

Being passed around from relative to relative didn't help my psyche, and if anything, I felt out of place because of the stress I endured, but fully understood that my parents were calling everyone they knew out of desperation. The relatives I stayed with all had decent lives and were going on about their daily routines when *boom*...there I was sitting in their respective dining rooms eating dinner while contemplating making my next move.

While staying in Corona, I rode with my uncle Kingston who rebuilt old Scouts and Broncos, while my aunt Penelope was busy teaching and my younger cousins attended school. My uncle Kingston had a little shop in South Tucson, and I ended up just smoking weed and waiting for the Mexican food trucks to arrive for lunch because I had the munchies.

After a few months of not doing anything but hiding from my life in Virginia, I moved into the city of Tucson with my cousin Kyler and his friends. I quickly found connections in the apartment complex and had sexual relationships with many of the girls that resided there. But I stuck out like a sore thumb. I wore Timberland boots and fatigues, and though I was born in the state, I spoke differently than the locals and carried myself in a different manner. I was quickly known in the area as "D.C." short for 'Drama City' or Dale City, Virginia.

I was quickly befriended by an older gentleman named Levi from New Jersey that resided in the complex. He and I spent a lot of time drinking on his balcony, while looking over the neighborhood and talking about life on the east coast. It was nice to share knowledge and understanding with someone from across the country that understood that way of living, and his apartment became the only place that made me feel sane after being around the younger individuals throughout each day.

A few weeks after my arrival, my cousin Kyler moved out of town and the consensus among his roommates was that I was welcome to stay if I chose to. But instead of finding a job and utilizing my time as a reliable young man, I continued to steal, have sex with multiple girls, and drank heavily and smoked weed, all while continuing to set up new connections throughout the complex.

I also learned that Tucson was infested with drugs, and figured it was because Mexico was just south on Interstate-19 where drugs were sold at seventy-five percent less than they were on the east coast, so I began selling to support my habits. I'd done LSD on multiple occasions in the past, and always enjoyed myself, so when one of the roommates was planning on purchasing a 'sheet of acid' for the 4th of July, I chipped in to make a profit while being able to use the product.

After we divided the LSD among those who purchased it, we started the party and many of the residents were high, or 'tripping balls,' within the first hour. One of the drunkards in the complex walked over to purchase a few squares of LSD, and when we opened the front door, he began hollering at me over someone's shoulder because we'd already sold it all and he wanted to get high. I walked to the door to confront the angry drunk, but one of the roommate's jumped in front of me and punched the neighbor in the face, knocking him out. I stood on the front porch looking over the unconscious man as the neighborhood folk were drunk and high and out of their minds. They were cheering and yelling out profanities at the dazed man as I assisted him to his feet. I felt bad because I'd been hit in the head a number of times, and knew he was obviously drunk, so I suggested that he go home and sleep it off before the situation got worse.

As the night went on, people from all over the complex were standing outside and celebrating our Independence with their friends and neighbors. While I was outside talking with Levi from the east coast, I looked over his shoulder and noticed the angry neighbor walking toward us. "Go back home. You're drunk, brother." I suggested respectfully but as a warning. As soon as those words left my mouth, the man disrespected me, and Levi turned around and placed his handgun in the man's mouth. "Turn around, go home, and leave D.C. alone. This is my only warning, son." As the crowd began to get rowdy, the drunk man was being escorted back to his apartment by his two roommates.

The two men apologized on his behalf and were heading home when the angry man broke free and charged at me. Without a moment's notice, men from the neighborhood jumped on the man, beating him brutally and dragging him back to his apartment up the concrete steps. Time and time again, the stubborn, drugged and drunk man, would exit his apartment during our celebration, and attempted to attack me for not selling him a few squares of LSD. I continued to advocate for the poor soul as different men took turns beating him. I witnessed on multiple occasions, men dragging the bloody man up the concrete steps while assaulting him because he refused to listen. It was sickening. I felt his pain through my own experiences, but the locals that knew me, respected me and seemed to do whatever it took to keep me safe from anyone trying to cause harm to me.

Later, during the early morning hours, I walked over to the apartment to check on the injured man. When his roommates welcomed me in, the room was cloudy, and I immediately noticed drug paraphernalia on the table. I looked over toward a sofa and saw the defeated man sleeping in his blood drenched clothing. He was swollen from his chest up and the pillow he was resting his head on, was stuck to his face because the blood had dried.

The man that rented the apartment, Jax, told me that once the wounded man was to wake up, he was evicting him from the apartment because of the disrespect and didn't want any problems from the young men in the complex. As I was leaving and expressing how tired I was from staying up all night, Jax asked if I would like to smoke some "Speed." He then pulled a large bag from a dresser drawer containing a substance that didn't quite resemble cocaine.

Someone in Scottsdale showed a bag of "speed," but this bag was much larger and looked like ice. It wasn't a popular drug on the east coast, like heroin and crack were, so I didn't quite understand the dynamic of the drug. Jax told me that it was a street term for Methamphetamine and that it was nothing like either of the other two drugs. Of course, me being me, I sat down when the drug was freely offered before glancing over to the injured man on the other sofa. He hadn't moved a muscle and I began to question if he was still breathing. Jax then pulled out a broken light bulb and told me that his 'Meth pipe' had broken, but that using a light bulb would give us the same high.

The experienced addict placed what looked to be a scoop of glass shards into the broken bulb before handing me a straw, and suggested that he light it for me since it was my first time and he didn't want me to burn the Meth. I questioned the situation internally and knew that it was a bad idea, but my self-will ran wild at every opportunity. At that point, I had no hopes or dreams of becoming a successful young man, so I sat back and continued to self-destruct around complete strangers that somehow took a liking to me.

As Jax grabbed a torch from the floor, I began to take deep breaths. I was nervous while still coming off the LSD and really didn't know what to expect. He told me to kick back and relax and that I wouldn't be tired after my "first blast." He lit the torch and began to slowly burn the shards in the bottom of the light bulb and said, "Alright, hit it." I took a long, deep breath, and began inhaling the substance that was circulating inside the glass bulb. "Hold it. There you go. Hold it in…now exhale, brother," he instructed me. As I exhaled the smoke, my entire body felt wet.

I was in a place of euphoria. I couldn't move, nor did I want to. I'd never felt anything like it in my entire life and couldn't begin to understand how or why I was feeling that good. He asked, "How do you feel, home boy?" Still in euphoria, I replied, "I'm…I'm… I'm good, bro." "I told you this would wake you up. Here, hit it again," he continued to instruct me. I was still coming to terms with the first hit, then the second one absolutely had me stuck. I was on another planet and the men might as well have been aliens because I'd forgotten their names. After a few hours passed by, I grabbed my suitcase from the other apartment and moved into Jax's apartment moments after he and his friend realized the injured man was alive and kicked him out onto the streets.

Neighbors were questioning why I switched apartments and I made up some lame excuse, but it was because I was addicted to the feeling that Methamphetamine had given me. The euphoria was different than any of the other drugs that I'd used, even though alcohol had me feeling like a superhuman the first day I drank it. Formaldehyde got me so high that I thought I was a prophet and would speak to angels, and huffing paint just didn't work out for me like I'd hoped.

I quickly began riding through Tucson with Jax and he introduced me to a group of men in the complex. The men were rough and rugged, and I could feel the negative energy around them as soon as I entered their apartment. Either way, they had good dope and I wasn't going anywhere. I spent a lot of time doing drugs in both apartments and did what was necessary to support my habit.

One morning while I was getting high with the men upstairs, their telephone rang. The bigger man answered the phone while the rest of us were snorting huge lines of Methamphetamine off their table. I heard the big man pleading on the phone about something, and then he began walking in my direction saying, "The phone is for you, kid." "Excuse me? What do you mean it's for me? I don't know anyone out here," I questioned. "Take the phone, kid," he demanded. *I answered,* "What the f…hello?" A voice was sternly saying, "Don't leave that apartment! Do you understand me?" I toughened up and said, "Who is this?" "It's your uncle Eli. Don't move," he commanded. The big man looked at me nervously as I handed him the phone, saying "Why didn't you tell me who your uncle was?" *I replied,* "What do you mean? Am I supposed to go around telling people the names of my family members? Who cares who my uncle is?" "I do, kid," he insisted with fear in his voice.

A few moments later we could hear a motorcycle pulling into the apartment complex. "That's your uncle; go downstairs and speak with him," the big man replied. When I went to speak with my uncle, he expressed how angry he was. Not with me, but with the big man upstairs that was providing me Methamphetamine. He told me he loved me, said he would check on me later, and had me send the other man outside. After that day, I never saw the man again. I didn't know my uncle Eli's affairs, nor did I wish to know. All I knew is that I was getting involved with people that gave me an evil vibe the moment I'd met them, and I was ready to fly back to Virginia before something happened to me.

I went back to the apartment where my suitcase was, packed the few belongings that I owned, and gave my blessings to everyone I'd met in the apartment complex. As far as Jax, I wished the man well before I walked into the airport, but as my life continued to amaze me, the two of us would cross paths again close to twenty years later, in the place that would save me from a life of addiction and chaos.

CHAPTER 7

WHAT GOES AROUND
COMES AROUND

I landed at Baltimore-Washington International Airport, in Maryland, and still hadn't slept in three days. And though I was heading back to Virginia, I knew living with my parents wasn't an option, so one of my brothers from the gang named Lincoln, who was from New York, picked me up in Baltimore and we crossed state lines back to Prince William County.

On the way to reunite with the gang in Dale City, he and I were driving past my parents' house when we noticed fifteen to twenty vehicles parked outside their home. He quickly pulled his emergency brake and we hydroplaned around the median before pulling into their driveway. I'd never seen that many vehicles at my parents' house, and we were both anxious to see what was going on.

As we exited the car, he placed his .38 caliber pistol in his waistband, and we approached their front door. With Lincoln standing closely behind me, I pounded on the door as we heard loud music coming from inside. The door opened, and a young man that I'd never seen before answered, "Who are you?" The oblivious stoner asked. Before I could swing at him, and as Lincoln was pulling his pistol from over my shoulder, a much larger man rushed to the door and pushed the disrespectful youngster from the inside saying, "My apologies, brother. Please, come in. Hey! Quiet! Your brother is here."

The entire house froze.

The youngster that was on the ground, quickly apologized while Lincoln looked at him placing his handgun back in his waistband. "I didn't know... I didn't know, bro. I'm sorry" the youngster pleaded. It was if they'd seen a ghost when we entered the house. They must've known we were violent and affiliated because they didn't move until my sister approached us.

She was shocked to see me and came to the front door trying to play the situation off like it wasn't a big deal that they were partying in our parents' house. For Lincoln and me, we were one second away from pulling that youngster out of the house for opening my parents' front door and doing so in a disrespectful manner. My sister and her girlfriends quickly pulled us into the kitchen to butter us up with alcohol and Hash, in an attempt to ease the tension. As I walked through the house, I looked at everyone's face because I was still paranoid and wanted to see if I noticed anyone that I didn't care for.

As the partygoers looked and whispered, the much larger Irishman approached me and reached out his hand in a sign of respect. The man named Ronan and I acknowledged one another while shaking hands, and because I was sleep deprived and coming down from the Methamphetamine, the offerings of alcohol and Hash didn't sound like a bad idea. Lincoln and I drank and got high with my sister's people, but my parents were on vacation, they weren't aware of the festivities, and I was used to my sister being in a relationship with Dre ever since I'd attended Garfield. But I quickly saw how things had changed since I'd left for the southwest.

While the party continued and the tension eased, I had a sudden urge to walk upstairs to check the bedrooms. While no one was paying attention, I grabbed a large butcher knife and crept up the stairs. I searched through my parents' room and fortunately for everyone, the room was unoccupied. I checked my old room and my father's gym, and they too were empty. I walked over to my sister's door and opened it slightly, so the hall light would faintly enter. There were bodies spread out across the floor and as I was closing the door to give them their peace, I noticed someone sleeping in my sister's bed. I stepped over the drunken bodies and glanced at the person to see if it was a male or a female, and it was a young man.

I walked on to the bed and placed the knife at his throat. As he slowly opened his eyes and realized what was happening, I quietly asked him, "Who are you…and why are you in my sister's bed?" Startled, he replied, "Holy shit man. I'm your sisters 'boyfriend. My name is Patrick. We were just having a good time and I drank a lot. She said I could sleep in here with the others." I removed the knife, stepped off the bed and exited the room.

I needed to come to terms that my sister was not with Dre anymore, and with some much-needed sleep, was able to gain understanding that it was her journey and not mine. I also had to come to terms with my situation with Nora, who was calling me while I was in Arizona, and writing me letters, even though she hid the fact that she was pregnant by another young man while I was away. Even with me sleeping with many girls in Arizona, I had a resentment and wanted to hunt the young man down for getting her pregnant. I had the desire to let him know who I was. Nora was the first girl that I fell in love with, and though I wasn't good to her, I felt disrespected by the unknown father more so than I did her because of who I was. All the alcohol, weed, and Formaldehyde did was fuel my inability to let situations go. I wasn't a reliable young man that held jobs and faced my responsibilities head on. I was quite the opposite, and knew I had nothing to lose by hunting the young man down and burying him.

Lincoln and his mother were gracious enough to allow me to rest my head at their place, but like me, Lincoln wouldn't let situations go. Resentments got the best of him as well, and he was sent to prison for four years after shooting at a man in Northern Virginia. One-by-one, my brothers in the gang either lost their lives or were sent to the penitentiary for not letting situations rest. It was our egos and pride that led many of us to face consequences that removed us from society or from life in general.

While my self-will continued to run wild, my existence was to be determined by either becoming a responsible human or perishing in the streets with no place to call home. After being homeless and struggling mightily, my parents eventually found it in their hearts to give me another chance and opened their door to me once again. Our agreement was that I was to enlist in the Military and get stationed elsewhere or get a full-time job and enlist into the Virginia Army National Guard. Since I'd obtained my GED in Phoenix, I had what I needed and agreed to enlist in the National Guard so I could stay in Virginia. I went to MEPS, (Military Entrance Processing Station) for my enlisting process and was sworn-in the summer of 1998. I became a 92 Yankee in the 116th Brigade Special Troops Battalion in Fredericksburg, Virginia.

Due to my color blindness, and my scores on the ASVAB (Armed Services Vocational Aptitude Battery) test, I became a Supply Specialist. Responsible for supervising or performing tasks involving the general upkeep and maintenance of all Army supplies and equipment. I issued and received small arms, secured and controlled weapons and ammunition in security areas.

My new job reminded me of my mothers' cousin Miguel in Scottsdale, who drove me through the desert to show me his unit in Casa Grande. I was a smart young man who made poor choices but knew in my heart that I could do anything if I put forth the effort and stayed clean and sober. I had a great experience in the battalion and I even knew a young man from Woodbridge that decided to change his life and wisely left his troubled past. Unfortunately for me, I wouldn't step up and keep my end of the bargain with my parents. Months after I was sworn in, I was discharged for failing a drug test.

It was short lived, and my mother fell apart, having to make the decision to turn her back on me as my grandfather did. I knew it devastated her because I was a 'momma's boy' and she loved me with everything she had. When I went home after they heard the news, I walked into my room, and she'd destroyed everything. My pictures were broken, posters were torn from the walls, and the furniture had been thrown across my room. Once again, due to my lack of being responsible and obedient, I was out of a home, with no money, no car, and walking the streets again. I immediately turned back to a life of crime and did what was necessary to get food. I was able to travel from house to house while living out of a bag, and grateful for the folks that allowed me to take showers in their homes.

I travelled with the "Point-Blank" Go-go band to stay busy and carried equipment just to have places to go. I was on a suicide mission without acknowledging it at real time speed. I continued to drink heavily and used every substance in my arms reach, to numb the feelings of self-pity.

Then on November 8ᵗʰ, 1998, my life would change forever.

I rode with the band to King George County, Virginia for a show. I smoked two joints of Formaldehyde, swallowed two pills of ecstasy, and consumed a bottle of Canadian Mist before the show even started. Before the band performed, one of my older brothers, Prophet, showed me where the weapons were hidden in case a fight were to break out. As the band performed and as folks were having a good time, a fight ensued outside the doors. It all happened so quickly as it always did. Gunshots were fired, and Prophet loudly gave the distress call. I walked over to the stage, unzipped the keyboard bag, and began passing out handguns. As I was turning back toward the stage, I witnessed a friend of mine holding a seventeen-inch police issued Maglite, like a weapon, and charging toward another man. As he attempted to hit the man kneeling on the ground, his own brother Dayton grabbed it out of his hand and threw it as hard as possible trying to break it against the cinderblock wall.

BOOM!

Lights out. I was out. I heard the gunshots, but I was physically unable to move. "Omen got shot! Omen got shot," I heard girls crying for help. I heard my gang fighting in the distance, but for the life of me I couldn't move or think. My spirit was in turmoil, my body was freezing, then it became extremely hot as my motionless body stayed on the floor. I heard first responders asking me my name while bags of ice were being placed on me, but I literally didn't know who I was. They rushed me to a hospital in Fredericksburg to the emergency room, where I laid still in a bed, until a doctor entered the room with my older brother Prophet.

The doctor asked Prophet what happened, and my brother told him it was an accident. I could understand what the two men were saying but wasn't able to speak yet. The doctor walked out of the room and while Dayton attempted to enter the room, Prophet denied him access.

Prophet closed the door and looked down at me saying, "Damn, little brother; I can see your pearly white skull. You're going to be alright though, little bruh. One of our own grabbed a large flashlight at the show and threw it trying to break it against the wall. Unfortunately, your hard ass head was the wall, baby boy." While Prophet continued to console me, I could hear a disturbance in the lobby.

The doctor returned and Dayton attempted to enter the room once again, but it was to no avail. As the group was becoming more distressed in the lobby, the doctor shaved my long hair where the fracture was, cleaned it, pulled my skin over the fracture, stitched my head up, and sent me on my way. No CT scan, no MRI, and no more assistance from the hospital even though I couldn't speak and knew the blow to my head was life altering.

For months, I stuttered and the freezing temperatures during that winter fed me the worst pain I'd ever felt. Being initiated, fighting multiple brothers at a time on several occasions, having a dislocated jaw, a fractured collarbone, and the beat down I took in D.C. combined, couldn't compare to the blow I suffered by that Maglite. There was a dent in my head, and the sharp pains were unbearable, and they were internal. My body was in shock and the winter weather pierced the left side of my brain every time I stepped foot outside, so I was afraid to leave a warm house.

I stayed at a friend of mine's house named "White Boy Rick" that winter and he allowed me to rest in his basement. Because I was so stubborn, I didn't seek medical assistance after the hospital released me prematurely. Instead, I began loading blunts of weed with cocaine. If that didn't numb the pain, I snorted as much Cocaine as I could get my hands on and continued to drink as much liquor as possible. I knew life was moving on with or without me, so I began to leave Rick's house again because I was growing weaker by the day. With having so much physical and mental stress, and not wanting to get hit in my head, I stayed away from large crowds, especially where people were drinking. I also acknowledged that with as many people as I'd harmed in the past, life was getting back at me ten-fold. I was learning firsthand that "karma" was in fact a bitch, and life was her sister, so life was paying me back for being the menace I've been.

During my adolescence, my father would tell me, "Nothing good happens after midnight. There are no logical reasons to be out past midnight unless you have an overnight job." Though I agreed with what he was saying, I chose to stay out past midnight and bad things kept happening to me. *What goes around, comes around* was always a phrase that was thrown out there in the lifestyle we lived. And as far as the fighting went, I had to be extremely cautious and mindful of my surroundings. If I was confronted by a situation where someone wanted to harm me, I used other means to harm them first. I wasn't, under any circumstances, taking another blow to my head by anyone.

As time passed, and the stuttering went away, I met a nice girl named Janine while going out one night with Rick. I was still moving slowly physically and didn't peel back too much of my past because I didn't want to scare her away. Our conversation was a nice one, and after the night was over, we exchanged phone numbers and agreed to see each other again. Around that same time, another girl named Sadie, who I'd known for years, wanted to visit me—this after she and I hadn't seen each other in a while. We were never in a relationship, but we'd slept together countless times, and that's exactly what happened when she came to see me. No deep conversations, no talking about life, just stopping by and doing what we always did, and then she left. Even though I slept with my old friend, Janine and I were seeing each other on a regular basis.

One month later, while recovering from a drunken stupor after drinking myself into a coma the night before, Rick's telephone began to ring and continued ringing. I finally woke up and answered it, "Hello?" The caller replied, "Hey it's Sadie." I said, "Yeah what's up?" Then she shook me, "I'm pregnant, Joel. Joel? Are you there?" I was stunned and managed to muster up, "Okay, yeah…um…yeah, okay. I'll come see you tomorrow and we'll talk." "Okay, Joel…you'd better," she demanded.

After we hung up, I closed my eyes, laid back, and the phone rang again. I reached over and answered it. "Yeah, hello? Hello?" This call was different. All I could hear was a soft voice, crying in the background. I said, "Hello? Who is this?" "It's Janine. Joel… I'm pregnant," she said. I sat up slowly and rubbed my eyes in disbelief. "Are you okay?" I asked in all sincerity. She cried, "No-no, Joel; I'm not okay." As she continued to cry, she said, "My family, my dad… oh, my God. What am I going to do?" I couldn't come to terms with what was unravelling before me. I mustered up, "I…I will support you and be there for you. I'll do whatever you need me to do. Don't worry; we'll figure it out. I'll call you after I shower. It's going to be alright. We're going to be alright."

As I hung up, my head began throwing sharp pains through my entire left side as the anxiety began to take over.

It was necessary for me to calm down within because I didn't have any drugs or alcohol to numb the pain or the anxiety. I was deeply concerned because I had nothing to offer either female, both of whom are certain they were pregnant with my child. I was homeless, jobless, just endured a traumatic brain injury, self-medicated and in the worst of ways. I had no means to provide for myself, let alone two girls and two babies.

As I picked up the phone to call Rick, because I needed more liquor or Cocaine, I heard someone banging on the back door. It sounded like a swat team or a bounty hunter. We were selling drugs out of his basement and I immediately thought someone ratted us out, but all I was worried about was getting tackled to the ground and hitting my head again. The pounding continued as someone else was running down the stairs inside the house. Then it went silent. I heard the basement door open then a scuffle in the next room. The bedroom door flew open and Rick was pushed against the wall and punched in the head by a young man I'd never seen before.

Another young man entered the room with a handgun yelling, "Where's the dope? Where's the drugs, bitch!" As he pointed the gun in my face I replied, "I don't know what you're talking about" while sitting in the corner by the bed covering my head because I was paranoid about another head injury. As I took a second glance at the young man pointing the gun at me, we both slightly turned our heads and squinted our eyes. I knew him from somewhere, and by his reaction, I believed he knew who I was as well. After Rick and I continued to deny that we had drugs, they opened a small closet door, grabbed everything in it, and ran out of the house. As luck would have it, everything in that closet was everything I owned. That is how my karma and life worked on this journey.

The next morning, I went to visit both pregnant girls in two different locations. Though I hadn't learned to become an honest and reliable source to any girlfriend throughout my life, I pledged to be responsible and gave my word that I would provide them with whatever they and the babies needed. Later that evening, I met with a few of my brothers from my gang and a good friend of mine from Waco, Texas. We spoke about what happened the night before and how my priority was finding the two men that did the home invasion and pointed a gun at my face. After driving around and finding no leads to the intruders' whereabouts, we agreed to call it a night.

As the van was heading in the direction to drop me off, blue and red lights began flashing from a Prince William County police vehicle that switched lanes to pull us over. As my friend from Texas pulled into a popular strip mall, more law-enforcement vehicles drove into the parking lot and surrounded us. One-by-one the officers pulled us out of the crowded van before placing handcuffs on us and sat each of us down on the ground next to one another.

As this was unfolding, across town, Rick and the three Bonilla brothers were pulling into Rick's driveway. As they were walking around the house to enter through the back door, the two men that robbed us the night before jumped out of the bushes to attack my friends. Unbeknownst to the two intruders, the four young men they attempted to ambush weren't intimidated and attacked back.

After close to an hour of being interrogated by the police, they finally released us, and we were back on the road. When we arrived at Rick's neighborhood, we noticed emergency personnel from a few hundred yards away. The van came to an abrupt stop, and my brother Prophet opened the side door and let me out. Without another word, the van drove away in the opposite direction. The lights flashed brighter as I walked over the small hill toward the house. There was caution tape wrapped around the property and as I approached, an officer said, "Excuse me! You can't walk in this direction." "I'm home-less, officer, this is where I'm staying for now," I responded. One of the officers lifted the yellow caution tape and I headed down the driveway toward the back gate.

While I passed Rick's white sports car, I noticed blood all over the concrete. The stains continued throughout the grass and as I glanced toward the front of his car, I saw what looked to be an eyebrow hanging from his license plate. As officers were exiting the backyard, I stopped to observe the landscape. There was blood splattered across the entire right side of the yard, and the beautiful wooden shed with white shutters looked as if someone flung red paint all over it with a bucket. As I walked around the corner, I saw that the patio furniture was broken, bent, and tossed around the yard. I could hear a group laughing and boasting from inside the basement, "Omen! Omen! We got them punks! We destroyed those bitches!" With my head hurting from the freezing temperatures, I stepped across the threshold and entered through the back door into the warm basement.

Once again, my life had been spared, and I avoided another major blow to my head. If I were to have been dropped off as planned, the two men would have ambushed me while I was by myself, and as small as I was and as slow as I was moving from my injury, they could have ended my life with ease. But because we were pulled over and interrogated at the same time, I merely dodged another traumatic event, as I did when Joker was shot through his window years prior.

The two men were beaten so severely that their entire faces had to be stitched up. There were no criminal charges for Rick and the Bonilla brothers on the grounds of self-defense, but when their day in court came, I was denied access in the courtroom. *It was odd.* Rick, the Bonilla brothers, along with many acquaintances from Dale City, attended the hearing, and though I was the one they pointed the gun at that night and whose belongings were stolen, I wasn't granted passage at the door to look at the men before they were sent to prison.

A few weeks later in Rick's backyard, a scuffle broke out over drugs, and a young man that lived on the same street, a friend of mine, was shot three times. Miraculously, he was grazed by each bullet, including the one to his head. Violence continued to ensue throughout Prince William County, and I now had two babies on the way. Though I was aware of that, the lifestyle consumed me to the point of me needing to leave town once again. Both concerned girls questioned why I was leaving for another state, but hiding my transgressions and not expressing my feelings, sent me spiraling down a path of destruction as always. When my nervous system was activated, the three traits I was confronted with, were to fight, flight, or freeze, and that showed true after I committed more retaliatory acts of violence and vanished soon thereafter.

The Bonilla brothers, one of their girlfriend's, another young man, and me and my pit-bull Chino, all crammed into a 1985 Chevy Cavalier with a broken windshield and headed south on Interstate-95 to Florida. The only things I took with me were my dog, marijuana, and a twenty-gauge shotgun.

We drove thirteen hours before finally arriving in the "Sunshine State." The weather was amazing compared to the winter weather in Virginia, and though the pain in my head was very much there, it wasn't as debilitating due to the warmer climate. Our first stop was in Lakeland where the Bonilla brothers knew some folks in a rundown neighborhood. Lakeland was full of small ghettos and trailer parks. Drugs seemed to have taken over here, especially "Crank" which was a low-purity form of Methamphetamine. Crank was much more popular here than up North. Girls were walking up and down the streets as if they were lost, dope dealers pulling up serving junkies, while neighborhood dogs were barking at everyone erratically while chained to trees.

It was no more than an hour after we arrived, that I was high on Crank and drinking Corn Liquor. At that point, it didn't matter if I'd moved to another planet alone. I was an alcoholic and an addict looking to score. If a wild, unidentified substance would have found its way to me while sitting on the moon, I would've certainly tried it.

When we entered their friend's trailer, I was sickened. I witnessed maggots moving paper plates across the filthy counters as little kids were running through a maze of clutter. I looked around at my boots to make sure there weren't any critters trying to attack me, but with all the mess, the critters were surely hiding under the piles of debris. We stepped outside to get fresh air and I was still puzzled at the amount of hoarding inside the trailer. When I turned around, one of the Bonilla brothers whistled at a beautiful girl walking down the road. They said she lived nearby. While she was walking past, we locked eyes long enough to know that she wanted my attention. I was a sucker for beautiful girls, and I didn't have an on/off switch, so before long I approached her, and we ended up seeing each other whenever my friend's and I drove to Lakeland.

The same evening, the six of us drove to Haines City where the Bonilla brothers reunited with their mother and relatives. Their aunt was married to a redneck that owned the home, and though it was a learning experience living with Puerto Ricans and good old boys from the south, we had Moonshine, so I was content with the living situation. I learned to play chess, worked in the orange groves planting small trees and we even hog-tied a five-foot alligator in the neighborhood. I wasn't living though; I was almost nine-hundred miles away from Virginia and spent the majority of my time drinking, using Crank and sleeping with older women I met in different towns.

That may have sounded good to some men, but I was lost inside, alone among people. Janine called me from Virginia and told me she'd contracted a sexually transmitted disease, and I was the only person she'd slept with in a long time. I was embarrassed, and believed it to be true, because I'd been sleeping around and wasn't protecting myself. She was caught off guard by my actions and didn't understand how I could live that way. I couldn't begin to tell her why I was the way I was because I had no clue myself. As months went by and I'd realized that I was dying from the disease of addiction in an unknown environment, I decided to return to Virginia where at least I'd die around people I knew.

As soon as I returned, I went to visit Janine. I was sober that day and grateful for it because her father wanted to meet me. I was full of anxiety without my vices. I was entering uncharted waters and didn't know how to present myself to a respectable military man whose daughter was having a baby with a low-life gang member. It was obvious I had been gone a while because her belly had grown significantly, and though I was nervous about meeting her father, I survived the uncomfortable meeting. He was very kind, and just desired what was best for his family, including his pregnant daughter, who didn't have a clue about what kind of individual I was.

I was still reluctant to share my story with Janine and unfortunately neither of us knew what was coming next. As she continued to worry throughout her pregnancy, I gravitated to the chaos as usual. The young men from the neighborhood formed another Go-go band while I was away, and I heard they were performing at a house party in Woodbridge. When I arrived, with one of my brothers, I was acknowledged by the band when the young man on the microphone yelled out "Omen" in a welcome home gesture. I walked into the kitchen and an old friend handed me a large bottle of liquor as we spoke about why I went on the run down south.

I was sober all day up to that point, but I was off and rolling again, and the anxiety that I battled while not having my vices, was finally gone. I began chugging right out of the bottle as blunts were being handed my way. I noticed a large pit-bull in a side room off the kitchen and I recognized him from somewhere. As I walked closer, I realized that it was the dog two of my brothers and I found tied to a tree—months prior in Massaponax. As I crouched down to greet the chained-up dog from a respectable distance, a girl that I knew from high school screamed with joy and tackled me from behind. The dog immediately felt threatened and attacked the first person he could get his mouth on. Fortunately for the drunk girl, it was me.

The dog grabbed me by my jumpsuit and attempted to drag me into the dark room. His teeth punctured my arm, then my leg, then he grabbed a mouth full of the suit, and began to pull me out of the kitchen. There was no flight or freeze at that moment. It all happened so fast and he wasn't slowing down by any means. As he chomped down on my boot, I could feel his teeth trying to puncture it at the toes. I snapped. I grabbed the liquor bottle by the neck and went to town on the vicious beast. I fought the dog with everything I had, not allowing him to lock his jaws on me. He went for my face, my neck, anywhere he could, but the chain was saving me, and I was gaining ground on him. I continued beating him until he realized that I wasn't going to stop, and then he let go and walked back into the dark room and laid down.

While I was gathering my pitiful self, I looked up and the entire place was silent. I saw the drummer holding his drumsticks with his mouth wide open and the homeowners were looking at me and asking everyone who I was. The girls that didn't know me were looking at me as if I'd assaulted a kitten for no reason, and then to top it all off, one of my brothers, Diego, who I never seemed to get along with, picked me up and threw me against the wall for being disrespectful in his friend's house.

Our brother Beast pulled us apart and told Diego what happened. I brushed myself off, picked up the bottle, and took a swig as everyone carried on listening to the live band. I walked outside as the party continued and the intoxicated girl apologized for jumping on me. Then the man and woman that owned the home, along with two of the girls that gave me nasty looks, walked outside and I was able to apologize for making a scene in their home.

After that night, Waylon, who was the homeowner, along with his wife and her two friends, became extremely close to my gang and me. But they would quickly learn that we were a wild bunch, and that their decision to welcome us into their home, would complicate their lives and have them scrambling to find a new place to live, as I scrambled to find peace on a journey that continued to test my self-will.

CHAPTER 8

WHAT'S IT GOING TO BE?

As I continued to deal with the pain in my head, I took another blow to my head in a minor car accident involving two vehicles from our own party. As Joker crashed into the other vehicle, my forehead slammed against the windshield, causing enormous swelling to the back of my head. Once again, declining any medical assistance, I self-medicated, using drugs and drinking away any logical thought to seek help from hospitals because of a resentment I held toward the one in Fredericksburg.

It wasn't always the criminal element that delivered the pounding. The lifestyle itself would prove enough as, at any given moment, our careless behaviors would ignite a "butterfly effect" triggering situations to unravel while putting ourselves in harm's way without even realizing it. By associating with individuals that had no regard for human life, or not being mindful of our surroundings or having concern of the repercussions, many of our acquaintances were sent to the grave before they were twenty-five years old. And because I was in fact self-destructing, I continued to hang out with people that I told myself I wouldn't because I wasn't in a position to transition to a safe and healthy lifestyle.

After the accident, I kept going and continued pushing forward while self-medicating. I received a phone call from Sadie, and she was at the Fort Belvoir Army Base ready to deliver our little boy. One of my brothers quickly dropped me off and I walked into the hospital in hopes that I wasn't too late. When I spoke to the front desk clerk, she phoned the room for authorization, but my access was denied by Sadie. I was confused and didn't understand why she would call me and upon my arrival, deny me entrance to the delivery room.

After pacing in the lobby under duress, I searched for a payphone, "Hello? Hey, it's me; I'm here, but the crazy lady up front said you didn't want me back there. What's going on?" As Sadie began crying, she hesitated to answer my question but finally said, "I'm... I'm sorry, Joel. He's not your baby. I'm so sorry; I really wanted him to be, but..." I ended the call.

With one more possibility of being a father, I moved in with Waylon and his family. They moved to a new place down the road from where my soon to be daughter would live, and I was ready to break the pattern of being hopeless. I began working with Waylon and his father renovating beautiful homes on the countryside, and my intentions were authentic. I was ready to save money while cherishing the opportunity to prove to myself that I could be a reliable man before my baby girl was born.

I continued working side by side with the men until our services were, unfortunately, no longer needed. My work ethic was second to none when I put forth the effort, and my superiors made that fact be known wherever I got an opportunity to prove my worth.

While searching desperately to find employment, my brothers Dre, Branch and Casper moved into a large high-rise in Alexandria and offered to let me stay with them if in fact I did find a job. An opportunity did present itself, in the much larger city, and I quickly became a cook at a popular steakhouse on Duke Street.

Even though I left Waylon's house, in Woodbridge, due to the lack of job opportunities in the area, his family and I stayed connected, and my relationship with him would open many avenues for me down the road when I needed them most.

My intimate relationship with Janine grew much closer during this time as well, but temptations soon got the best me and I was sleeping around again. As much as I tried to do the right thing by her or attempted to save money, I was weak, not disciplined, and my choices derailed any chances I had to secure those savings or provide her with a stable relationship.

I didn't reside in Prince William County anymore, but I continued to see other girls in different counties. I made the careless decision to drive a stolen car that I borrowed to drop off a girl in Woodbridge on a night I wasn't scheduled to work. After dropping the girl off at her house, I met with one of my brothers to talk business. As we pulled on to his street, multiple unmarked law-enforcement vehicles surrounded us. It seemed as if they were watching me and knew exactly where I was going. I looked over to my brother and suggested that he step out of the vehicle as I contemplated driving off and initiating a high-speed chase.

As he wisely listened and exited the brand-new car, guns were immediately drawn on me. I also made a wise decision and followed their instructions, and they booked me on the charges of Grand Larceny, Fictitious License Plates and Operating A Motor Vehicle Without A License.

The morning after, I woke up in the Prince William County Adult Detention Center and used the jail's phone. Though I had multiple female friends at the time, the only one that was responsible was the one about to give birth to my daughter. Janine agreed to post my bail and gave me a ride back to Alexandria and I immediately went back to work. I still didn't have it in me to sit down with Janine and explain everything that I'd been through, and she never asked. All she was asking for was a relationship that would benefit our two families because our daughter was about to be welcomed into the world.

I stayed in the state as my lawyer suggested, and before I reached the courtroom for my pre-trial hearing, he approached me using profanities and fussing at me, "What the hell is going on with you, kid? You told me you stole the car and that you were prepared to do the time. You didn't steal that car! Someone in another state stole that car and you're covering for them? You could've served years for covering their ass. Get out of here. All your charges were dropped with the exception of driving without a license. Pay your fines and attend the classes. And hey—grow up, kid. Change whatever it is you think you're doing and live a good life before you do end up doing real time."

I was still shocked about how he approached me coming out of the courtroom.

He was mad. He was more upset than I was at the whole ordeal. It didn't matter to me that I wasn't the one who physically stole the car; I was the one that was careless enough to allow the law to find me. I was just responsible for keeping my mouth shut, and grateful that Janine was kind enough to bail me out when she had every reason not to.

On September 26th, 1999, our beautiful baby girl Selena was born in a military hospital in Bethesda, Maryland. Unfortunately, since I didn't have any transportation, I missed my one and only opportunity to welcome her into the world when she was born. I should've figured as much, I made it in time for the child that wasn't mine and I was hours late to welcome the child that was. I couldn't have written an essay on karma if someone offered to pay me, but that is what I felt I was presented with time and time again. I lived in shame because I failed even when I thought I had the will to succeed. I struck out every time I stepped up to the plate, and Selena being born into the world was no different.

My parents kindly gave me a ride up the beltway, and I didn't need a wise man to tell me that it was because of their grandchild being born and not an act of kindness on my behalf. The two were anxious and excited to meet my beautiful baby girl and I was so grateful that was the case. The moment I laid eyes on her *I knew God was real.* She was precious, and though I was embarrassed and ashamed of who I was, I faced her family that day and held my daughter for the first time while praying with everything I had that I would be a good father to her, and that a miracle would take place and I would change.

I'd wished there were a pause button to my life. I was attempting to take a deep breath from all the movement around me, trying to grasp that I was a father and doing whatever I could to stand still, while Dre, Branch and Casper were being arrested on serious charges. The apartment was gone, and without any place to rest my head in Alexandria, I was forced to abandon an amazing job at the steakhouse. I quickly moved back to Woodbridge with Waylon and his family and their house had become another hot spot for my gang. Though they were extremely kind for opening their doors, I thought it was foolish to allow such folks as us to walk in and out of their home while raising small children. I wasn't one to regulate another man's home because I was the one without money and no meaningful way to earn it. I was homeless, just had a child and I was simply grateful that he and his wife allowed me to seek shelter under their roof.

After a while, it seemed things were slowly getting better for me. I was still looking for full-time employment but fortunate to have cash paying jobs with Waylon and his father. I was also able to visit Janine and Selena as much as possible since their family was only living a mile or so down the road. The one thing Janine needed from me though was one of many things I didn't have to offer—stability with a job. I had little money coming in and that stressed her to the point of interrogating me about how I was going to support them. It was a serious issue, and her points were valid, but I wasn't used to being badgered about finances and stability.

I battled the urge to not do anything ill-advised for money because I didn't want to jeopardize my relationship with Selena, but the more Janine complained and bickered, the more I felt belittled and worthless. I knew, in my heart, that I deserved every word that came out of her mouth, but I was just an okay cook with a GED. The only thing I was superb at was stealing, and after a while, I just couldn't find it in myself to sit back and listen to the criticisms while being rejected by the businesses where I was seeking employment.

A few nights later, while the devil himself knew I was uneasy and vulnerable, I was approached by Diego and Dayton who had been scoping out a jewelry store in Lake Ridge. I didn't trust Diego because I felt his motives were to only look out for himself. And though his character may have never been questioned by others, this never swayed what my spirit was telling me about him. I contemplated my feelings toward him versus the need for me to make quick money—a lot of quick money, to hold us over until I was able to secure a job and provide for Janine and Selena long term. It weighed on my mind as she called again and again complaining about diapers, wipes, formula, bottles, clothes, doctors' appointments, and the list went on and on. She truly needed my assistance and without any signs of hope, I began to go mad.

I was conflicted spiritually as Joel battled Omen—good deeds versus evil doings. But it was time, and they approached me again with the same proposition, "Are you with us or not? We're going with or without you and evidently you need the money. What's it going to be? My spirit literally told me to say no, but the flesh opened my mouth, and I agreed to suit up.

We drove to Waylon's house and changed into our black gear. We gloved up, laced our boots, grabbed our tools and masks, and headed up the stairs. Waylon asked, "Omen, you alright?" "Yeah, I'm good…just gotta take care of some things. I'll be back" I replied. Waylon was concerned as we walked out of his front door and into the car.

We drove to the strip mall and one of our female friends Mae agreed to be our eyes on the outside. My stomach was torn because I knew in my heart, I didn't trust certain individuals when it came to committing crimes. I'd committed many crimes with certain young men, but this specific situation felt much different, and different wasn't a good thing.

We pulled into the parking lot, shut the engine off, and looked each other in the eyes. *There was no going back now.* We handed Mae a radio to keep us informed of any movement outside, the three of us exited the car, and we jogged to the location. Once we were in, we walked over to the diamonds. But as soon as we were going to work, Mae's voice came across our radios, "Holy shit…shit, shit, shit…we have company…hurry we have…"

Her radio went silent.

Mae warned us and that's all it took for me to head for the exit. I didn't care about anything but making an amazing escape. As I crept out, I crouched down into the shadows and headed south around the building. Sirens were approaching from all directions and I heard people yelling from where Mae was sitting in the car. I stayed low as I hid under a small bridge and contemplated submerging myself into the pond, but the December temperatures began to freeze the surface. I heard a helicopter closing in and multiple dogs barking near the jewelry store and knew that time was against me. I observed my surroundings and quickly planned my escape route, anticipating how I was going to make it back to Waylon's house. I glanced across the road and noticed a small school with trees on the other side, and I quickly ran for it.

I noticed two small school buses parked by the trees and without hesitation, I pushed one of the doors open and crept up the steps. While staying low, I pulled the lever to close the door and removed my mask because it was difficult to breathe. I looked toward the shopping center and it was infested with law-enforcement. I saw K-9's sniffing around the bridge and the helicopter was circling over with the large spotlight.

I quickly stashed my black clothing and my mask under a seat. I had a laminated prayer card in my pocket that my grandmother had given me, and I pulled it out knowing it had my fingerprints on it. Though I only prayed during times of desperation, I looked at it, squeezed it with my trembling hands, said a quick prayer, and thanked my grandmother who believed in the Lord.

I didn't feel secure in the bus, so I took off between the trees and ran toward the main road. It was brutal trying to breathe while sprinting in the freezing conditions, and I was running out of steam due to my unhealthy lifestyle. I became clumsy and stubbed my boot on a curb, causing me to tumble directly under a streetlamp. *Hell no! You're not going out like this! Get up! You're almost there dammit.* I was exhausted and could barely catch a breath. I got up without looking back and made it across the road to a tree line where Waylon's neighborhood began.

I crouched down again to gain some energy when my brain began hurting really bad. I wasn't giving up though. I jogged toward the townhomes, but they all looked the same. I was confused on what street it was on and began to panic when the helicopter began searching the neighborhood. Finally, I heard, "Omen! Omen! I'm over here. Let's go. Come on! Let's get you inside." I collapsed at his front steps with blood coming from my ears and nose. Waylon carried me up the stairs to the bathroom and turned on the shower, stripped me down and set me in the tub.

The next morning, I woke up on the living room floor and heard a voice talking about what we'd done. I turned around, and it was Diego, sharing information with a girl sitting next to him. For the life of me, I couldn't wrap my head around why he would share that information with her regardless if he were sleeping with her or not. I looked at him, got up off the floor, walked into another room, and grabbed the phone to set my plan in motion. I called Felicity a girl that I'd known for years and trusted enough to know that she would help me. She was on her way to work and without saying anything that would incriminate myself, she turned around and agreed to pick me up. I called another girl Kai, set up a ride with my brother TJ, and the two of them agreed to drive me to the Greyhound station not putting Felicity in harm's way if law-enforcement questioned her. I then called one of the women I'd slept with in Florida and she agreed to meet me at another Greyhound station in Polk County.

There was no need for me to speak about my offenses to anyone, because at the end of the day, I wouldn't trust a soul to keep their mouths shut if interrogated and their freedom was put at risk. Nobody was going to benefit from me saying where I was going and why I was leaving town again. I grabbed my duffle bag, packed my belongings, and walked out of the front door before putting Waylon and his family in harm's way.

When I arrived in Florida, my friend Kora was waiting as she said she would be. I noticed one of the Bonilla brothers was with her, and the two were in a relationship and I respected that. I was in no way planning to cross him or disrespect either of them for that matter. I was in Florida laying low until I could find out more information about Diego, Dayton and Mae and to find out if my name were being mentioned to authorities. The next day I made some phone calls and was told that all three had been captured and arrested. Going with my instincts and the fact that Diego was found after I heard him sharing information with the girl the morning before, I figured my name was already in a detective's file. I also reached out to Janine and to my parents notifying them that I was moving in with a friend out of the state, and I'd return to Virginia soon.

That evening, while I was sitting on the front porch drinking, a neighbor walked outside and grabbed something out of his Oldsmobile Cutlass. I glanced over and noticed the artwork on his back. He was cut from the same cloth I was. We were affiliated with the same gang, and as he walked toward his house, I introduced myself and the two of us acknowledged one another as brothers.

Later that evening, while talking with Zion, he told me that he was under the impression that the lone Bonilla brother in Florida was jealous that I'd returned to Winter Haven. He quickly offered to let me stay with him and his family to quash any speculation that I wanted to be with Kora, and I wisely accepted that invitation.

Zion's older brother was also on the run from the law, after he too committed a crime in another city. A crime serious enough, that if caught, would lock him away for the rest of his life. And though the three of us had the same affiliations, we all had ties in different states, and his brother declined to acknowledge me when we were introduced that night.

The next day I got word that Mae was released from jail for having no prior convictions. She also had no ties to our gang, and detectives more than likely saw that she'd just made a poor decision and was possibly pressured into being our look out. But that in no way meant she didn't say my name, and I knew how manipulative and confusing detectives were, so I assumed she shared information to help her own personal cause. As for the other two, Diego was released because authorities had no proof that he was even at the jewelry store. It was just hearsay. Dayton and Mae were the only two caught at the crime scene and because Dayton had prior convictions and didn't have money, he was sitting in jail waiting to face a judge.

I called my parents again and my father told me that detectives and Prince William County authorities were seeking information as to my whereabouts. Worse than that, the Pentagon warned him that he would lose his security clearance, relieving him of his duties after twenty-five years, because I was a known gang member with felony warrants.

After those conversations and acknowledging the fact my intuitions were true, I went back into Zion's house and sat on the couch.

As I was contemplating my next move, his older brother walked in and sat next to me, "What's troubling you, young man?" He finally acknowledged me as family, and I began to explain my situation. "I've been ratted out after hitting a jewelry store in Virginia. I can't believe they told on me. I just had a baby girl, Selena, and couldn't provide for her and her mother, Janine, financially. I just wanted to help them. Damn! I can't believe they told on me. I've been through a lot, brother…we all have, and I knew in my heart if we were to get caught, whoever got arrested, would look out for themselves and talk to detectives. I went against my spirit, and now my father's telling me that he's going to lose his security clearance at the Pentagon if I don't turn myself in. I've never done anything to help my family, but if I turn myself in, and find out who's talking, I'm gonna to do something stup…"

The man interrupted me and said, "Hey, look at me, gangster; it's not worth it. Trust me; I know. That's why I'm sitting in Florida having this conversation with you. I'm done. I'll never have a life again. And when folks told on me, I did that very same thing you're thinking about doing. Don't. Life has a way of coming back around and punishing those that do wrong. It may take a week, or it may take twenty years, but they will get what they have coming to them with or without you being the one doing it. Do the right thing by your father and serve your time, but don't act out on a resentment that will have you looking back at this conversation twenty years from now in a prison cell." The older and much wiser gangster got up and walked out of the room.

I truly felt the way he and I met under disastrous circumstances was for that conversation alone. And though his wisdom was warranted and appreciated, I knew it wouldn't be a simple task to just allow individuals who had betrayed my loyalty to walk around as if nothing ever happened. After a wild night of unknowingly smoking "Angel Dust" with Zion and we'd lost our minds, before his family and my friends had to bring us back to reality, I listened to his older brother's advice and walked onto a bus destined for Richmond Virginia.

Joker, along with three girls, woke me up as I slept on a bench in the bus station then drove me back to Dale City. During our ride north on Interstate-95, Joker and I made a deal. He would provide room and board for one week if I agreed to turn myself in at week's end. Though the feeling of walking into a locked-down facility was nerve-racking, it was the only way he was allowing me safe passage for those seven days. It was a dangerous move for him to aid and assist me while law-enforcement was searching for me because I was the lone remaining suspect and everyone knew. And though I still had a resentment toward him for running in the opposite direction while I got beat down by a dozen grown men in D.C, he showed his loyalty toward me by assisting me in my time of need.

The entire week he blessed me as he opened his doors to girls that I wanted to sleep with before turning myself in. The thought of not caressing a woman's body baffled me. Another privilege that I took for granted was good food. I ate as much food as possible, acknowledging that if all went south during my trial, I wouldn't be eating good food for a very long time.

The last, and most important business I needed to tend to before going away, was visiting Janine and Selena. It was a stressful situation, but it was necessary that I broke bread with her and her family and wanted to explain the allegations against me. I knew that's all I could've given that family. It wasn't money, support, time of day, or even hope. It was simply the truth of what kind of young man they were dealing with.

When I arrived at their home, it was uncomfortable for everyone. But Selena had a way of shining a light through even the darkest of moments. As I held her and sat with the family, I felt feelings that I'd never felt before. *I was heartbroken.* Not the same heartbroken as when Nora became pregnant by another young man, but a real and true sadness took over my life. The thought of not being able to provide for my precious little angel was defeating. That another man may be the one she called "daddy" when she fell or became frightened of the dark. I didn't want to let her go, but I knew the family was expecting an explanation about why I ran to Florida and hadn't been there to support them.

I looked around the room at everyone and exhaled. "Alright, I'm sorry. I'm sorry for not being around. I know it may seem like I don't care about you guys, but I do. I've been through a lot, and though that doesn't excuse my behavior or actions, I'm trying to do what's right by the people who are most important in my life. I'm the one the police are looking for—for the jewelry store down the road. I didn't have any money for you and every time you called for support for Selena, I had nothing to offer. Not like it matters because I'm never around anyway, but I may be going away for a long time. I'm turning myself in."

The family was in shock.

Their jaws dropped, and all of their eyes were wide. This was a decent, loving, good family that wasn't ready for their daughter to give birth to a child. And though they were blindsided by me crashing into their lives, they never judged me. They never disrespected me or belittled me for being a useless and unreliable young man. I was grateful for being able to make my peace that night and was honest about my wrong doings. I kissed Selena and held her for as long as I could, before handing her over to Janine, and walking out of their front door.

CHAPTER 9

DRAG ME TO HELL

T*he next morning, my brother, TJ, picked me up and drove me to the Adult Detention Center in Manassas to turn myself in. When we arrived, we sat in his car and smoked some weed and shared a bottle of liquor while talking about life. As the blunt of weed came to its end, I knew it was time for me to go. I knew there was no more contemplating or procrastinating, and that it was essential I did what was right by everyone who loved me.*

As I walked through the doors, I took a deep breath and headed toward a sheriff standing behind a window, "Yes, sir. I'm here to turn myself in for a crime they say I committed back in December." "Yeah, okay. Take a seat, kid" he said calmly to me. I looked toward the aluminum bench where he was pointing, looked back at him in disbelief, shook my head and exited the building. I couldn't believe after all the energy and resources law enforcement expended trying to hunt me down, the Sheriff casually told me to sit down and wait. Waiting was not what I had in mind and each second that passed, the little, "itty bitty shitty committee" in my head, was giving me reasons why waiting was a very poor suggestion.

When I walked out toward the parking lot, *I heard,* "Nah! Nope, no sir. Turn around and get your ass back in there. I am not leaving until you go in." TJ was patiently waiting by his car and must've been anticipating me walking out. I said, "Do you know that the Sheriff told me to sit and wait? I'm not waiting!" TJ replied confidently, "Oh yeah you are. Here—sip on this and then take your wanted ass back in through those doors. You know you can't be out here. You're bringing heat to everyone. We love you G, but you're going in there and you're staying in there." He was absolutely correct; I was bringing heat onto others, and after a few minutes, I walked back in and turned myself in.

They took my fingerprints, changed me into an orange jumpsuit, and had me wait in a cell until a detective was able to come in and question me. Sometime around midnight they woke me up and a female detective sat down with me face to face in a small glassed-in room. She told me it was difficult to gather information on my whereabouts, and she had used a lot of resources trying to hunt me down. Before she was able to say another word, I heard, "What up, Omen! Oh shit! My G is here! Whatever you need, I got you. I got you, G! Much love, G; I'll see you inside." *I couldn't believe it.* My brother, Hops, was mopping the hallway, working as an overnight trustee, and less than one minute into the interrogation, he's throwing up gang-signs and calling me by my alias.

The detective turned her head and looked at me with curiosity, "And...who...was...that?" I turned my head towards her and replied, "I...want...my...lawyer." I knew that opening my mouth and saying another word would've been incriminating, so I plead the fifth Amendment and with my highly energetic brother letting it be known to the world that I was affiliated, I had them escort me back to my holding cell where I slept until they woke me up later that morning.

As I walked through the hallways, carrying two plastic totes of linens and hygiene products, I saw my niece's father, Dre, playing basketball like he always did on the outside. His greeting was much more appropriate under the circumstances and let me know I would be taken care of. As I continued down the hall, inmates that didn't know me kicked their cell doors and yelled profanities in an attempt to frighten me, but I wasn't going to be intimidated.

As the corrections officers were opening the door to my new living quarters, my brother Beast banged on his door and looked out of the small window, "What up, G? You alright? Let me know if you need anything." I acknowledged Beast as the officers tapped my shoulder, letting me know it was time. As I entered the cell block, I was immediately confronted by an extremely large youngster named Big Coop from another gang. As the metal door locked behind me, I dropped the totes and looked around as all seven men turned their attention toward me. The block was quiet enough that we could hear conversations going on in the surrounding cell blocks and I knew in my heart that I was about to get tested.

My heart was pounding through my jumpsuit as I was preparing for the worst, acknowledging that another blow to my head would be debilitating. The other six men sat back anticipating blood from the way the Big Coop reacted when I entered their block, "O Dawg! Come to the wall, G. Let them know that I need to speak with you through the vent in the closet cell. They know who we are. They know what's up." My brother Beast in the next cell block deflated the situation in seconds, and I was relieved at his impeccable timing. My young rival took a deep breath as I walked my belongings to my two-man cell, and two other men escorted me to their cell where I was able to speak to Beast through their vent.

Each day the sun rose, and I adjusted to my new means of living. The seven men and I became close and the more Big Coop and I spoke, the more we respected one another and what we both stood for. We also became partners while playing cards and while holding conversations, learned that we knew a lot of the same people around the metropolitan area.

When it was time to sit down with my lawyer, I assured him from the beginning that I had nothing to do with the jewelry store. I told him I was in Florida at the time and regardless of what the other suspects may have been saying, I wasn't involved. I then questioned why I was incarcerated without physical evidence placing me at the scene of the crime and told him I had people in Florida willing to vouch for me.

As for Mae, Dayton and Diego, only Dayton was incarcerated and happened to be in the same complex as I was transferred to. I didn't trust anyone's word, and it was necessary that I had no contact with him or show any connection to him or even that I knew him before I saw the judge. Within weeks, I began receiving letters from other brothers in different prisons and found out that more brothers in our gang were talking to detectives in other cases that were pending. It made me sick to my stomach to know that grown men that agreed to commit criminal acts would give authorities information granting them an early release for testifying against our own family.

The longer I stayed, the more people heard where I was. I began receiving letters from people inside that barely knew me but wanted someone to write to. It was lonely there. I opened one letter from a young man named Filip from Dale City, and he explained he was in a program that housed dozens of men, and how the living quarters were much nicer than where I was. He went on to explain the guidelines, and how it was mandatory to take classes, participate in all areas of the program, and agree to obtain a GED in order to be selected from a long list of candidates. The most significant thing he wrote was that the judges looked highly on the idea of inmates receiving an education and that it could possibly reduce sentences if they were to graduate with good behavior.

I was comfortable where I was. Big Coop and I were on good terms and being around the fellas helped me to stay out of my head at least until the lights went out. But the thought of attending fatherhood classes and whatever other classes they facilitated to help reduce my sentence didn't sound all that bad.

A few days after I read the letter, the chaplain approached our cell block with his rolling cart full of books and asked if I was interested in the program. I was confused about how he knew about the letter and respectfully told him that I wasn't certain of what I was doing moving forward. After he walked away, I took some time to meditate on the thought before I would write Filip back with a decision. I met Filip through White Boy Rick and had a feeling that he meant well due to the fact he took his time to write to me, specifically about the opportunity. Weeks later, I sent a letter letting him know that I was interested, but after quite some time passed and I hadn't heard anything, I accepted the outcome and was content with staying where I was in the eight-man cell block.

One afternoon, after the fellas and I returned to the block after playing basketball, I went to my cell to release some air out of a lotion bottle that I was making hooch in. A few of the fellas and I had been adding ingredients to our homemade alcohol for weeks, and it was finally time to raise our cups.

I called them to my cell and as they were rubbing their hands and licking their chops, we heard our main door open. "Put it away; put it away," one of them whispered while walking out the doorway. "Carroll! Pack your belongings," a corrections officer shouted. *One of the fellas questioned with concern,* "Pack your belongings? Where in the hell you are going, brother?" "That's a good question," I replied as I peeked my head out of the cell. I asked the officer, "Where am I going, sir?" His only reply was, "I said, pack your belongings, son." I was just as confused as everyone else in the block.

I whispered to the fellas to keep the hooch as I packed my hygiene products and letters. As the impatient corrections officer was waiting, I went around the cell block shaking hands with all the men I grew close to. I saw it was fit that the last man waiting was Big Coop, the large young man that almost went to blows with me upon my arrival. I dropped my totes and hugged the big youngster before I made my way out the door. As I exited, the men held one hand up in the air, insinuating they were about to drink the hooch in my honor, and it was bittersweet knowing I wouldn't be joining them after that day.

As I was escorted down the hall, the corrections officer informed me I was being transferred to another facility on the complex that housed dozens of men. We walked out of the main facility and across the complex to a large building that sat alone. As we continued through the building, I noticed multiple dorms filled with dozens of bunk beds, and my anxiety crept in because I didn't know if I was ready for what they were offering.

When we arrived, the dorm was dimly lit with emergency lights that helped the lone corrections officer on duty to see the inmates at night. I glanced through the officer's window and noticed only one bed was vacant, and it was on the top bunk. My fear of heights was much greater than my fear of death, and that alone was enough for me to back out of entering the program.

As I began to inform the officers about changing my mind, the officer who walked me over exited the office, and the officer on duty, who watched over the inmates, asked me to sit in a chair next to his desk. He asked me if I knew what kind of program this was and how long it took to graduate. I told him I was aware of taking classes but wasn't aware of the length of the program. "This is the Life Learning Program we offer the men here at the ADC (Adult Detention Center). It's a six-month faith-based program, son" he said to me. I opened my eyes wide, put my head down and began rubbing my hands across my forehead and eyes.

That information was clearly not in the letter I'd received from Filip, and I didn't anticipate serving six more months anywhere. *I said to him,* "Yeah…about that sir… I wasn't aware of the faith based and six-month deal. I don't plan on being locked up for six months, and with all due respect, sir, I don't feel that this program is what I need. I seriously doubt that God can fix what's wrong with me." He wasn't about to send me back across the complex that night and I knew it. He calmly said to me, "Sleep on it, son. You look tired. Go grab that top bunk and get some rest. Try one day, and if you feel the same, we'll transfer you back to the main facility. It's a lot nicer here and you will be absolutely shocked at what God can do in our lives." As I shook my head in disbelief, I grabbed my totes and exited the office.

As I walked toward the bunks, someone called my name out in a low voice. Then another person said it, and then another. I heard my name coming from every row of bunks, but they were whispering, and I couldn't tell who it was. As I arrived at my bunk, my stomach twisted. I was not excited to climb to the top bunk just to fall off onto my face while I was sleeping. But I did climb up for the sole reason of keeping the peace between the officer and myself.

When I tried to lay down, my body began to tense up and I said, "Nope! I'm not sleeping up here. sir. Hell no; take me back! Take me anywhere." I hopped down and headed toward the officer, but he wasn't changing his stance, "Relax and take this opportunity to gain wisdom, son. You're battling a darkness that we cannot fight alone." The officer was big, built, had a chiseled face and looked like he could've been on the cover of a GQ (Gentlemen's Quarterly) magazine, but his spirit had a calmness about him, and it was pissing me off.

I paced back and forth between two bunks and didn't care how ridiculous I looked to whoever was awake or knew me. I was terrified. I tried reasoning with the officer to switch me out with someone else, but he said that was unnecessary. Then I brought up the fact that he was a child of God and to have some compassion for my fear of heights, but he didn't even smirk. I explained how I'd had multiple head injuries and was afraid to hit my head again, and he just pointed toward the bunk.

Finally, after a long thirty minutes, I climbed back up to my three-inch mattress. As I looked around for a moment and laid on my back, I began thinking about my old cellmates and how comfortable I was in the much smaller, confined area. I thought to myself, *God isn't going to help a liar and a thief—a gang-member that hurts people, uses drugs and drinks liquor like a lunatic, sleeps around with multiple women and only prays when I'm in trouble. Plus, I don't need this program anyway. Who are they kidding? What are they going to do, throw the Bible at me and have me sing Kumbaya? Hell no…not this guy!*

I made my decision and was going to have the corrections officers transfer me back after shift change and open the bunk up to another man who wanted it. As soon as I closed my eyes, I got cold chills. It was as if I was thrown into a walk-in freezer. I opened my eyes and started seeing shadows coming from the walls. I sat up quickly and began to panic while everyone else was sound asleep. I noticed the shadows climbing up through the floor and I opened my mouth to get the CO's attention, but his office was dark and empty.

I slammed my fists down again and again in an attempt to wake the man on the bottom bunk, but no one could hear me. The shadows were coming directly at me and I didn't care if I looked crazy to everyone else, so I began yelling as they scaled the bunk, but still, no one could hear me. I got up on my feet and was about to jump to another bunk, but the shadows wrapped around my entire body and slammed me on to the concrete floor.

I reached out for a man's legs, but the dark beings were swallowing me up and quickly dragged me toward the exit. I scratched and clawed, but they held my arms tight and began to suffocate me as they slammed my head and body against the door frame when we entered the hallway. "Help me! Help me! Please! Someone please," I screamed so loud and pleaded for them to let me go as the dorm light faded and they dragged me away into the darkness.

My body jerked violently. I opened my eyes, sat up, and noticed all the inmates were sound asleep. My heart was beating through my orange jumpsuit and I was sweating profusely. I looked over toward the office and the large Hispanic corrections officer was standing in the doorway motioning his hand as if he wanted to see me. I slowly hopped down from the bunk and wiped the tears from my face as I looked around for the shadows. As I entered his office, he closed the door behind me and reached for a book. He told me to sit down but I was hesitant. I continued to shake while looking over my shoulder, checking to see if the shadows were coming from the dark hallway.

While he searched through his book for a specific page, I glanced through the windows because I was paranoid, and I sat next to his desk before he turned to me saying, "Joel? The darkness is coming for you, son. But don't be afraid because the Lord loves you. This was meant to happen. You are not here by mistake. God wants you here. He knows you're struggling personally, but without God's armor, Satan will continue to attack you with everything he has. Son, look at me. Did you know the name Joel is in the Bible? And do you believe that Jesus Christ died on the cross for your sins?" I nodded in a "yes" motion as the tears poured down to my jumpsuit. The CO asked, "And do you believe that God will impart eternal life to your spirit? *I was bawling.* I couldn't stop and my entire body shook as I sobbed uncontrollably. I nodded again, acknowledging the kind man's question about God.

The corrections officer and I spoke for what seemed to have been hours. We spoke about life, what my intentions were toward Selena and Janine, and the reasons why I struggled with myself and why I couldn't control my actions despite the brutal consequences I faced constantly. The events that occurred that night and the corrections officer's way of handling them changed my mind about the program and my decision to transfer back to the main facility.

As for the shadows showing me, they were ready to drag me to Hell, I was grateful it was only a vision of what was to come if I didn't change and not my eternal ending. Life had shown me plenty of times that evil existed in both our world and in the next, and because I was entering a faith-based program, I truly believed the officer's wisdom about how Satan wanted me back in the dark before I could get any closer to God.

From the moment I awoke the next morning, I was taken care of by the inmates in the large dorm. Filip, the young man who wrote to me and suggested this opportunity about the program, was still participating in the program along with a half-dozen young men that admired me and were aware of my affiliations on the outside. The classes began early and lasted until the evening with meals in between. I created relationships with every man in the building, leaving no man to feel unaccompanied. I respected all and became a reliable source of assistance to anyone in need.

Every day, during down time, a group of us worked out together, pushing one another to our max. I gained twenty pounds rapidly and was stronger than I'd ever been. When it was time to play basketball, with my ball handling and passing skills, I was picked onto a team every day, even against some of the larger men that had been there a while.

During one of our pick-up games, I crossed over an arrogant and self-assured man the other men called Bonney, in reference to William H. Bonney, also known as "Billy The Kid." I caused Bonney to trip over his own two feet and I scored a game winning jump-shot. As everyone else lost their minds and celebrated the successful sequence that ended the game, I reached out to help Bonney off the floor, but he aggressively pulled his arm away.

We played again with the same ten men on the court, and I guarded the distressed man as I did in the game prior. After I made another jump shot and Bonney missed his shot attempt, I dribbled the ball up the court and he elbowed me in my jaw, dropping me to the ground. The men on the court along with the men that were exercising on the sideline, ran to my aid and the group grabbed Bonney forcing him to leave the court. I shook it off and despite Bonney being much larger than I was, I followed him into the building. We piled into our dorm and I confronted him while he was walking to his bunk. He quickly turned around and the two of us went at it, but it was cut short, as the other men broke us up, reminding us both that we would be sent to the "Ice Box," and removed from the program.

After the two of us calmed down, he approached me and made his amends. He explained that he was a competitive person and that he didn't have any coping skills to deal with his anger. He went on to say that being embarrassed was one of his triggers for violence. I expressed to him that I understood his struggles, and that I too had no positive coping skills for any situation that irritated me.

After we broke bread, the two of us became closer that day. We attended anger management classes and made the wise decision to play on the same team. But a few months later, as we all anticipated, Bonney was transferred to the penitentiary where he was to serve many years for the crimes he'd committed.

After his departure, I contemplated all the poor decisions I'd made and if those decisions would keep me incarcerated for years like the other fellow. I questioned why I was the way I was. I had loving parents; I had an opportunity to get a good education but chose to make a name for myself by acting out, and I drank rigorously and sold drugs instead of opening textbooks to become more intellectually stimulated. I thought about if I would've applied myself and put forth the effort in the National Guard, how I could've used basketball as my hobby and my greatest coping skill instead of using drugs, drinking and stealing.

I wondered why I walked away from everything that was positive in my life, stretching and dismantling every relationship I ever had the blessing to be a part of. Why I chose to sleep outside in the cold without shelter or food instead of respecting my family's wishes of being an obedient son and following simple rules. *It was insanity.* The thought of making decisions that inflicted so much physical and mental pain on myself and others was unfortunate.

I'd been fighting since I was ten, had a gun pointed at my head a half dozen times, been shot at and almost shot, had my clavicle fractured, a fractured jaw, cracked ribs, multiple concussions, took a brutal beat down in DC, was initiated by my gang and that wasn't fun, fought my own brothers while high on formaldehyde numerous times to toughen me up, injured my head in a car accident, and took a major blow to my brain causing me to stutter, triggering severe pains that left me worried about dying every time I was under stress. I caused so much pain on others, so why wouldn't I expect the same painful results in return. I caused emotional, financial, physical and spiritual discomfort to hundreds, all while fighting myself internally and plotting to send certain men straight to Hell for what they did to me.

On multiple occasions, I was with someone that was killed soon after I left them. *Was I a bad omen like some said? Were people dying around me because of me?* I stopped counting the number of brothers and sisters that we'd lost to disease, car accidents, murder, or suicide. I knew my personal choices were to blame and nobody forced me to take part in any of it. I was homeless by choice, an addict by choice, been kicked out of the military and my home by choice and gave away every girlfriend I ever had due to my poor choices and now there was a child involved. As unfortunate as it was, the weight fell onto the families as I continued to do whatever it was I did to fill the void created from each of those misfortunes.

Many of us signed up for the lifestyle but were unaware the people we associated ourselves with weren't as trustworthy as they lead us all to believe. Now I was sitting in a locked-down facility by choice, and the three individuals I committed the crime with, were more than likely doing whatever they needed to help their own personal cause. Regardless of whether I was in a God-fearing faith-based program or not, accepting it and moving on, like my brother in Florida insinuated I should do, was weighing heavily on my mind.

Through the struggles I battled within, I managed to graduate without incident and received a certificate of completion. I learned many things about myself and my faith in God became stronger. I also learned my name was in the Bible, with "The Book of Joel" being in the Old Testament. The only scripture I memorized was from *Matthew,* "But seek ye first the kingdom of God and his righteousness, and all things shall be added unto you." I wrote that scripture on the folder I carried everywhere, so it would be instilled in my spirit. It was a reminder that if I were to seek God in everything I did, He would bless me with 'all' the things that were necessary in my life.

A few days before I was transferred from the program, a large group of middle school students were walking through the facility to participate in the "Scared Straight" program. As my fellow inmates intimidated and literally attempted to scare the youngsters straight, I recognized the teacher who was chaperoning them. When the intimidation strategy came to a halt, the men spoke with the students in all sincerity, offering knowledge and wisdom and speaking to them from the heart about their own personal journeys that led them to being incarcerated at one point. When a moment of silence presented itself, I took center stage and focused my attention to the teacher and said, "Ma'am, do you recognize me?" The teacher nervously shook her head in a "no" motion. I said, "My family and I moved from Arizona, years ago, and I was one of your students. You are an amazing teacher, and I just want to say thank you." The teacher began to cry and covered her mouth as she nodded her head in a "yes" motion insinuating that she remembered me.

I then took the time to speak with the students about my consequences after years of making poor decisions. About peer-pressure and how the choices they made in school could influence their future as young adults. How being cool around their peers wasn't what was important in life but being honest and reliable during their adolescence is how they would benefit in a society that lacked authentic people. I let it be known that they were the future, and they could have dreams and aspirations to follow instead of following in their friends' footsteps simply because they wanted to fit in. I told them that being different meant they were unique in their own way. I only knew this to be true from my own personal experiences, and ultimately my surroundings had a major role to play in my life because I wanted to fit in myself.

Two days after we shared our testimonies with the students, I was transferred to another dorm in the main facility where I became a "Trustee." I worked on the kitchen crew and immediately reaped the benefits because we were able to eat more food than the other inmates. It also helped me to stay busy and to focus on the task at hand, rather than sitting around and battling the long list of resentments I had floating around in my head.

One morning, before my shift, I was told that a lawyer was there to visit with me. I'd already seen my lawyer that week, so I was confused about the timing and began to think that they'd found physical evidence that placed me at the scene of the crime. When I sat down in the small booth, there was a stranger sitting on the opposite side of the plexiglass window. He slid a stack of documents under the window and asked me to sign my name everywhere there was a highlighted "X."

The first stack read, "Division of Child Support Enforcement (DCSE)." I was being charged with child support every second I was sitting behind bars. I asked Janine's lawyer how I could possibly pay child support while being incarcerated, and he responded with, "Not my problem." The next stack of documents was about Janine taking full custody of Selena. I was resentful at the timing. Life was getting serious and I was on the bottom level of it. I understood that she needed to get support somehow and had to do what was necessary for the two of them, and after throwing my own pity party, I came to the conclusion I had no logical basis to be upset with her after everything I put her through.

I continued working in the kitchen and began writing letters to DCSE about my child support payments. I wanted to be proactive and show the courts that I was willing to help the cause, but it was to no avail and they never responded. A few months before my court date, a young man named Amari was transferred to the Trustee work program. He was affiliated with another gang in Northern Virginia, and though we'd had run-ins in the past, the two of us acknowledged one another and never showed signs of disrespect. While working together, I learned that he was incarcerated for robbing a business next door to the jewelry store just one week prior to us committing our crime.

Law enforcement had been patrolling the strip mall after the first robbery and my brothers obviously didn't do much research while planning our great heist. The more information I was learning, the more I wanted to distance myself from everyone, but I knew I had to keep it together because my day in court was near.

The morning of my pretrial services, many of us were escorted to a library where they had us wait before we were taken in front of the judge. As soon as I entered the dimly lit library, I noticed Dayton sitting in the back of the room and our eyes locked. It was the first time I'd seen him since I exited the jewelry store. I sat in the empty desk next to his and immediately began questioning him about his intentions while in the courtroom. "I didn't say a word about you, O. They questioned me countless times and I refused to speak with them. If I would've said anything, I would've been out a long time ago. Someone else must have said something, but I didn't…trust me, O," he pleaded.

As much as I wanted to believe him and trust his word, I couldn't find it in myself to do so. Even if he did tell authorities my name, with his criminal history, they wouldn't have released him on a deal until after his day in court—his court date and not my day in court. I knew there was a reason why he was attending my court and before I could speak on my speculations, corrections officers entered the room.

At 7:00 a.m., the officers began calling us out into the hallway where they shackled us by our hands and our feet. Close to thirty of us were taken under the facility to two holding cells. As the large group was split into two, I questioned Dayton again about his intentions as the iron door locked behind us. Moments later Dayton was escorted out of the holding cell and I knew in my heart he was going on the stand. When my name was called and I entered the large courtroom, I stopped and observed the crowd, searching for any one of my brothers to be a witness to what was about to happen, but not one was in attendance due to our affiliations. I sat next to my lawyer, and moments later the prosecuting attorney for Prince William County began calling witnesses to the stand. I was concerned because they spoke about witnesses, and not *a* witness. I felt weary, and my head was on a swivel looking around with curiosity to see who the first witness was.

As I took a deep breath, Diego walked through the aisle and sat next to the judge. *I was as vulnerable as one could be.* I looked behind me in hopes that someone in our gang arrived, but there were too many people in the large crowd to see passed the first row. I did however notice Mae's father sitting directly behind me.

As the prosecutor questioned, Diego answered him verbatim. "I dropped them off that night in front of the strip-mall but have no idea if they were involved in any crime. I drove away after that and haven't spoken to any of them since." As the prosecutor continued, my legs were shaking under the desk anticipating for the bomb to drop. He named the two other suspects that were supposedly dropped off and then out of nowhere, named an acquaintance of the gang that was never connected to the case in any way shape or form. The other suspects must've told detectives there were three men who committed the crime and since Diego pulled his name out of mix, it was necessary for him to put another random name in the mix. My lawyer was confused because our acquaintance from the 'K' streets had the same last name as I did. I believed this had everyone thinking I had a brother connected to the crime. So, I imagined my lawyer thought I was more likely to be involved because I had a brother involved.

I leaned over to my lawyer and assured him I didn't have a brother and that the witness's story was fabricated, but I knew I was powerless. I had to sit there and witness what was taking place. I looked Diego in the eyes as the prosecutor asked him to point out the person of interest and he lifted his hand and pointed directly at me and told the court my full name. My lawyer looked at me and shook his head out of frustration because I'd been adamant that I was in Florida during the crime and now his defendant was being placed at the scene of the crime plus he thought I had a brother that was involved.

After he testified, and as he stepped off the stand and walked past me, I shook my head in disbelief. Not thirty-seconds later the prosecutor called on another witness to step forward. A sheriff opened the door and Dayton walked across the floor and sat next to the judge. This time the prosecutor immediately asked his witness to point out the person of interest. As I took a deep breath and exhaled, my brother, who just told me he wasn't going to tell on me, pointed directly at me and told the court my full name.

The prosecutor asked Dayton how I was involved in the crime, and he answered verbatim. "While the rest of us were in the jewelry store, Joel was outside being our lookout." Again, my lawyer leaned in and whispered in my ear, "What is happening, young man? You're telling me that two different men get on the stand under oath and lie to the courts about your involvement." But I stood firm in my stance that I wasn't involved and hopelessly watched as another brother testified against me as my spirit told me they would.

When officers walked me back to the holding cell, they separated Dayton and me. When it was time for us to walk back as a group, they stopped and opened the two doors. This time, they escorted over two-dozen men into one holding cell and placed me in the other large cell by myself.

I lost it.

I kicked the cell door over and over hoping the corrections officers would come in so I could let some aggression out, but they never came. I knew Dayton and the other men could hear me through the walls, so I began singing. I used the aluminum benches as a drum and sang as loud as I could while singing a song that was a message for my brother that betrayed me. I was escorted to a room to meet with my lawyer and he reminded me that if I were to take the case to trial instead of taking the plea bargain, I could be incarcerated anywhere from five to twenty years. I understood the severity of my situation and though I was scared, I just didn't have it in me to tell on myself.

As the long days passed, all I could do was play the mental tape back, watching my brothers as they testified against me in the courtroom. I made phone calls to my gang on the outside and wrote letters to different prisons, to gain some insight on what the hell was happening to our gang. But without any witnesses to observe what went down that morning, I would need the paperwork on both brothers' statements for there to be proof of my accusations.

The way they tried to avoid telling on me while telling on me, was their way of justifying their testimonies. Diego stating he "just dropped me off," and Dayton stating I was, "outside as a look out," was their attempt to clear their name, and not place me in the jewelry store. But they said my name. They pointed me out to aid and assist a Prince William County prosecuting attorney, after I clearly and specifically told them both I was in Florida during the crime. To me there was no justification.

When I sat down with my attorney the morning of the trial, he asked me again if I wanted to come clean and told me that my friends in Florida weren't returning his calls. I confidently told him that we had nothing to worry about. As the two of us entered the courtroom, I looked over and observed the men and women of the jury, and reality set in and my stomach turned. I instantly realized that my fate was in the hands of men and women I'd never met. And with statements from both of my brothers on the stand and probably a third statement from Mae that wasn't in my pre-trial service, I felt my smartest move was to come clean.

I leaned into my lawyer and whispered, "I'm out. I'll take the plea. I apologize for wasting your time, but I didn't know for sure if my brothers were going to identify me or not. The man's name that Diego said during my pre-trial service had nothing to do with the crime and he isn't related to me. I don't know why he would place him at the scene, it's ridiculous. He has absolutely nothing to do with this. I want my plea deal and I'll call my people in Florida and let them know that I took the plea." With the judge patiently waiting, my lawyer walked over and told him that I requested the plea deal.

Before sentencing, I spoke a lot about my situation with Amari. He understood my frustration and he and another inmate shared their insight as I tried to come to terms with being betrayed. We agreed my next choice was pivotal for the outcome of the rest of my life and that regardless if my gang believed me or not, I knew what happened in the courtroom that day. One way or another, life would deal with all of us on life's terms, not ours.

During our long conversations, the two of us realized we had a lot in common. We committed crimes at the same strip mall, had the same sentencing date, the same judge, and would eventually have the same release date with the same probation officer.

When my day came to face the judge, he looked through my paperwork and saw what I'd accomplished while being incarcerated.

He granted me time served for graduating the faith-based program and working as a 'Trustee' without any incidents. Without any major prior convictions, he set a five-year probation period and suggested that I never entered his courtroom again.

As the bay door rose slowly, the humidity took over and the smell of freshly cut grass was oh so sweet. As I held my large garbage bag with everything I'd accumulated during my incarceration, Amari and I crossed the threshold into society and set out to meet with our new probation officer across the road.

With the bright sun beaming down on our eyes, we walked across the parking lot until we heard someone honking their horn at us. We turned around, but the sun was too much for us to see who it was. "Hey, you need a ride?" A soft voice came from the driver's side and Amari and I were both confused.

As we approached the car, I noticed a beautiful baby girl in the backseat, but I couldn't see who the driver was through the reflection. The two of us walked around to the driver's side and put our hands up to block the sun. "Who is it?" Amari asked. I replied, "I can't tell. It's…wow." I couldn't believe my eyes. It was Janine and the beautiful little girl in the backseat was Selena.

After everything I did, and all of the stress I caused Janine and her family, she was there waiting for me upon my release. She drove me to my parents' house that evening and I spent some much-needed time with the two of them and was blessed to eat a home cooked meal before holding my baby girl as tight as ever. I was also eager to share my 'Fatherhood and Life Learning' certificates and my family seemed to have been proud of my accomplishments, but as my track record indicated, and as they were all crossing their fingers, only time would tell if I'd matured enough to become a reliable father, son, brother, and man, to the families that wanted nothing but the best for me and my future.

CHAPTER 10

My Spirit Told Me So

I *managed to control my emotions when I returned to the streets and patiently considered taking the lives of those who intentionally partnered with the prosecutor. Without having proof of what happened in the courtroom, I wasn't in a position to request a thumbs-up from the higher ups in the gang even though there were some loyal brothers out there that were conflicted. I quickly learned that more people were associating with the ones that testified against me than I'd expected, and I was at a loss for words. It fueled my resentments and I struggled trying to come to terms with how and why people would believe their version of the situation over mine. It drove me mad and my focus turned to vengeance instead of building a solid foundation for my new family, but it ended up being a disaster.*

I reached out to Amari and had a proposition for him in regard to my retaliation. Though he was affiliated with another gang, I trusted him enough to know he disliked certain individuals I was resentful toward and the two of us planned to sit down over a few drinks at a local club. Unfortunately, as the ominous pattern of my life continued, he was murdered before we were able to have those drinks and I was left back at the drawing board scheming up a new plan.

While the two of us were locked away, we'd talked about being vigilant and how essential it was for the two of us to be mindful of our surroundings coming out. We also understood that life never stopped when we were locked away and acknowledged that our enemies would be waiting for us to return to the streets, so we needed to be mindful at all costs. But the truth was—the streets didn't respect anyone; no matter how tough you thought you were, and because he didn't practice what he preached, his adversaries were able to find him soon after we were released. For me, it was just another person that I was close to that disappeared from the face of the Earth before they were the age of twenty-five.

While I was secretly plotting, my brother Casper was kind enough to allow me to stay with him and his family because I was struggling to find a place to sleep. My first day in their home, I ended up having sex with his sister and it made for an uncomfortable situation to say the least. My intentions when leaving the program were to please God in everything I did, but I was failing each test mightily and was baffled at how weak I was even after giving my life over to God. Soon after, I reached out to my sister and her husband Patrick. They kindly agreed to let me stay in their basement with the agreement that I worked a fulltime job and stayed out of trouble. Patrick was the top salesman at an appliance warehouse and because of the respect he had from his peers, he was able to get me a job in the warehouse shipping and receiving hundreds of appliances a week.

Having a stable place to rest my head and working long hours helped me to stay out of trouble from the law, but as always, good things always came to an end with my foolish behaviors. My drinking got the best of me again and my sister grew tired of me being around my nieces and nephew while intoxicated. Patrick and I had become good friends after my introduction with the butcher knife in my sister's bed years prior, and though I needed to find another place to stay, he and I continued working together and I was able to save a few hundred dollars.

Luckily, I found a room for rent across the street from the appliance company and it was convenient being only two minutes from my job. I also picked up another pit bull puppy to keep me company and though I was working a fulltime job, I started selling weed for extra cash after my brother Marley moved into the same building. As convenient as it was to have my first place, Marley and I were evicted, months later, due to the amount of traffic we had coming in and out of our rooms. I was fortunate to quickly find another place with a friend of mine named Cobb. He and his mother were extremely kind and even allowed me to keep my pit bull, Phoenix, since Cobb raised pit bulls himself.

I continued to struggle with my addiction to alcohol and no longer worked at the appliance company. I began working at a swimming pool company with friends of mine from 'K' street and was finally off unsupervised probation. I quickly started smoking weed again, and though it induced paranoia; it alleviated the pain in my head as long as I didn't consume too much alcohol with it.

One afternoon while finishing up on a job site, I received a phone call from my mother, telling me that my cousin Kyler was in a boating accident in Arizona. She said his female friend died at the scene, his buddy who I knew while I was in Tucson was in the hospital with multiple injuries, and Kyler was in a coma. All I knew during times of grief was to get wasted and it gave me another excuse to 'use.' I prayed for Kyler and his buddy to pull through but used the tragic event to get high on LSD, Microdots, smoke weed and drink as much alcohol as possible while my peers fed into my pity. Fortunately, both Kyler and his buddy survived, and I was left searching for more excuses as to why I wasn't being a family man like I told everyone I would be after being released.

A few months later, Lincoln was released after doing four years in the penitentiary. His mother owned a beautiful condo off the Occoquan River and when the opportunity presented itself, I accepted the offer and moved in with the agreement that he and I would maintain a healthy lifestyle and pay the bills. The condo sat on the river and we had an amazing view from our third story balcony, something I hadn't been privileged enough to experience before or calling such a nice place home. It was no secret I lived at Cobbs's house way longer than any of us anticipated, but there was one downfall from me leaving his house, and that was I wouldn't be able to keep Phoenix at the condo, and that crushed me.

Though I was unstable for years, I truly thought, in my sick mind, I would be able to provide for my amazing dogs and I hated letting them go. I cried more for Chino and his nephew Phoenix than I did for my deceased brothers and sisters but was glad to learn my brother-in-law Patrick's twin brother and his girlfriend were willing to raise Phoenix and give him a better life.

When I settled in the condo, Janine was kind enough to drive down to visit, but her visits were few and far between because she was putting forth all the effort while working a fulltime job on top of raising Selena alone. The two of them moved with her family to the Virginia and West Virginia border and I rarely spent time with them due to me not being responsible. So my relationship between Janine and Selena became non-existent as time passed.

When business slowed down at the pool company, I quickly found employment next door to the appliance company, I previously worked for, at a popular flooring business. Again, I did well at work while operating forklifts and doing the shipping and receiving of merchandise, but temptations got the best of me again. Two weeks into me working there, I was offered cocaine in the back of the warehouse, by two employees, and the strength I thought I would have after acknowledging Jesus died on the cross for my sins still never surfaced. I contemplated every reason about why I was going to get high instead of just saying no. Within days I was high as the gas prices and every penny I made that wasn't going toward child support or bills, went towards cocaine and it got out of control immediately.

I vigorously searched for new ways to supply my habit and became hyper focused on getting as much as I could while being oblivious to the fact that the drugs were changing me. Drugs trumped all logical reasoning and I continued getting high, pushing to the furthest depths of my mind, the agony of not being a good father and not wanting to allow those who snitched on me to continue living. Soon after, two new young men were hired in the warehouse and I got them high as soon as they clocked in. We would drive across the bridge to D.C., smoke formaldehyde, drive back to snort as much cocaine as possible, while different girls would be waiting for me at the condo, and at times I totally forgot they were there waiting for me.

There were moments where I forgot I was there. I was lost. I entered a small Asian owned store one evening with my co-workers and the cashier sounded like a demon and I couldn't move. I was stuck on stupid. It was as if someone hit the pause button on me in front of the checkout counter and the other customers had to walk around just to squeeze in to pay for their groceries. I could hear my heart beating and my pulse was pounding through my face. The combination of formaldehyde, cocaine and liquor must have had a conflict of interest in my body because my buddies had to turn me around, escort me out of the store and sit me in the car before someone called the law on me.

On an early morning, in September of 2001, while I was "only" high on cocaine and was carrying carpet pads to the back of the warehouse, I noticed a commotion in the owner's office. I stopped and looked through the large window where a group of wealthy men were hovering over a small television and grieving about something on the news. I turned around and shrugged it off as I began to hear cries from inside the office. *What the hell is wrong with these guys,* I asked myself while anxiously waiting for my cocaine to be delivered. My dealer hadn't shown up yet, so I continued unloading the truck when I realized I was the only employee working. "What the hell, gentlemen! Hello! There's a truck over here full of padding! It's not going to unload itself," I yelled. One of the managers must've heard me and shouted something back at me. I was too high to understand what he was saying.

My brother-in-law Patrick frantically approached me from next door, "Joel! We have to go!" I said, "Go? What the hell are you talking about? I'm not going anywhere! I have some cocai…" He yelled, "Airplanes are flying into our buildings. One just hit the Pentagon." Shocked, I replied, "What? What are you talki…" He then reminded me, "Your…father…is…in…the…Pentagon! New York got attacked too. We need to go to your parents' house and see what's happening! the cell phone towers are down, and we need to check on your mother." It finally hit me why nobody was helping me. The entire warehouse was empty because everyone was watching the news.

Arlington was down the road and the fact that my father was in the Pentagon made it personal, but I was an addict, and an addict always waited for their dope no matter what was going on around them. I was certainly going to get my dope from the dope man, before I flew an airliner up that man's ass. "I'm not leaving, Patrick. Check on the family and I'll catch up later," I demanded.

Shocked, he replied, "What? Are you serious right now?" I'd been through so many violent situations in my life that it didn't shock me like it did billions across the globe. As a child, I was pulled from class many times over the years while terrorists attacked Belgium. Though it was terrifying, chaos and tragedy were something I was used to seeing, more than many of my American brothers and sisters.

In total, 2,996 Americans lost their lives that day and over 6,000 were injured, including 125 casualties during the attack on the Pentagon. I was truly grateful my father was physically unharmed during the explosion and that he was able to make it home to my mother in one piece.

That night, two of my brothers and I parked on a road, overlooking the Pentagon, and sat on the trunk of the car passing a bottle of liquor as we observed the aftermath of the attack on my father's workplace. There was a large American flag hanging to the right of the destruction and a number of spotlights, running from generators, that illuminated the devastation. We witnessed multiple agencies working side by side to piece together how such an attack could take place at the most significant government building in our country.

My brother and roommate Lincoln had family in New York, so he was anxiously waiting to see them after the attacks took place in the financial district of New York City. When the two of us drove north to spend the weekend with his loved ones, his father took us to downtown Manhattan. We rode the subway and as soon as we boarded, we immediately felt the sorrow in the atmosphere. We witnessed firefighters sobbing and it was evident many of the other passengers were intoxicated and depressed while in a state of shock.

The most intriguing aspect of our trip was how the New York natives came together to aid and assist one another and began rebuilding the city in honor of those that lost their lives. It was also how the firefighters were holding their brothers while they continued to grieve, and others waved American flags across the city representing our country with pride.

I would never forget the morning of 9/11 and the fact that I was more concerned about getting cocaine rather than running to my family's aid. I made the decision to cut back on the hard drugs after that day and it didn't help that I crashed a nine-foot pole, attached to the forklift, through an office wall in the warehouse while I was high.

When the weekends approached, and I wasn't spending all of my time snorting cocaine, Lincoln and I would go out to meet girls, this was after he and his girlfriend split up. One of our longtime friends told us about a party in Alexandria and said a bunch of girls would be there, so we drove across county lines anticipating getting laid later that night.

When we arrived at the neighborhood, there were dozens of men outside, rolling dice and selling dope. I had an ominous feeling about going in the building and suggested we go back to Prince William County to play pool at the bar where his mother worked, but my two counterparts insisted we were safe. The lights were dim as we entered the project building and the smoke from the marijuana was so thick that I couldn't see. I became extremely anxious, but my company already walked into the crowd. When I met them at the back wall, they were already looking for girls to take home with us, but my intuition from the beginning expressed the urgency to escape before we were targeted by the Alexandria gangs.

I noticed a group of men looking at us from across the dark room and then another group turned their attention towards us as well. Lincoln and our friend noticed the groups combining into one large group and they finally acknowledged the reasons for my anxieties. Every man in the crowd joined together and began throwing up gang signs and yelling out their affiliation while the Go-go music got louder. As soon as I saw the men outside selling dope and rolling dice, I knew in my heart the building was governed by one family. But my sex driven companions weren't thinking with the heads that gave much thought and now they were being as mindful I was.

We looked toward the only exit and it was blocked off by the crowd that was becoming more aggressive. I felt evil manifesting as it did in D.C. before I was brutally beaten. I whispered a prayer under my breath in hopes of a miracle as a man approached me before his crew followed suit. As the three of us prepared for the chaos, I heard, "Omen? Oh my God! What's up baby?" We had no idea where the voice was coming from and the entire crowd stopped pushing toward us. "Omen! Move… I said move. Get out of my way," said a girl who was moving through the group. It was evident she was in charge, as every gang-member in the room respected her demands.

She made her way to me and hugged me before turning her attention to her people, "This is my brother Omen! He is family! Now show him and his boys some love and get them something to drink." Lincoln turned to me in disbelief, "Who the hell is that?" The truth was I couldn't remember who she was or why she showed me respect, but evidently, I did something to impress her in my past, and with the help of a small prayer, God used her as my angel and our lives were spared that night.

A few weekends later, my brothers Malcom and Marley were going to D.C. with the young man that had his name falsely placed at the crime scene during my criminal case, and I decided to ride with them to have some drinks and gamble. Everything was going well, but like most nights, I couldn't control my drinking and it sparked off a chain of unfortunate events. While we were hanging out in a basement with a group of men, I saw a beautiful girl walk by and she asked me to follow her into another room. I took another swig out of the bottle, handed it to Malcom, and gladly accepted her invitation.

I walked around the corner and we immediately began making out while she was sitting on a washing machine. The more lustful our intimacy became, the more my clothes came off. I placed my leather coat on top of the dryer, and she said she had a condom upstairs. As she exited the room, I walked around the corner and took another swig from the bottle. While I was all worked up and expressing my excitement, I realized my leather coat was in the other room, so I quickly returned only to see that she had taken it along with her clothes.

I'd been deceived. The beautiful girl played me like a fiddle. My wallet and prescription eyeglasses were in the coat pocket and as much as I wanted to say something, I knew I needed to accept it because retaliation wasn't an option. We were in someone else's territory and there were plenty of handguns laying on the floor while the men were rolling dice. As I was pacing back and forth and imagining shooting the place up, my brothers teased me because they knew I'd made a poor decision following a complete stranger while dozens of her men were standing around. The only wise decision I had was to learn from it, so I drank the resentment away as my brothers suggested I slow down, but I respectfully declined and drank myself senseless.

Swig after swig, I drank the night away until I felt like I was going to be sick. I stood up and attempted to exit the basement, but I began to vomit in my hands, and it gushed onto the floor. The D.C. natives were telling me to run outside and I accidentally kicked two dice in the middle of a serious crap shoot. The men jumped off the ground and grabbed their guns. I knew the severity of gambling, and I gambled myself, but I was trashed, and my brothers came forth and humbly negotiated with the men not to hurt me.

I was a horrible drunk and everyone I knew had no shame in telling me so. I hated the taste of alcohol but as soon as I drank one, I drank whatever I could find, and my brothers continued to suggest I stop. I was a mess. I would puke daily then drink another ten hours, not once eating because I wanted to feel the buzz all day. "I can drink all y'all under the table," I often said, and I ended up saying it whenever someone suggested that I put the alcohol down.

I quit the job at the flooring company and became an auto-detailer at the strip-mall where the jewelry store was located. Mae moved in with us to help me and Lincoln financially, but I still carried a resentment toward her though my bitterness wasn't justified. She had no clue what she was getting herself into, in the grand scheme of things, and had never committed a crime in her entire life.

A few months later, I met a beautiful girl named Rai when I was in a limo with White Boy Rick and some other guys from Dale City. While the majority were partying and having sex, she and I sat near the front and talked for hours. I asked to see her again, and our relationship grew closer; then we became intimate. She was the first girl I dated since I dated Janine and she quickly became family to all my people. We spent a lot of time at the bar where Lincoln's

'Ma' worked, and many of us in the gang gambled while shooting pool and drank into the morning hours. Times seemed to have been decent as relationships were made, but the more we connected with different people, the more traffic came through the condo and my sense of peace began to fade.

Lincoln grew closer to Diego and it created a huge wedge between Lincoln and me. I expressed my concerns and warned him not to trust Diego, but my warning fell on deaf ears without having the paperwork on the court case. I was baffled that not one person would believe such a well-respected gangster would testify against me in court, and that reality tormented me. I decided to reach out to a friend of mine named Alden that I'd known since high school to talk about my plan to retaliate.

On the first day of 2002, while in bed with Rai, she questioned why I wasn't aroused, and it was because I was hyper focused on vengeance. And though she was a beautiful girl, my mind was in a dark place and I had no desire for sex. So I lied to her, telling her I wasn't feeling well.

When the phone rang, I knew it was Alden, so I rolled out of bed and walked out of the room. He gave me the location where he wanted to meet, and I left the condo and Rai behind, promising her that I would return soon.

I drove to a popular club in town and the two of us sat down at the bar to discuss my situation at great lengths. Though he didn't know the facts, he never questioned my integrity. He respected me, and knew if I was feeling conflicted, the sit down was for a good cause. He agreed to assist me in whatever way I needed.

After our lengthy conversation, a girl we both knew approached us at the bar and I was invited to join them at his apartment to play Dominoes and cards. I agreed to follow, but only for a few hours, telling them about my girlfriend Rai who was waiting for me at my place. Before we exited the club, something came over me. It was as if my spirit was telling me not to follow them. I didn't know why, but my stomach was in knots, and a sharp pain went through my head. I quickly altered my decision and told Alden that I suddenly didn't feel well and wanted to check on Rai. We wished one another a 'Happy New Year', agreed to meet up soon, and went our separate ways.

Later that morning, as I woke up next to Rai on the couch, I turned on the television and it was on the local news. I immediately recognized the apartment complex that was swarming with Prince William County Police and other first responders. Rai asked, "Hey, are you going to cook us something for breakfast? Joel?" "Hold on," I responded. She asked again, "Are you cooki…" I interrupted her saying, "Hold on, please!" As I watched the news unfold, I knew something horrible had happened. I felt it in my spirit as I did earlier at the club. The knots in my stomach returned and my head began to hurt again. Seeing my concern, she asked, "What's wrong? What's that on the news?" As I contemplated every scenario in my mind that could've taken place, a picture of Alden, his roommate, and another young man were posted on the center of the screen.

The news anchor said all three men had been shot execution style in his apartment. He continued saying that early in the morning, after gunshots were heard, Alden and the other two young men's bodies were found shot, lying naked in the bathtub. As I struggled with the fact that another person was killed soon after I left them, Lincoln and I wanted to pay our respects to our friend at Ebenezer Baptist Church. When we entered the church that winter morning, hundreds gathered during his service. I felt something was amiss though as we searched for our seats.

Though it was a blessing to pay our respects, I felt animosity in the air. Lincoln may not have acknowledged the same feelings, but I saw a number of men in the crowd turning their heads as we walked in. As we sat near the back row, the heads continued to turn our direction and my spirit felt their concerns. I felt they might be thinking I had something to do with their close friend's death. They must've known he and I were sitting at the bar having drinks moments before he was gunned down in his apartment. Since I was the last person seen with him, besides his other friend that was shot, their concerns were valid.

It was quite an uncomfortable feeling, being looked at like a suspect, so I convinced Lincoln to drive me back to the condo where we passed a bottle back and forth until I felt a little more at ease. We returned to the chapel a half an hour later and that made the situation even more suspect. I could only imagine what they thought of us leaving, only to return minutes later.

As the pastor continued, the chapel doors opened, and a young girl walked past each aisle and handed the pastor a note. He shouted, "Hallelujah! Praise God! The suspects that took this young man's life have been arrested in New York. Praise God! Now this child of God may rest in peace and please allow the families of each victim to find closure, good Lord." Any suspicion of wrongdoing on my behalf was instantly absent, and I felt the Holy Spirit taking over the chapel as everyone's focus turned toward the celebration for Alden's life instead of focusing on Lincoln and me.

This is how it went down: after Alden and I separated at the club that night. The two suspects entered the apartment with the intention of robbing Alden, but as the situation unfolded and there were never any drugs to be taken, one of the suspects demanded the three victims undress and lie in the bathtub. When one of the victims refused, a suspect shot all three, leaving them for dead. Unbeknownst to the suspects, Alden's good friend Larry survived the incident and was able to assist authorities in the investigation. The suspects were caught during a long crime spree that left many families burying their loved ones.

For me, I knew I'd dodged another date with death, but felt a sense of responsibility because every person I spoke to about plotting revenge against certain men ended up losing their life. So, after Alden was laid to rest, I made a promise to myself that I wouldn't continue feeding the pattern of unfortunate events one after another. *I made the decision to keep my thoughts of planning my vengeance to myself.*

CHAPTER 11

D.C. SNIPER

Though Lincoln and I attended Alden's service that day, our relationship was diminishing due to him showing loyalty to both me and Diego. I lived at the condo longer than I'd lived anywhere else since I left my parents' house as a teenager, but my mind was set, and I was looking to move out as soon as possible.

My girlfriend Rai was working at Potomac Mills Mall and was planning to attend college with a girlfriend of hers from high school, so the two of them began searching for an apartment. It couldn't have come at a better time for me, because the traffic at the condo was becoming an issue, and the paranoia constantly made my head feel like it was on a swivel instead of my neck. My older sister's friend, Ronan and another guy named Tony, who I went to middle school with years prior, became reliable business partners with us in the drug game. I trusted the young men because they weren't known for having ill-intentions; it was strictly about making money to them. I knew if I ever needed anything, apart from the drugs, they would be there for me out of respect, and even more so, for the love of my older sister.

I arranged a face to face meeting with Ronan, the most respected young man from their group. I wanted to speak to him alone about purchasing a firearm and kept the promise I made to myself and didn't speak of my intentions about what I intended to do with a gun. As I anticipated, he respected me enough not to ask questions and agreed to help me out. Shortly after our sit down, I dropped Rai off at her job and made my rounds through town to make money. I stopped by the Gomez brothers' house on 'K' street and had some drinks until it was time to pick Rai up from work later that evening.

I made my way through town and came to a complete stop at a stop sign while heavy traffic passed on the heavy populated road. I took a long swig from the bottle, turned up the Go-go music and as traffic receded, I stepped on the gas. Then I heard it. *BOOM!* Startled, I yelled out, "What the f…?" Something slammed into me, but I didn't see anything. I checked the rear-view mirrors and pulled to the side of the road. I rolled the windows down and noticed a man laying across the sidewalk with his bike mangled on the grass. "Oh, my God! Sir! Yo! Are you okay?" He said to me, "Yes, I'm okay you assho…," but I didn't stay long enough to let him finish the sentence. I put the car in drive and put the pedal to the metal. There was no way I was catching another charge. I stepped on the gas as the busy parkway was filling up again and I gained high speeds as the pack of cars were approaching. The man clearly said he was okay and that was enough for me to drive away in an attempt to save myself from going to prison. I felt horrible that we collided, and I truly didn't see him in the dark, but that wouldn't mean a thing if the law caught me drinking and driving in Rai's car without a license.

Luckily for me, the bottle of liquor had the lid on it and didn't spill everywhere. I pulled over in the mall parking lot and tossed the bottle and checked the car for damages. Rai's driver's side headlight was hanging out, so I quickly fixed it before I drove up to the mall's main entrance to pick her up.

Later that night, I went to a club in Georgetown with Tony. This guy was in the first class I ever attended in middle school, in Virginia, after I moved from Arizona. We'd seen each other off and on throughout the years, but our relationship grew closer when Lincoln and I decided to open the connection for higher grades of marijuana and cocaine. After I tested the product to ensure it was worthy of purchasing, which I always asked because I was an addict, we sat at the bar and talked about life over a dozen drinks or so. As the night turned to morning, I received a call from Rai, and she was not happy with me, "Why are the police at my mother's house looking for a young Hispanic man who was involved in a hit and run? What did you do, Joel?" Playing dumb, I responded, "What? What Hispanic guy are you hanging out with?" I was an idiot. I always flipped the script on any situation when I was questioned about my wrong doings. I said, "They must have the wrong car. There would be damage to the car or something. I'm telling you... I didn't hit anyone with your car. It'll be fine." She yelled, "Umm...no, it won't be. The officer just said my headlight is hanging out and the victim got my license plate as you drove away."

I couldn't believe it. I was in trouble with the law again, but because it was dark that night, I would fight the case on the grounds that there would be no possible way the man could identify me as the driver. The court date was set for the man to testify against me, but it wasn't scheduled for a few months. I moved out of the condo soon after and rested my head at Rai's apartment in Manassas that her and two other girls rented. She wasn't crazy about the idea of us living together so early in our relationship, but I had a job opportunity at a pool company close by, and she agreed to let me reside at the apartment against her best judgment. Although she didn't understand the severity of my circumstances, allowing me to stay with her helped me to get away from the other side of the county.

The job offer came about when I spoke to my friend Waylon. After the jewelry store incident, he and his wife moved out of the townhouse where the police found Diego hiding in the attic and moved south with their kids to get away from all the drama. When I showed up for my first day of work, I was caught off guard when Dayton was working there as well. Waylon and Dayton kept in touch after Dayton was released, and a small group of guys I knew were already working for Waylon's father building swimming pools.

I was conflicted once again. Everywhere I turned I had a situation that would test my will. I wanted to harm Dayton in the worst way, and I moved out of the condo specifically because Lincoln was associating with Diego. I didn't know how to handle the situation and was uncomfortable from the start, but I needed to pay child support and wasn't going to be mooching off Rai while she worked hard toward her future. I ended up staying at work that morning to focus on my own future. Prison and death weren't on my 'to do list' as far as goals I wanted to achieve. I wanted to spend more time with Selena, but my circumstances, along with many failed attempts to get past resentments, had me moving further away from her and her mother. Selena was always on my mind, and my intentions were to save up enough money to buy a car so I would be able to drive north to see her more often.

As time passed, I began selling ecstasy pills on the side to make more money. Ecstasy was a powerful psychoactive drug made from MDMA. The drug heightened people's energy and after I tested the pills, I became addicted to the feeling it gave me. It was different than any drug I'd ever used. I was truly happy when I was high on it. I was in a state of euphoria. I loved everyone around me. It wasn't like LSD, Cocaine, Formaldehyde, Methamphetamine, Weed, or alcohol. It created a sense of companionship between people and at the time, I wanted to stay in that euphoric state.

As I continued using the "happy pill," the resentments I had toward others faded away. Even though it was mind blowing to accept, I continued working with Dayton and even purchased ecstasy from Diego because he had a great product at a great price. I just felt good all the time, regardless of my past afflictions, and it felt wonderful to not feel angry after everything I'd gone through.

I started going to Rave's in D.C. to sell my product. The environment was foreign to me because I was a gangster that was used to violent clubs. These people were dancing to Techno music under black lights and waving glow-in-the-dark things around, while others were enjoying themselves in a gigantic room that was like a bubble bath foam party. I witnessed people having the time of their lives and not once did I witness violence, and that's when I realized it was the perfect place for me to sell ecstasy.

As I continued working and selling the drug, news spread across the Metropolitan area that innocent people were being shot by someone using a .223-caliber rifle. Authorities said they were looking for a white van, but in and around the D.C. area, there were tens of thousands of white vans and they couldn't find leads fast enough as to who and where the suspect or suspects were or where they were going next.

On October 2nd, of 2002, two people were shot in Maryland and one of the victims died. On October 3rd, four people were killed while going about their daily routines, and that same night, the only victim who was shot in Washington D.C., was killed while walking down the street. On October 7th, a thirteen-year-old boy was critically shot outside of his middle school. Two days later, on October 9th, a tarot card was found close to the crime scene. The card was said to have been a 'Death Card,' and it had a message that read, "Call me God."

As the government and law-enforcement continued to place the pieces together on the world stage, millions of us in society were cautious about our every movement outside our homes. While pumping gas, I would literally dance around to Go-go music and move enough to where it would be an irritant to any sniper, but I couldn't have been cautious enough. On October 9th, during the evening hours, I was in the apartment cooking dinner for the young ladies I lived with, while listening to a Major League Baseball Playoff game over the television. As I continued to cook, I heard a gunshot, followed by a loud echo. I knew it didn't come from a handgun and quickly asked the girls to quiet it down. As they continued to talk, I asked them to turn the TV down and knew in my heart the lone shot was from the .223-caliber rifle that was used in the recent killings.

I took the food off the stove and walked over to the balcony. I opened the screen door and looked across the street where there were many businesses lit up in the night. Across the main road that ran through Manassas and connected to Route 66, was a gas station where a man was laying on the ground next to his vehicle. It was a fifty-three-year-old Vietnam Veteran that was walking back to his car after paying for gas when he was fatally shot from a long distance. The suspect, or suspects, targeted our area because Route 66 was a main highway that connected to many other areas, and the opportunity of fleeing the scene unnoticed was significant.

On October 11th, another man was killed while at a gas station in Fredericksburg, where my sister and her family lived. On October 14th, one day after my birthday, another woman was shot and killed in Falls Church, Virginia at a home improvement store. On October

THE BOOK OF JOEL

1^{9th}, another man was shot outside a restaurant in Virginia, and the bullet that was retrieved from the man, connected him to the same rifle used with the other shootings. On October 22nd, a bus driver was shot while standing on the top step in his commuter bus in Maryland, he later succumbed to his injuries.

Two days later, on October 24th, after three long weeks, authorities arrested two suspects found sleeping in a Chevy Caprice at a rest stop in Maryland. The suspects weren't in a white van at all, and my friend Nokes that I worked with, swore he and I witnessed the two suspects standing next to the blue Caprice outside of a school in Manassas, after seeing what the suspects looked like on the news.

It came out that an older adult male trained a seventeen-year-old male to use the rifle and had him carry out many of the killings. It also was said the two suspects killed many others across the country, including a man who was shot and killed while playing golf in Tucson, Arizona—on the same side of town where many of my relatives lived.

After the chaos of the 'D.C. or Beltway Sniper' came to an end, life quickly went back to normal for those of us that didn't lose any loved ones during the killing spree. I continued working at the pool company and sold drugs while feeding my drug habit. Rai and I weren't doing well, due to my poor choices and choosing drugs and alcohol over being a reliable boyfriend. While the relationship was in turmoil, the two of us tried our best to mend our relationship out of love for one another, but my transgressions would get the best of me once again. Whenever we went to the bar to shoot pool with the gang, I would get hammered and not want to leave until the bar closed. When we attended night clubs in D.C., she acted responsibly and made sure she left early enough to get rest and be able to make it to work every morning. While she went home by herself, I continued to use drugs and drink myself comatose.

After a while, my lack of self-respect and respect for her wishes became too much for her and she wanted me out of the apartment. I stayed away most nights and was able to seek shelter with Waylon or his cousin Nokes from work, but when I returned to the apartment in an attempt to plead for her forgiveness, the situation became violent. She was so fed up with me that she used physical violence in an attempt to push me away and I knew I was destroying her life and she didn't know what else to do.

Rage and disturbing behavior were the outcome for me for many years whenever someone disrespected me, but I didn't put my hands on her. I broke things, I was disrespectful verbally, and I even threw my pit bull Prince during an altercation we had. That in itself was grounds for me to step back because I loved my dog and would never want to hurt him. All she wanted was for me to move out and I didn't want to leave. I loved her but not enough to put the drugs and alcohol down. I became jealous when she would go play pool around the gang. And when they didn't tell her to leave, it created more animosity in me toward some of the people I grew up with. Rai was a cool girl. Everyone liked her and enjoyed her personality, and when I began to fall apart, other men began to close-in just like the boys in high school did with my first love, Nora.

It came to a point where I needed to leave the apartment before I caught another charge and was sent to prison. I didn't believe in hitting females, but if the environment were toxic, anything and everything could go wrong. When we finally decided to call it quits, Rai immediately began hanging out with Diego. He was confident and girls were attracted to the way he carried himself, but I knew him for what he truly was and that turned me into a lunatic while he reaped all the benefits.

I moved my belongings to my sister's house in Fredericksburg and her and Patrick allowed me to store everything I owned in their basement while I looked for a place to go. I started using cocaine heavily and my drinking got even worse. My head began to hurt again and with the ongoing stress, the pain became debilitating.

Waylon and Nokes both offered to open their doors to me, and I went from house to house between both cousins and grew close to all their relatives that lived around the region. I kept my dog Prince, after Rai and I separated, and was able to house him with Nokes who had pit bulls of his own.

I got word, soon after I left Manassas, that the other girls Rai and I lived with, went to Rai's job at a dental office with more girls and assaulted her while she was working. I was told they didn't like the way she handled our situation, but she quickly blamed me for the assault and thought I conspired to create the whole situation. I truly had nothing to do with them acting out in that way.

I was lost mentally and spiritually without a clue about where to turn next. Without means of transportation and then moving even further away from where I grew up, I still wasn't able to visit Janine and Selena and every emotion continued to suffocate my life as a whole. I drank and used as much as possible to counteract the desire to retaliate for my many situations. I functioned well enough to keep my job at the pool company and that covered the child support, my drug habit, and the alcohol, but money was hard to come by because I quit selling ecstasy.

Luckily, my family reached out and asked if I wanted to go to Tucson, to visit our relatives and attend a family reunion in Puerto Peñasco, Mexico. Again, my family came through during my times of struggle. They never knew the severity of my situations, but knew my ex-girlfriend Rai well, and knew that our breakup affected me in the worst of ways.

My time in Mexico was exactly what I needed. Though I continued to drink, use drugs, and smoked weed while visiting with my relatives, I was able to relax a little. I wasn't able to block out the resentments I had back East, but I partied like a rock star during the festivities, dancing with beautiful Mexican women and relishing the time I had there. I did everything I could to forget what I left behind, even if it were only for a few weeks, but it was to no avail. I sat on the beach for hours each night, staring into the ocean while contemplating each scenario, and mulling whether or not I was ready to retaliate on everyone who disrespected me.

It always came down to where I was spiritually and whether I was willing to lose my own life for the cause. That was the conflict I had within. At times, the thoughts seemed justifiable and rewarding, but I wanted to see Selena again and needed to find a way back into her life. Thankfully, that was the one scenario that stuck with me through all my deliberations and retaliating truly wasn't worth it… *even though the stress was killing me.*

CHAPTER 12

GET IN THE TRUCK

When I returned to Virginia, I isolated myself from everyone I was affiliated with. I still couldn't find it in myself to build up enough confidence to show my face in Dale City knowing Rai was seeing Diego. I couldn't have imagined how people who ratted others out could walk around with their heads held high while others continued to associate with them. It just baffled me to my core.

I ended up seeking shelter with Nokes and his family south east of Manassas. It was nice reuniting with my dog Prince again and during this time, Nokes and his wife were taking care of his grandmother before she went to be with the Lord. Their place was out in the boondocks, and that was exactly where I needed to be due to my homicidal ideation.

It was going on eight years that I felt a strong desire to get revenge on those who turned on me. Going back to the mid-nineties when I was at Garfield High School and students were rioting. With my head trauma and substance abuse, I knew myself well enough to know that if I did go home, someone was going to lose their life. I was aware that it could be my life taken if I went back, but with all the plotting and contemplation I'd done, I felt I was years ahead of any of those men as far as planning the acts out.

The longer I stayed in the woods, the more country folk I met through Nokes. He and Waylon had an extremely large family. The street was named after their family and their blood ran deep throughout the Metropolitan area. They weren't gang affiliated, but with a family that big, they didn't need outsiders to create numbers. And the fact that they welcomed me in with open arms, showed me that I was still a charismatic young man regardless of what I told myself throughout my years-long meltdown.

When the day came for me to sit in court, I asked the family if they would go with me as they were an intimidating presence. Even though I was a basket case compared to most people, others didn't see me as intimidating by the way I looked. The name "Omen," and the stories people heard intimidated them, but my size surprised many once they'd met me.

I cut all my hair off and purchased eyeglasses after I hit the man on his bike, in hopes he wouldn't be able to recognize me on that dark night. As we sat in the courtroom, I thought about Selena and prayed I wouldn't return to the confinement of the corrections system. I knew I deserved whatever consequence was cast upon me, but I'd hoped that God would see whatever goodness I had left in me and would spare me from facing that reality.

When the judge asked the victim to identify the suspect, the victim looked directly at me, looked at my company, and told the judge he didn't recognize anyone in the courtroom. I was shocked to say the least but didn't make any obvious movements to express my relief. The judge asked him if he was certain, and the man nodded his head and answered, "Yes, your honor, I am certain. The man driving that night is not in this courtroom." The man spared me, and I'd never know why, but I was truly grateful for his mercy. I understood my chances of ever being a productive member of society were fading with every poor decision I made.

I hid in the woods for over a year, staying clear of everyone I grew up with. My depression sank to uncharted levels, and though I was in good company, I eventually found myself seeking out those in the family that drank and used drugs. This strong-willed family supported themselves by supplying the small town's addict population. Because the family was spread-out and well established, it was structured to succeed without disruptions from outsiders. Initially it seemed cruel to me that family would serve dope to their own family members, but I soon found out how that protected the family, and didn't harm them, when outside influences would attempt to take over the drug currency deep in those woods.

Nokes had an older cousin named Niles who lived down the hill in a tiny red trailer. Niles was known to everyone in the area as a lifelong addict. His sixteen-foot trailer sat on another man's land, which was strange to me, because the landowner had a sixteen-room mansion built in the woods that was never occupied. The exterior of the mansion was never painted and looked creepy as hell from the outside.

Since Nokes wasn't an addict or an alcoholic, I found solace at Niles's trailer a few hundred feet down the hill, as it gave me somewhere to drink without feeling uncomfortable. The lonely man looked to be in his eighties, but when I asked his age, I was dumbfounded when I learned he was only forty-eight years old, and that crack cocaine was what debilitated him to the point of living like that. I ended up drinking with the Niles, daily, and when his family made their rounds through the country, he would quietly walk into his trailer, close the door behind him, and smoke his rock cocaine in peace.

Eventually, I began purchasing the dope because it was easy money. Alonzo, who was the main source, lived outside the area and would travel south weekly to serve his clients. He would sell me what I could afford, and I would make a profit, helping me, him, and the addicts along the country road when they needed a quick drop off while he was at home in Maryland.

One evening he called and asked if I would serve a particular client of his, so I went down the road to sell a few bags at a house I'd never been to. When I walked in the front door, a large woman greeted me and began questioning who I was and where I came from. I could tell she was paranoid, and because she didn't know me, she was skeptical and thought I was a "narc." As I began to explain who sent me, a man approached from the back of the house. He was as paranoid as she was, but when I took a second glance at him, I knew him. "Yo! What up, little man," the man acknowledged me as he looked over my shoulder and out the door. "I was locked up with this young man. He's cool, come on in, brotha," he said. He was correct. Buster and I worked as trustees together while I was away, and though he was an addict, this man was built like a Rottweiler on steroids.

I sat in their kitchen and explained how I knew Alonzo, and that I was staying at Nokes's house down the road. They knew the family well, and once they felt comfortable with me, they asked me for the crack cocaine. As the woman pulled out her glass pipe, I got up to leave, but she hollered out another woman's name and said, "Before you leave sweetie, go in the back and hook my sister up. Go on now... she won't bite." "Come on youngster; I'll introduce you," Buster said as his girlfriend lit up the crack rock. "Oh yeah...this some good shit," I heard the woman say as I followed Buster down the hall.

I followed him to the bedroom, and he introduced me to the other sister. Her name was Wynnie, and she was definitely more attractive, much nicer, and didn't seem to be as paranoid as her sister. We talked in her room as I broke up the dope, and the two of us ended up making a connection that evening. I hadn't been around many females since Rai and I split up, and I felt comfortable in the presence of this woman. She wasn't the stereotypical crack head that I'd been around. She had a career, goals, and carried herself as the respectable hardworking woman she was. It caught me off guard though, because I'd never seen anyone smoke dope and function in that manner. It truly blew my mind. I gave her my phone number before I left that evening, and she agreed to call me the next time she needed a sack.

Later that night, after Nokes and his family were settling down, I walked down the hill to Niles's trailer with my dog Prince. Niles and I drank a while as we talked about life. Then the questions came, "What are ya hidin from, young fella? Why in da hell would a bright 'sta like yaself, willingly come to 'da woods and banish yaself from life itself? Dees woods ain't fa ya. Whe's ya daughta? Why ain't ya takin care of ha? Why ya hangin wit dees fools out in dees woods? I don't mean to pry, but ya somethin' special. I can feel it. Ya gonna be some-thin big one day, young man. I'm tellin ya...as God is my witness. I can feel it." The sincere man patted my shoulder as he slowly walked into the trailer to get high.

I sat outside in the dark with Prince, as he placed his face on my lap, and I glanced through the trees where the distant porch light from Nokes's house up the hill was barely noticeable. I began thinking about Selena, Janine, my family, Rai, Nora, Dayton, Diego, Mae, being incarcerated, everyone who passed away, not graduating high school, being discharged from the National Guard, all my injuries, and lastly…all my wrongdoings. The more I thought about Niles's words, the more shame I felt.

He hit me in the gut with his subtle lecture and I wasn't prepared for it. I felt his spirit, and it was that of a broken but wise soul. He was wise from experience, his words were deeply rooted, and it affected me to the point of wanting to use to get away from it all. I reached down to the twelve pack I brought with me, but it was empty. I rubbed Prince's head, though I could barely see him in the darkness, and took a deep breath, "Oh Lord, forgive me for what I'm about to do. Come on, pup." I stood up off the chair and turned toward Niles's door and knocked.

When the door opened, Prince jumped in and I closed the door behind me. A faint voice told me to lock it, as the struggling man held a nebulizer mask over his mouth and nose. Niles had emphysema, so he had to use that machine before each time he smoked cocaine. It was truly a sad thing to witness and proof of how bad the drug could affect people. But I was already inside my head and the only coping skills I knew were to use and drink. I pulled a sack of rock cocaine from my pocket and sat it on his small table. As I began to break it up, Niles shook his head and said, "Young man, whateva ya think ya know, ya don't. Dis shit is killin me if ya hadn't noticed. I know ya lost these days but dis ain't gonna fix it. I don't wanna be da one folks lookin to when ya all high and losin ya mind. Don't be like me." I answered him, "I hear you brother, and I appreciate your concern, but hiding here in your woods isn't enough for me to escape my reality. I won't get stuck on it forever. It may take me down for a good while… but it won't get me forever." I continued to break us off a good portion for the night because I knew once I started, I wouldn't be able to stop.

He turned his machine off and walked to the back where his small kitchen was, opened a drawer, and pulled out an antenna he'd broken off an old truck. Next he reached under his sink and grabbed a steel sponge and dropped them both on the table. He cut off a piece of the sponge and placed it in the antenna, put a crack rock in it, and shook his head. He looked up at me. "Fatha, have mercy on dis young fella," he prayed as he handed me the loaded pipe.

Prince started whining and climbed on the chair next to me. He sensed something evil was about to take place and he didn't like it one bit. He licked my face as I flicked the lighter, Niles was loaded and ready, "Alright, brother. Cheers to you, my friend." I placed the metal pipe to my mouth, took a deep breath, exhaled, and put the flame to the rock. I could hear the drug cooking as I inhaled slowly. I held in as long as I could and after I exhaled, my ears rang louder than a locomotive through a tunnel. I thought I was going to defecate on myself. Prince crawled on me and licked my face as the concerned Niles looked at me from across the table then he said, "I hope ya know...ya gonna be chasin dat hit till ya put dat shit down. And I hope ya right... I hope ya don't get stuck on it foreva." I opened my eyes wide as he was talking to me, and my insides were like, *w-h-a-t...t-h-e...f-u-c-k*. I couldn't move and ended up being stuck for hours, until well after the sun came up.

In order for me not to get stuck in his little trailer all hours of the day and night, I ended up going to Wynnie's house where it was more comfortable. The first night I spent over there, Buster was searching under beds, the couches, in the closets, in the cabinets. When I asked him what he was doing, he said, "Did you see that man? I know he's in here. He came in while we were in the rooms. Oh yeah, he's in here... I know you're in here! I'm gonna find you... and when I do... I'm gonna smash you." And he just kept going. He was on a mission like I'd never seen. I peeked my head into Wynnie's room, she nodded and said, "Does Buster think there's a strange man in the house? It happens all the time." I just looked at Buster, shrugged my shoulders and went back in the room.

From the moment I smoked the first rock, selling it became impossible. It had a hold on me, and like Niles said, I chased that first high anticipating the same results. It got so bad so fast, that the men I knew, and their families, were worried about me and Waylon even drove up from the south and asked to see me. He didn't know how to confront me after he'd heard the rumors of my new addiction. But I made it easier for him after I pulled out a crushed beer can, flicked the ashes from my cigarette onto it, placed a crack rock on top and smoked it in front of him. He was both shocked and saddened because he knew I was self-sabotaging while being bitter and depressed.

Multiple people attempted an intervention and Nokes's mother took me to her church because she said my heart was pure. I didn't know if that was the truth or not because I hadn't been clean and sober in years. When I was locked away, yes, my heart seemed decent enough, but when I was on drugs, I'd lose control and began doing things that led people to question my character. I was addicted to smoking cocaine. I liked smoking cocaine, because it alleviated my sense of shame and blurred out all the resentments I had. It also stabilized me as far as wanting to harm others. But when I mixed it with freshly brewed corn liquor, I would end up embarrassing myself because it turned me into a sex fiend.

If I weren't around a female, I would call everyone on my phone list, hoping a female would answer and if they did, I would attempt to have phone sex with them. I did have a way with words, I thought. But after I'd wake up from long high, reality would set in when I learned who I'd called and what I said to them. Many times, I called my own relatives across the country while high and drunk, talking dirty and being perverted. I just didn't care about anything including my morals. I smoked my morals through a crack pipe. I called a friend of mine's mother and attempted to have phone sex with her and that didn't work out so well either. He and his father ended up confronting me about it and though they felt betrayed, they knew I was battling demons and reached out in an attempt to save me.

The only person I called to have phone sex with, who wasn't someone's wife, sister, mother, aunt, or hell, even grandma, was a girl that I worked with at the carwash when I lived at the condo. Her name was Olivia Rose and she was one of the girls that used to braid my hair before I cut it all off after the hit and run. The two of us stayed in contact throughout the years and I often reached out to her when Rai and I separated. She must've thought I was a pervert because every time I called, eventually I turned our conversation into a lust driven, over-the-phone porno call.

No one outside of the people I knew in the woods was aware I was addicted to smoking cocaine. I was known to drink a lot and to use drugs recreationally, but none of my family, Janine's family, or the gang knew how hard I'd fallen. I wasn't willing to admit to everyone that I was acting foolishly because I was a junkie. They may have thought I was a creep for things I did but I wouldn't be confessing my transgressions to anyone anytime soon.

I received a phone call from my mother telling me that one of my uncles was arrested for trafficking drugs from the southwest to the state we resided in. And then my sister called to tell me Ronan, the one that I got the gun from but never questioned why, had shot himself in the head. Soon after, his biological brother, who I'd worked with every day as his helper installing appliances, overdosed and died.

I thought I was numb on the inside, I was wrong. The news of Ronan's suicide affected me. He was a true leader of his people. I'd been depressed many times for long periods of time. Though I didn't physically show it to people because I fled and isolated myself, his death proved to me that no matter how strong we may be perceived by others, no human truly knows what another person is going through mentally or spiritually.

Wynnie kindly drove me to the wake in Woodbridge and though I was anxious after not showing my face in months, I wanted to pay my respects to a man that respected me. My sister immediately questioned me about the woman who accompanied me. She had suspicions of my wrong doings with drugs because I didn't look well, but we ended up staying a while and I shared my condolences with Ronan's mother. On our way back to the boondocks, we stopped by my parents' house because I hadn't seen them in a while.

As soon as I entered their house, my mother questioned why I was with an older woman. She was also saddened to see how hard life had been going for me. My family was used to me being in trouble, they questioned my lifestyle many times, but also knew me to be a confident young man. One who always had beautiful young girlfriends that my mother welcomed with open arms when I brought them around. I respectfully asked Wynnie to wait in the car while I answered the questions that continued to pour in from my concerned mother. Even so, we were back on the road in no time.

Shortly after Ronan's suicide, Hurricane Isabel smashed into Virginia leaving close to two-million Virginians without power and ripping thousands of trees from the earth. We weren't able to leave the woods until the roads were cleared and this was a problem. Wynnie and I were on a mission to score dope and the main access roads were blocked off. Without access to Alonzo, from Maryland, we agreed to meet up with two men who'd recently settled in the area and had immediately made it known they were the new drug dealers in those parts. Though their settling here created animosity between them and Alonzo, all we cared about was getting high. Since the hurricane cut off our supply, we did what was necessary regardless of who sold it to us.

Without the new drug dealers Rocky and Ron, I would've been chopping every tree that blocked the country roads in order to get our next fix because drinking moonshine throughout the entire storm wasn't going to be enough. My body craved drugs as well as booze.

As the days passed and the roads were finally cleared, one of the functioning addicts in the area asked if I wanted to earn some money assisting him with a job. He told me he was in the flooring business and that's how he supported both his and his wife's cocaine habit. He needed extra hands for his next job, and I accepted his offer before he picked me up early the next morning. Knowing the way, my journey through life continued; the house we drove to, 129 miles away, was on the same country road Janine and Selena lived on with their family. Out of all the houses we could've been working near in the state of Virginia, we were in walking distance from where my daughter lived and I knew there had to be a reason why.

So, around noon, I told the man I was going to visit with my daughter regardless of how bad off I was. I didn't look healthy because I wasn't healthy, but God had the man ask me to help him with that specific job for a reason and it wasn't because of the wood floors. I believed it was so I could be close to my daughter and maybe, just maybe, seeing her and holding her would save me from a darkness that was only getting deeper.

I approached the beautiful home that sat at the top of a hill and said a prayer as I rang the doorbell. I took a deep breath and looked myself over, knowing I was much thinner than I had been in years. I was extremely pale having been indoors smoking dope and I hadn't slept in days. It didn't matter to me while I was around other addicts, the way I was living, the way I looked and always being edgy, but as soon as I stepped foot on their property, I felt a calmness I hadn't known in years. I felt as though good spirits were present and that's exactly what God intended for me to experience that day.

As I thought about what words I wanted to say to Selena, and that in moments I would witness for myself how much she'd grown, I wondered whether or not I would be scolded by the family for showing up unannounced. I rang the doorbell a number of times, but it was to no avail. I sat on the top step hoping Janine and our daughter would drive up the hill at any moment, but no one ever showed, and I felt a crushing disappointment. I just didn't understand, I thought this was meant to be.

I couldn't believe it. I questioned why God sent me 129 miles away to a job site just seconds from their house if I weren't there to see my daughter. I was so close to holding her and telling her how much I loved her and how sorry I was for being absent. I guess none of those words were meant to be spoken that day and I thought it might be possible this was only to show me I could be too late.

That evening, as the man and I pulled into Nokes's driveway in the boondocks, we noticed Rocky and Ron standing with Niles by his old red trailer. The driver said, "Don't go down that hill until Wynnie pays them for the cocaine they fronted her yesterday. Do you hear me, boy? Don't be stupid. Hey...seriously...look at me. Wait until she gets home from work and pays them before you walk down there." The day before, Wynnie asked the drug dealers to front her some dope and assured them she would pay them as soon as she got paid the next evening.

When I opened the van door and steeped out, the two men looked up the hill and turned their attention toward me and yelled,

"Omen! You're just the young man we wanted to see. Come down and have a drink with us, young G." "Don't go down there! You'll get killed! Wait until she pays them or go inside and get Nokes and your dogs first. Are you hearing me," the concerned driver pleaded. I felt in my spirit that harm was coming my way, but I wasn't jeopardizing Nokes's freedom or the safety of his family.

It would've been easy to walk ten feet through Nokes's front door to give everyone a heads up on what the situation was, and he most definitely would've been walking next to me stride for stride down the hill to confront the men, but I knew it would've started a war because his family had been running the dope down here for years. Nokes had nothing to do with the drug deal, or my lifestyle, and I wasn't about to have his entire family surrounding these men because of my choices, so I closed the van door and headed down the hill as the van reversed out of the driveway.

The sun was all but gone when I approached the men. My debilitated old friend Niles was sitting in a chair and he appeared to have been injured. "Sit down, Omen, and take a swig of that" Rocky said, while handing me a half-gallon of whisky. I took a long swig before I sat on a cinderblock next to Niles. "Where's your lady friend Wynnie," Rocky asked. "She said she would have our money today and she hasn't shown yet. Have you seen or spoken to her today?" I turned to the two men as I handed Rocky the bottle of whisky, "I've been working all day up north and haven't spoken to her. So, no, I haven't seen her today. But I know she'll pay you when she gets back, and I know she gets paid today…it's Friday." Rocky responded with, "Well…how do we know she isn't going to rip us off?" "I don't know," I replied, "But what I do know is that she's a good person and I haven't seen anything to make me say otherwise." Then Ron chimed in, "Listen, little G…and listen very carefully…we both like you. You're a solid young man, and our old friend Niles here in this chair feels that you are a special person. Says you have a gift. But we're here for our money…and we're going to need that money right now, so I can go to the city to get more dope. As the men turned to one another, I looked over toward Niles and he shook his head. At that moment I felt evil manifesting and it was closing in fast.

I heard Prince barking furiously from the house on the hill and I began praying that Nokes would let him out, knowing that my dog would run to my aid as soon as the front door opened. Then Nokes's porch light turned on and for a split second, I thought it was happening, but it wasn't in the cards I was dealt that day, because nobody opened the door, and my dog wasn't able to get to me.

I looked up at the men and pulled my phone from my pocket, "I'll call and see where she's at." "For your sake, I hope she answers," Ron mumbled while walking to his truck. "She didn't answer; I'll try again," I said. I pressed redial, but it just continued to ring. I pushed it again and nothing. I looked over to Ron while he reached into his truck and I pushed it again, then again.

Niles began pleading with Rocky, as he must've felt the evil surrounding us as well, but it was too late. As I pushed redial again, Rocky punched me in my head where the flashlight hit me long ago. While I tried to figure out how to escape, he picked up the cinderblock I was sitting on and hit me in the ribs with it. He lifted it again and did the same. As Niles yelled out for help, Ron opened the back door of the truck and his cousin hit me again so hard that I defecated in my pants.

I started crawling toward Prince's barks when Rocky picked up a piece of bamboo from the ground and started to force it down my throat. My defense mechanisms from being attacked in the past, didn't allow him to succeed. He threw the stick with fury and Ron calmly walked over to me pointing his handgun in my face, "Open your mouth. Omen! Open your fucking mouth! We said we liked you, but we're going to fucking kill you because your lady friend played us. Now get up. Get the fuck up and get in the truck. Get… in…the…truck…Omen!" Poor Niles tried to help me, but he was too slow and too weak, he was pushed to the ground with ease.

I got to my feet and though I had been hit multiple times in the ribs with the concrete block, my head was all I felt. Rocky sucker punched me perfectly on the dent in my head and it rocked my world. I felt like I was going to die, still I wasn't going in the truck willingly. They began pushing me toward the truck and I attempted to flee but the larger men overpowered me dragging me through the dirt. I hadn't slept in days and my energy was dissipating fast, but I fought back with everything I had; I wasn't going out without a fight.

I was so small that I was able to escape their grasp and pushed off Rocky making him trip. As I turned around to run toward the hill, I heard Ron cock his handgun and it was pointed directly at my temple saying, "I...am...not...fucking around. I will blow your fucking brains out...right here. Now get in the goddamn truck!" I looked at Niles who was still on the ground and glanced up the hill toward Nokes's house because they usually had multiple people over and they would've been outside smoking weed, but as everything else played out that day, nothing was going my way.

The two frustrated men were finally able to get me in the truck and Ron sat next to me in the back seat, "The child safety locks are on, so there's no point in trying to escape." I could smell the shit from my pants and apologized for the smell as we drove away, and I watched as Nokes's house faded away into the darkness. I wiped my face and noticed there was blood coming from where Rocky was trying to pry my mouth open with the bamboo stick and my head and my body were in really bad shape.

I was so close to seeing Selena earlier in the day, but she wasn't there and all I wanted to do was tell her that I loved her, regardless if she or their family believed me. It was as if I was in a dream state looking at myself from the outside, watching this young man reaching out for the doorbell just wanting to hold his little girl one last time and nobody answered. Looking in as this young man was calling a woman continuously, and if she'd answered his phone calls just once, his life would've been spared. I saw myself listening to the dog barking, knowing that his owner was in trouble but was unable to run to him because even though the porch light turned on, the front door never opened.

Small snippets of my life flashed through my mind and in the tick of a clock, that life would soon be over without the presence of a divine intervention shielding me from a bullet to the head. I quickly asked God for forgiveness, but my sins were piled so high that I wasn't able to focus on any of them and all I could think of was my family.

As the truck turned off the dirt road and we headed to a more remote area in the backwoods, Rocky received a phone call, "That was her; she'll meet us in twenty minutes. What do you want to do with Omen?" "Wow, isn't that something? Unbelievable," Ron chuckled softly while looking down at his gun. "A hundred more feet and my cousin's phone service wouldn't have been able to receive that call. I think your crippled buddy Niles may be on to something. And maybe you are blessed, and God really is looking out for you. That's crazy. When we get the money, let him out." I held my head low and sobbed uncontrollably as we passed the remote wooded area where they were going to shoot me and leave me for dead.

Rocky made a U-turn through a path as I saw my death in those woods that night and it was extremely vivid. I could smell the dirt being tossed onto my face and envisioned my lifeless body lying in hole with insects crawling all over it. I immediately thought about my brother Conor who was executed in the south and how his body was found months later because some random person walking by noticed a piece of his shoe, knowing that poor soul would have to live with that picture in their memory for the rest of their life.

I thought about my parents and Janine, and how they would've thought I'd just ran off again, or how they would've reacted to the news of my body being found months or even years later when a housing development or school was being built. As the tears continued to fall and I wiped my face with my shirt, the dirt road ended, and the truck drove on to the paved street. I looked through the trees toward the moon and shook my head in disbelief and asked myself how I'd managed to survive everything I'd been through up to that point.

I knew there was only one explanation for how that phone rang a hundred feet from my burial ground, and though I continued to stray from God and His word, I thanked him for His mercy in the back seat of that truck. I knew it was by His grace and His grace alone I was still alive, even though I knew in my heart I didn't deserve it.

CHAPTER 13

REALITY WAS TRICKY

W*ithin minutes of exiting the truck I was back at it—smoking crack again. The blow to my head caused more physical and psychological trauma. My ribs may have been broken, but because of the lack of trust I had toward hospitals, I chose to stay away and immediately turned back to self-medicating.*

One day later, I wisely chose to retreat from isolation without having to be physically removed from the backwoods. The kidnaping was enough for me to realize I was going to perish in a world where I didn't belong, just as Niles forewarned.

Unfortunately, before I would join the crowded world, to stay with Waylon and his family, I learned I wasn't going to be able to keep Prince. I took another gut-wrenching shot to the heart when I had to leave him behind, abandoning him as I did his brother Phoenix and their uncle Chino because I wasn't in a position to care for him.

When I arrived at Waylon's house in the city, it was as if I'd woken up from a nightmare, but I still had the injuries I'd sustained while trapped in it to remind me it had all been real. While I was slowly recovering, Waylon introduced me to his aunt and uncle who lived in the neighborhood and I was fortunate to get a cash paying job with his uncle doing subcontracting work. It was convenient all the way around because they smoked dope and I was able to continue self-medicating while having a few dollars left over to purchase my alcohol each day.

I stayed in contact, by phone only, with my lady friend, Wynnie, I used with in the backwoods. Though she was a loving and kind soul, we stopped hanging out once my transition back into life was in motion. A few weeks later Olivia Rose, the girl I'd worked with at the car wash years prior, came to visit me to see how I'd been holding up.

I instantly felt a sense of normalcy when I was around her because she wasn't an addict and was the sort of female I was accustomed to being with before my isolation from the world. I didn't know it at the time, but I needed a strong woman to guide me out of the darkness and one who despised the drug infested criminal lifestyle.

Olivia Rose was from Covington, Louisiana, and lived with her mother in Lake Ridge where I went to middle school. Every week when she came to visit, I hid the fact that I was an addict, but I always kept alcohol close by to help me through the cravings. Though Waylon wasn't an addict either, he knew I was actively using with his aunt and uncle, and he and his relatives kept it secret from Olivia, allowing our relationship to evolve until she and I became exclusive. It was, unfortunately, no secret to everyone that Waylon and his wife had their own struggles throughout their marriage. Since the night I'd met them years prior, they'd been forced to move out of their homes at least seven times for a number of reasons. In the past, I saw how having an open door caused turmoil between them. Situations like law-enforcement finding Diego in their attic, after the jewelry store incident, began the pattern of unfortunate events. But even when the gang stayed away, their relationship continued to spoil, and at times, I chose to intervene in order to protect their children.

As time passed, the places we moved into grew smaller and smaller with each eviction, and when we were all forced to move into a small apartment, I knew it was time for me to move on. Olivia Rose and I didn't have to discuss my living situation, since she witnessed firsthand how we'd lived in three different homes in the past six months. She did think it was strange that I'd been living with different families as a twenty-four-year-old man who had a daughter and questioned why Selena wasn't in my life. However, she seemed to like me for who I was, and I was truly grateful because I had absolutely nothing to offer. She wouldn't have been able to fathom my struggles, even if I'd have chopped them up and fed them to her piece by piece. Still, she was always there for me, whenever she wasn't working, and she encouraged me while I continued to battle through my afflictions.

With nowhere to go and facing homelessness again, she quickly introduced me to her mother. After convincing her mother I was a good person and just needed to be in a healthy environment, her mother shockingly agreed to let me stay but under her conditions. She was a single mother who served in the military and when she retired, continued working at the Pentagon as my father did. Her terms for me to stay in her home were plain and simple. Olivia Rose and I were to sleep in different rooms, I needed to find a job and work as a man should, and she wanted to try my cooking because her daughter told her that I could cook a good meal.

That was an amazing deal for me, and I respected her terms with no need to negotiate. I hadn't slept in a comfortable bed in quite some time and wasn't going to disrespect her under her own roof. I was just grateful to be in such a nice home where I could enjoy their delicious southern cooking and had no doubt I could find a job. Olivia Rose found it to be humorous and couldn't compose herself. She ended up in my bed the first night, making me very nervous because I didn't want to end up walking the streets again if her mother found out.

Though I was beginning to open up around the women, I continued to hide my internal struggles and spoke to no one about my addiction, or the things that happened to me. Because I wasn't getting high anymore, I was quickly able to find employment at a car dealership and I purchased a minivan from Nokes to help me get to and from work.

After a while I grew tired of parking vehicles at the dealership, so I spoke with my brother in-law Patrick and went back to the appliance company where I became a full-time truck driver. A few days in, a group of employees invited me to Happy Hour at a bar across the street. I knew in my heart if I chose to join them all hell would break loose after my first drink. Sitting at the bar with the fellas ended up being an everyday excursion and though I was aware of what could happen, I was beginning to feel comfortable in my own skin again and was glad that I joined them. My new routine began to worry Olivia Rose, she called me and questioned why I was out later than the norm. Instead of simply telling her the truth on how I enjoyed hanging out after a long day at work, I blatantly lied to her. I still didn't know how to handle being questioned and I was horrible at facing confrontations.

As the men and I were leaving, after one of Olivia Rose's concerned phone calls, the group asked if I could drive to one of their friend's houses before going home that night. I thought nothing of it since it was on the way home, so I agreed to taxi two of them while following another co-worker.

When we walked into their friend's house, the homeowner was sitting on the couch smoking crack cocaine. I was pissed. Not at them, at my circumstances. I left the car dealership to make more money working with a company that I was familiar with and now I was in a strange person's house where they were doing exactly what I was trying to stay away from. When the aroma presented itself, it was as if my life was lifted up and slammed through the gates of Hell one hundred times over. I had the choice right then and there to walk away and do the right thing. Nope. Not me; not the junkie with nostrils that could smell good dope from a block away. Not the young man that was kidnapped and almost shot dead in the woods for smoking that same drug. I said, "Hey, brother…excuse me gentlemen what's his name? Excuse me, sir. I want some of that right there. I have money." "How much do you have," he replied.

Within minutes I was pushing hot pipes into my mouth and my co-workers had no clue as to what they'd ignited in me by asking me to drive them there. I was smoking rocks in the twenty-six-foot company truck while me and another co-worker were sitting in traffic on I-95. I would stay out for days while Olivia Rose and her mother worried about me and I lied every single time, knowing she didn't know the difference between a raging alcoholic and a pipehead. Instead of working and going home, I stayed with strange people all through town and smoked all their dope before taking off and smoking some else's. I would load the company truck with merchandise and sell whatever I could to whoever wanted it across the Metropolitan area, just to be sure I always had dope. I still had some goodness in me and gave some of the merchandise away for free to people that couldn't afford certain items, but the majority of it went to the teeny tiny little crack rock that I smoked out of a glass pipe.

The men I used with, at the warehouse, were self-sabotaging their own personal lives as well, but most of them had homes, they had bills, they paid those bills, and they went home to their wives and children. I was the father of a beautiful little girl who I loved dearly, and I had an amazing family as well. Once the dope was in me, I was under a spell and nothing would stop me from chasing that first blast I took back in the boondocks in the small red trailer.

After many failed attempts to detox myself, Olivia Rose and her mother sat down with me and asked if it would help, if the three of us moved out of state to Louisiana. I immediately shot the idea down once it was presented to me because my only thought was of Selena. I knew I didn't have what it took to be a father and that reality depressed me more than anyone would believe, but the thought of being in another state away from her was even more terrifying. It also terrified me because I knew it was a wise option. It wasn't like my other road trips where I would travel from state to state to smoke dope, drink moonshine and sleep with a number of females. It was me moving away with a girlfriend that saw something I didn't see in myself and who had the desire to live with me halfway across the country.

I contemplated the idea for weeks as I continued to self-medicate and talked with both of my families to get their insight. My mother and father saw zero hope for me in Virginia and they knew how much I loved my daughter. The reality was I couldn't function well enough to be worth anything to her while I was in Virginia. After somewhat agreeing with Olivia Rose, that it may be better for me to work on myself away from Virginia, I decided to show my face at a bar in town when I heard that my brothers were there playing pool. I hadn't seen most of them for over two years. I stayed in the parking lot and smoked a twenty-dollar rock before entering the doors because I needed a reboot after being awake for days.

I had no idea what to expect or who was even in the building, but it was necessary for me that I "broke bread" before leaving the state. When I walked in, I was wide eyed, and not only from smoking dope but because everyone stopped what they were doing and looked at me as if I'd just risen from the dead. Then as soon as one of my brothers called out my name, life continued and I was greeted with an overwhelming amount of love and respect by everyone that knew me.

I had thousands of scenarios play through my mind while I was in isolation in the woods and I had no clue what the moment would look like when I decided to show my face again. It wasn't because I thought I was frowned upon. If anything, it was me that frowned upon the circumstances and of how these scenarios played out. Basically I was just tired of looking at certain individuals and hearing their names.

I have never told on anyone and I always kept my mouth shut while being questioned. I never slept with any of my brothers' ladies and even though I acted a fool many times while drinking around them, I never crossed that line. I also never ran away when one of my brothers was being attacked and never found myself to be careless enough to throw a blunt object breaking one of their skulls. When I was told to do something, I followed orders and never questioned the ones that brought them to the table. I respected the code and everything we stood for and was honored to be part of the family. Yet—when many of those scenarios went the other way and the joke was on me, I began to lose faith, and that was unfortunate considering what I went through to become affiliated since day one.

I still had the utmost respect for many of my brothers, particularly the ones that stayed out of the limelight as well as those that were serving years in the penitentiary. So, I wasn't nervous entering the bar because of the things I'd done to my people in Northern Virginia; it was because of the resentments that continuously festered in my mind for as long as they did. I knew in my heart if I ever needed anything, those brothers would be there for me with no questions asked, and because of that, I wanted to show my respect and acknowledge Malcom who was sitting at the bar that night.

I wanted to share my plan of moving to Louisiana with Olivia Rose and her mother and wanted to hear his thoughts. I needed assurance that this was a wise move before leaving. I represented a family of gangsters and only those who were in the know, knew that we were a part of something greater than anything anybody could ever fathom.

I wanted to show my loyalty by asking if it was appropriate for me to leave before just picking up and vanishing, even though it was obvious that I hadn't been around for a while. The way I acknowledged the respect I had for Malcom was me approaching him and saying, "If you approve this move brother, I am leaving, and I may never come back. And before I do decide to move away, I want to be certain that you respect the decision." And that's exactly what I asked him while sitting on a barstool drinking my last drink with him.

After we talked for a while, he gave me his answer, "Go. If it's going to benefit you by moving away to find yourself, then go, Omen. I respect whatever you do and appreciate you coming to see me." I stood up, showed the rest of my people love who were drinking and shooting pool and walked out of the doors into the night.

It may not have been a big deal to anyone else, but it hit me hard. I was conflicted because I never sat down and spoke to anyone about my life and how much it meant to me to be a part of the 'G' family. The moment I was initiated, my life changed forever. I had amazing times with my brothers, but I also learned trust was something that was sacred and not everyone had it in them to be trustworthy. I learned wisdom that others who were locked away for years passed down to me.

I remembered walking the halls of Garfield High when a riot broke out and the principal got punched in the head. And when I was walking the halls with Nora and being in an all-out war with a rival gang member, who liked her, and it lasted for years. I'd watched houses burning to the ground and sprayed bullet shells all over the streets during that war. And the situation when other gang members put guns to my head thinking I ratted them out before I became affiliated.

I also remembered how all of us represented our gang to the fullest when we entered Go-go's across the Metropolitan area. On the other hand, I'd witnessed brothers holding their newborns in what seemed to be their most nurturing moments in life, and they witnessed how happy I was when I was around Selena.

All of those things were just memories though as I drove a twenty-six-foot box truck halfway across the country into Louisiana. The reality was that I abandoned my daughter and never had the courage to tell her to her face. The most important person in that whole situation was the little girl that never got the opportunity to be with her father. She never had her father tuck her in at night and if she was afraid, her father wasn't there to protect her from the dark. She wouldn't be able to run off the soccer field after scoring a game winning goal and celebrate with both of her parents like the other little girls were fortunate enough to do. The thought of her destroyed the chances of me ever having peace and it was heartbreaking that she may never believe I cared for or even loved her.

I may have been considered the "dead-beat-dad," but the truth was I was lost, and I didn't have the courage to figure out life's lessons. I allowed circumstances to get the best of me while in toxic environments I *chose* to be involved in, by my own free will.

The depression, due to me abandoning Selena since day one, didn't subside when I left the state. If anything, it carried even more weight and I fell into an even darker place in my new surroundings. Olivia Rose did her best to support me but couldn't understand what I was dealing with internally. She introduced me to her relatives from the south and they accepted me for who I was even though I was from a different race and I was fortunate because this scenario could've played out much differently.

Her mother didn't end up purchasing land as she intended but she did buy a nice home on Lake Shore Drive in Shreveport. Shreveport-Bossier City was home to many casinos called Riverboats that sat on the Red River and hosted the Independence Bowl in College football. The environment and culture were different than any other I'd ever experienced, and I could feel the energy of a state with so much history and mystery.

On one side of the railroad track there were big, beautiful homes and on the other side the structures were run-down and boarded up.

There were two categories of people from what I'd witnessed: those with money and those like myself who were struggling with addiction while trying to find their way.

It wasn't long after we moved that I was back at work, building swimming pools and staying busy. It was either going to be the restaurant industry I chose or the swimming pool industry. I knew both industries well but knew myself well enough to know I wasn't going to slow down on the drinking and if I chose to work in a kitchen, I knew they'd smell the alcohol on my breath as soon as I walked in. So I chose to work outside with the knowledge that most construction crews had alcoholics working amongst them.

My intentions to be clean from drugs were authentic and I'd moved close to twelve-hundred miles away in order to find my true self without the drugs, but reality was tricky. It crept in like a wolf in the night and devoured me if I wasn't grounded and prepared spiritually. I had no self-will, being clean for only one week, and the evil one was lurking while being fully aware of my weaknesses.

The first day I showed up for work I was still craving dope as I hopped into a truck with a group of men who had been in Louisiana their entire lives. These men stuck together like birds of a feather and though I was used to being in those situations, with as many places I'd travelled, it was quite uncomfortable because I was always depressed and wanting to use.

After we left the shop and were heading to my first job site, I looked out of the window the way I had many times in my life. As the men talked in the background, I observed my surroundings and admired the unique existence of the southern state of Louisiana before praying quietly for a new beginning. I prayed for guidance and envisioned living a decent and productive life, not once forgetting where I came from and what I'd been through.

Thoughts of my head getting a much-needed rest after years of trauma gave me hope for recovery. Hope for no more sharp pains or if the pains continued, I would finally visit a doctor for the first time since I'd dislocated my jaw thirteen years prior. But as I prayed for that better life and that my relationship with Selena would soon prosper, those hopes, and dreams came crashing down like a tsunami.

Two of my co-workers pulled out a crack pipe and a third was in the truck smoking Methamphetamine off of tin foil while hiding from the other two. It happened as quick as that—my vision of being a new man was obliterated. The promising data that was uploaded to my brain was immediately deleted from the files. As pleasant as becoming a strong-willed man, doing right by Selena, Janine, Olivia Rose and the rest of my family, it was all a joke. I was who I was no matter where I went. I was a weak man behaving like a child who didn't have the courage to fight the trials and tribulations life and humanity threw at me.

I blamed the drugs, but the drugs didn't find me, they didn't get in the truck with me in Virginia, travel across state lines, open up a box, and force themselves into my mouth. I lived on Earth, and there were drugs all over the world with billions of people that made the conscious decision not to partake in using them.

The reality was I travelled with my weak-minded, addicted self to Louisiana and nothing else mattered but getting high. I was back to sucking on a crack pipe in a foreign place and Olivia Rose was going through exactly what Janine and Selena were going through, all at the same time. Abandonment. I walked away from everything that was good in life once again, it wasn't easy, but I did it well and everyone who truly cared for me had witnessed it countless times. When reality jumped in front of me and said, *surprise,* I would quiver inside like the scared little boy I felt I was. Then karma, life and everything else would wreak havoc on my spirit.

I spent my entire time in Louisiana smoking crack-cocaine. Olivia Rose continued to be oblivious because I continued drinking daily and that was bad enough in a mentally healthy person's mind. During the same time someone in Tucson, Arizona used my social security number and I battled the IRS for what seemed to be forever because they said I owed thousands of dollars in unpaid taxes. A man had stolen my identity after I'd lost or had my wallet stolen eight different times around the country.

I was able to handle that situation, only with the help of my strong-willed girlfriend, but I repaid her by lying to her and staying out all hours of the night. The Division of Child Support

Enforcement in Virginia hunted me down because I was behind on my child-support payments. Since the economy in Louisiana was poor compared to Virginia's, I was losing ground and my payments were barely covering the ever so growing interest fees. I was only able to keep my job because I worked hard. Damn near every man I worked with was getting high with me and just like in Virginia, the men returned home to their families while my worried girlfriend searched the streets for me. I'd be hiding in some abandoned shack getting high with complete strangers.

My paychecks were so small, due to the low paying job, that after I'd cashed them and purchased more dope, I'd be broke within twenty minutes. I would lie and tell her I had jobs in other towns and that we 'had' to stay out. All the while, I'd be high in dark abandoned houses peeking out of holes in the walls because I was paranoid in these foreign neighborhoods. I ended up being the strangest person on the block.

Olivia Rose found me one morning laying on a bench under a bridge in the city close to where the casinos were located. The poor thing was miserable from staying up all night looking for me and not knowing if I were dead or alive. Another evening, when the pool business was closed for the weekend, she found me lying on the ground in front of the door where I'd been for hours. I was coming off the dope and so intoxicated, that I thought I was going to die while lying there detoxing in the sun.

I told her lies when I didn't show up for dinner and when I didn't have money for the bills. It came to a point when I just lied about the lies that I lied about. She grew tired of me wandering lost through the city and I was seriously losing the battle with my addiction.

All throughout this same period, Hurricane Katrina arrived in the Gulf Coast devastating everything in her path, while millions of worried families including Olivia Rose's family were reaching out to loved ones in hopes of finding them alive.

Thousands of people were left unaccounted for and many more thousands homeless. For me, it was just another historic event that I disregarded as I did with Hurricane Isabell and the attacks on 9/11. I was looking for another fix, staying up for days and worrying about nothing but the dope or booze I could score.

Less than one month later, Hurricane Rita dumped heavy rains in Shreveport-Bossier City and as before, I prepared and made sure I had my dope when I cashed my check. That same week I attempted to reach out to Selena to wish her a happy birthday, but Janine told me never to call again. Her ultimatum was that if I ever wanted to speak with Selena, I needed to move back to Virginia, West Virginia, DC or Maryland, where I could be there for our daughter in person.

It would've been amazing and beautiful to move back there for my little girl, but I knew horrible things would happen and that fact wouldn't change. I knew there was absolutely nothing I could say that would resonate to Janine to gain her respect or change her views toward me, so I buried my emotions deep—packing them down with more drugs and alcohol. That's when I began to have thoughts about taking my life.

When Hurricane Rita finally subsided, Olivia Rose pleaded for me to put the alcohol down. With my drug addiction still in the dark, her nor her family ever had the opportunity to meet the clean and sober Joel. The last time I was clean and sober was five years prior. I just knew in my heart her family thought I was an imbecile and my potential in life was that of a weakling who would settle for low-paying jobs and small apartments so I could feed my habit and not my family.

Then again, maybe my assumptions were wrong, and her family actually thought the world of me, truly wanting to see me succeed. Even after humiliating myself, time and time again, they continued to support me and opened their doors to me even when I ran ballistic. Then I would apologize for the one thousandth time for being a nuisance.

In the middle stressing her to the core and destroying my own, one of the Gomez brothers from Virginia called me and told me one of my brothers in the gang, shot and killed another one of our brothers during an argument. My brother Cook, who was killed on January 13th of 2006, served in the United States Armed Forces and was the youngest member of our gang in Northern Virginia. Some time ago he'd made the decision to change his life by enlisting in the Marines and upon his return home he was killed by another 'G.' Cook left behind his loving mother and two sisters who all of us in the family knew, respected, and loved.

The news of Cook's loss hit me hard and here I was not living responsibly or handling my business; as usual. I wouldn't be able to fly out to represent my brother during his service or console his family as I desired to do. It was an honorable and righteous path he pursued, and I respected the fact that he served our country. It embarrassed me to know that I wasn't man enough to make the choices he did when I'd had the same opportunity but was unable to seize upon it.

I was in a state of doom and had no idea on how to handle it. Olivia Rose's family members attempted an intervention, on my behalf, trying to help me change my negative behaviors, without success. Olivia Rose and I agreed we were going to move to Arizona in hopes that being close to my family would somehow change those behaviors. My mother and father, along with my sister and her family, all migrated to the Southwest to be closer to my relatives. But at the rate things were going for me, I was going to die before ever seeing the rest of my family again.

The culture in Louisiana was truly unique and special. I'd never experienced anything like it and no other culture in the world would compare to that of the people in that Southern state. Parade's for loved ones who'd lost their lives, crawfish boils on the corner for $1.19 a pound, cookouts and taking part in good ole fish fry's at Olivia Rose's family reunions—these were good times and good memories.

While thinking about the good times I'd had, even with the chaos I took to Louisiana, it was hard for me to imagine how life could possibly return to any state of normalcy after experiencing such destruction. After the devastation of two hurricanes befell the people of the South, and with assistance from many prominent people such as athletes, entertainers and hard-working men and woman from across the country, the Louisiana natives stood back up and came together as one like the people of New York did after 9/11.

I wished I were strong enough to kick my addiction when seeing how many humans came together to assist one another. I even thought about how I could've been of service to the communities when these catastrophic events occurred. But for the life of me, I couldn't get past my addiction. While being unable to conquer my own thoughts, and though there might have been a good person underneath it all who had the will and drive to help others, I just couldn't seem to help myself and I grew tired of trying since my addiction continued to pound me.

I didn't give up on Selena and I called numerous times before our departure to Arizona, even after being asked not to call. But Janine was done talking and the phone continued to ring and ring and ring. The negative self-talk took command of me and my depression sank to its deepest depths. Olivia Rose tried everything in her power to uplift me, but I was truly convinced I was a low-life and continuously told myself so while masking it from my peers.

I also began to realize that everything I'd done was finally catching up to me and the words I did speak held no ground because of all the lies I told. I continued to try calling because I was determined to hear my little girl's voice, when I did get a call through and tried to reach out, I was not allowed to speak to Selena. Janine and her family grew tired of the excuses and lies and came to the decision that cutting me out of their lives all together was the best solution for Selena's well-being and future.

CHAPTER 14

UNEXPLAINED PHENOMENA

*O*livia Rose and I got off to a rough start on our road trip. While *preparing to leave, her car slipped off the tracks when her brother and I were loading it onto a hauler. The next morning we departed and in the middle of nowhere Texas, the box truck got a flat tire. She was scared to pieces because we'd watched a scary movie the night before and she swore that she saw someone looking out the window of an old run-down trailer off to the side of the road.*

Having knowledge about disturbed people, in rural areas from my own experiences, I kept driving and managed to get our slow-moving truck to the next town. We were able to get our tire replaced there without incident. The rest of our trip was uneventful and that was a good thing because it gave the two of us time to talk while we travelled close to twelve-hundred miles.

When we arrived in Arizona, my family was anxiously waiting for us, not having seen us in over two years. But it was a bittersweet reunion for me due to my internal struggles since I continued to hide my secrets from everyone. The majority of my family were functioning alcoholics and I knew moving closer to them was going to be a true test of will. I already had connections in place here unlike the other places I'd travelled to where I had to make new connections.

Our first night in town, reality quickly set in as we gathered at a Mexican restaurant to celebrate our arrival. It was an embarrassing and shameful moment when I had to face those female relatives that I reached out to while high, drunk and I talked perverted to them.

It made for an uncomfortable greeting to say the least, but what was done had been done. That was just one of the many burdens I attempted to bury deep inside myself by using drugs and drinking. This caused me to make absurd decisions, which in turn got me to use and drink even more.

It was an endless cycle that appeared hopeless even when times seemed swell from the outside looking in. While I was dealing with the negative self-talk during our reunion festivities, one of my relatives initiated a toast and I was quickly reunited with the excessive drinking before going back to my parents' house.

Olivia Rose and I were both fortunate and grateful that my parents were willing to let us stay with them until we got on our feet. Within two days, I was able to help the cause by getting a job at a swimming pool company in town, servicing swimming pools.

The company provided me with a truck, work phone, gas card and a job route of almost seventy clients. Olivia Rose was hired on at a daycare almost immediately due to her experience in the field. Within a few months, we were able to move into a nice condo down the street on the eastside of Tucson.

The next year I serviced pools for some of the most prestigious people in the city. When my job was done each day, I rewarded myself by drinking to a hard day's work. Though I was proud of myself for being over one year clean from the dope, Olivia Rose wouldn't acknowledge the progress I'd been making because I drank so much and continued to hide my secrets that I'd been a drug addict for over a decade.

Again, I continued to lie to her about what I did or where I went after work and it became a pattern she was all too familiar with. Whenever the relatives I drank with were busy or out of town, I drove drunk to different bars to feed my cravings for alcohol. I physically couldn't stop the excessive drinking and eventually found myself waking up in foreign places.

For Olivia Rose to have left her entire family, over a thousand miles away, just to be left alone in a city strange to her while I attempted to drink my problems away, was humiliating for the both of us. I knew she was hurting emotionally but I was unable or willing to stop the negative behaviors.

I somehow managed not to lose my job or Olivia Rose, and the people closest to us were baffled at how I was able to carry on that way without consequence. Eventually we were able to find a nice house closer to my job's warehouse where I picked up my supplies, located off I-10. The neighborhood we moved to was so new only two other homes on our street were occupied, meaning both of the houses next to us were vacant.

The day before Thanksgiving, in our new home, Olivia Rose called me from work telling me she was feeling ill and that she was planning on going home early. But she was unable to leave because there was no one to cover her shift at the daycare. It turned out to be a good thing she couldn't go home that afternoon. After servicing my aunt and uncle's pool, completing my pool route for the day, they gifted me with a ham for the holiday before I met Olivia Rose at our house. After parking in our garage, I carried the ham into our kitchen and as I glanced toward the front door, I saw the door had been kicked off the hinges.

I immediately grabbed a weapon, shouted at her to stay in the garage and called 911 warning them that if there were intruders in my home I would destroy them. I ran through the house looking under beds, in every closet, threatening any and all possible imposters that death was coming if they were in fact hiding.

After searching the house, in its entirety, I told Olivia Rose that it was safe to enter. My rage got the better of me, I was so infuriated when I was going through the house that the sharp pains in my head returned. I hadn't been that angry in years.

Law enforcement didn't arrive, responding to my 911 call, until five hours later. As I paced the house trying to calm myself, I made a list of everything that had been stolen. Since no one lived in the two homes next to us, I knew from experience the suspects had no worries as far as witnesses and didn't hesitate to kick the door in and rob our house.

Thanksgiving morning, the news said there were multiple home invasions in our neighborhood the previous afternoon and I immediately recognized that God had protected Olivia Rose that day. She was literally walking out of the door at her job when her boss told her she couldn't leave because there wasn't another teacher available for coverage. If she were to have gone home and laid down on the couch or on our bed till she felt better, the intruders might have tied her up and shot her as they did other victims in our neighborhood.

Having lived the life of both predator and prey, I wasn't a stranger to the feelings of being a victim and I was completely aware of the kind of mindset these people had who were willing to rob and inflict harm on others. I lost a lot of sleep due to the stress caused by feeling violated after the break-in. I remained paranoid even after the neighboring homes were occupied with families.

My Aunt Gina's ex-husband, Dawson, and I quickly installed a security door and I also had an alarm system installed to make our home more secure. But when I'd close my eyes each night, I felt panicked and I would creep through the dark house with a weapon before sitting on our couch until the sun came up. Eventually it became such an issue for me that I went to a family member who sold Methamphetamine and picked up a sack just so I could work after staring at our front door all night. I was cautiously justifying my decision to snort small lines to keep me awake and alert. All it did was increase the paranoia and turn objects around my house into visual hallucinations of masked men attempting to break in through every door and window, all at the same time.

One evening while I was trying to hold it together and compose myself in front of Olivia Rose, our new neighbors walked over and introduced themselves. They were an older couple who were extremely kind. But when we returned their kindness, they took it as an invitation for them to walk over at any time throughout the week. They would ring our doorbell bringing us homemade cakes, pies, tortillas; you name it they cooked it for us.

It was an awkward situation no doubt, and though it made Olivia Rose totally uncomfortable every time they came knocking, I played it to my advantage because they always had alcohol and invited me over to shoot pool over a 'few drinks.'

One weekend, while their young adult son and his girlfriend were visiting, Olivia Rose and I were invited over for dinner and some drinks. As always, my girlfriend kindly declined the invite and

I used being off from work the next day, as justification to hang out with the neighbors, even against Olivia Rose's wishes. She asked that I not be gone long because we had plans set for the next day and she pleaded with me not to drink too much.

As soon as I entered their door, I was greeted with a beer and shot of liquor. I'd snorted a small line of Meth in my bathroom before I walked over and because of that, I was able to consume more alcohol without showing any signs of impairment. As our friendly neighbors continued pouring drinks, Olivia Rose casually walked over to check and see if I was drinking excessively.

To her surprise I wasn't vomiting, dancing on the pool table or threatening to burn their house down. In fact, she was polite about my being over there and simply asked that I be home by midnight. As shocked as I was that she wasn't embarrassing me in front of our neighbors, I assured her I was drinking respectfully, and I would be at home and in bed by midnight as she wished.

The truth was, she knew me even more than I knew myself and she knew that nothing would stop me from poisoning myself with alcohol. She was still afraid that I was going to overdo it and die. She was also aware that it never mattered what I said to anyone when I was drinking. I'd smile to everyone's face then turn around and forget all about what was said and continue to disregard their feelings and wishes while falling back into foolishness.

When she walked back to our house, the neighbors and I sat in their backyard and drank until the sun came up. I drank everything they had. All in all, I consumed dozens of mixed drinks over a sixteen-hour period. When Olivia Rose woke up and realized I wasn't in bed, she walked over and began lecturing me in front of everyone. I stayed calm because I didn't want to make a scene even though I didn't like being embarrassed in front of others. I kept my composure and walked back to our house where she really began to unleash her fury, behind closed doors.

I was at peace while holding conversations at the neighbors' house but when she continued yelling at me, I exploded. I picked up our coffee table and smashed it into a hundred pieces then I destroyed our bedroom doors. I had reached the boiling point and was transcending into a full-blown blackout when it all became too much, and I suddenly dropped to the floor. Though Olivia Rose was terrified and hyperventilating, she turned on the shower, stripped me of my clothes and helped me into the tub. As I lay still under the running water, I could hear her voice, but it faded quickly. I felt the cool water on my naked body but that too faded away and everything went into nothing.

For the first time in my life, I believed I'd passed away. It was much different than when the Maglite fractured my skull because even though I laid limp at the Go-go, my spirit never left my physical self. It did that morning and it hovered over my lifeless naked body in the bathtub.

Olivia Rose entered the bathroom while sobbing on the phone and as soon as I heard her cries, my spirit slowly re-entered my flesh. I drank so much while on Meth that I didn't keep track of how many mixed drinks I consumed. How much I drank wasn't a concern to anyone because I hadn't behaved like a maniac while my neighbors continued to pour drinks. I lay in the shower for a while and though I wasn't able to move, my spirit was completely aware of what was taking place. When it hovered over my body, even though it was only for a moment, I was at peace and not in pain anymore. If it weren't for Olivia Rose's cries while walking back into the bathroom to check on me, I may never have woken up again and she would've been left in a house with a dead man who'd never amounted to anything.

She called my parents and cried for help, begging them to make an intervention. But she knew her words would fall on deaf ears after they had spent decades watching me self-destruct while battling their own demons with alcohol.

Christmas Eve that same year, my parents, Olivia Rose and I left a Christmas party at my aunt and uncle's house and went back to my parents' house to play Texas Hold'em poker. All was well and we were having a good time, until my parents and I drank too much. Then all hell broke loose.

My father and I were in each other's faces, my mother was so drunk she tripped and hit her head on a large wooden Bible-stand and somehow they blamed me for it even though I wasn't near her.

While the chaos ensued indoors, I went out the back door and hopped their fence. Wearing only shorts and with no jacket, I began walking home fifteen miles away.

I was an idiot in every way. It was freezing on Christmas Eve and I ended up at a fire station where the firefighters allowed me to use their phone to call Olivia Rose who came to pick me up. Needless to say, there wasn't a family Christmas that year. A few months later, my parents quit drinking after my mother almost passed away from alcohol poisoning at a Pink Floyd concert.

Decades of consuming alcohol and it finally caught up to her. Doctors' told my parents that she would've passed away if she hadn't received medical attention when she did. It wasn't an easy task for my father to quit drinking, but he didn't want to be a bad influence on her or cause her to relapse into drinking again. So he worked vigorously and stood by his wife who he'd been in love with since they were in high school.

We'd gone through so much as family over the years and the one thing that almost took my mother and me out in the same year was an addiction to alcohol that was unmanageable for all of us. Even as my parents fought through their cravings, something that would save them both at the end of a decades long run with alcohol addiction, many of our relatives, who were alcoholics themselves, began to gossip saying my parents thought they were better than everyone else because they declined to attend holiday gatherings where everyone was drinking.

During these trying times, Olivia Rose continued to stand by my side even though she was confused about why I continued to consume the beverages that nearly killed my mother and me. But to those of us that drank heavily, she was considered a 'normy' and knew that it was impossible for her to fully understand the mindset of an alcoholic and what happened to us once we made the decision to pick up that first drink.

Instead of her bailing on me, when she had the chance, she planned a vacation for the two of us in hopes that it would alleviate some of the pressure our relationship was suffocated with. After everything I put the poor girl through and because she didn't take off on me, I felt it was appropriate to propose to her on a cruise ship headed for the Caribbean. I wanted to show my loyalty toward the person that stayed in my corner while sitting back and watching as I continued to battle my demons.

We planned on meeting her mother in Miami because she needed a vacation of her own and she hadn't seen her daughter throughout all the foolishness that was taking place in Arizona. But those plans quickly crumbled when our flight was delayed due to bad weather. I just knew things were too good to be true.

I'd finally made the commitment to propose to her after years of fighting the thought of marriage and I had the ring in my pocket, but our plane was delayed, and the cruise ship departed without us. I didn't know what to do at this point.

I have never handled confrontation well, so I chose to avoid any conversations with the airline staff, which might be what led to me feeling disrespected, even though it was out of their control. Olivia Rose on the other hand spoke her mind with ease and wasn't one to attack the opposition when she felt slighted and because of her patience, the airline booked us a nice room at a hotel in Miami for later that evening.

As soon as the plane took to the sky, I ordered an alcoholic beverage against my girlfriend's wishes. She was aware that I hated flying because of my fear of heights but did not in any way envision us starting our vacation with me having a drink to ease the anxiety.

In Miami, Olivia Rose was able to talk our way into two seats on a small charter plane that flew us directly to St. Thomas in the Virgin Islands. I was inspired by how she wouldn't take no for an answer and was able to stay composed throughout each conversation across the country while advocating for the two of us. It somewhat baffled me though as to why I didn't have that same tolerance. I began to see firsthand how she was able to withstand my shenanigans throughout the years.

As our dreadful three-thousand-mile journey to the Caribbean came to an end, the two of us were anxious to check-in to the hotel to unwind before exploring what the Virgin Islands had to offer. Our room overlooked the ocean and it was an amazing feeling to sit down and admire our surroundings. But as always, I took my alcoholic tendencies with us. After we dined at a local restaurant and enjoyed our night out together, I found myself sitting at a local bar drinking until I was plastered.

A few days later, after spending three nights drinking with random natives at different venues, I was hungover and ashamed for choosing booze over my lonely girlfriend. Her mother finally arrived on the cruise ship and that was a God send. The two were finally reunited after they hadn't seen one another in quite some time, and it was good for Olivia Rose to be with her mother after everything I'd put her through in St. Thomas.

When the three of us walked on board the gigantic vessel, I was amazed at how intimidating the ship was from the inside. It was its own world floating on water that hosted thousands of vacationers from all over the world. And while everyone else seemed excited and privileged to be there, I was feeling anxious being surrounded by so many strangers. I was also paranoid due to my fear of heights and the intimidation of the all-mighty ocean.

I quickly ordered an alcohol beverage once I'd learned we had a room on the highest level with a balcony. After I'd had a few drinks in my system and we sailed out to sea, I was comfortable enough and able to appreciate the amazing experience while standing on the balcony without the fear of falling. Though we missed the first few days of the cruise, we were able to visit the Virgin Islands, San Juan Puerto Rico and my favorite, because I was a drinker, one of Jimmy Buffet's Margaritaville Resorts.

After visiting the beautiful islands we returned to sea. On the last night aboard the ship, while heading for Miami, passengers were dressing up for the 'Captain's Dinner' which was the farewell dinner before we were to return to land the next morning. As soon as Olivia Rose stepped into the shower, I snuck out of the room and ordered two dozen long-stemmed red roses and requested they be delivered to our table after we were seated.

As we entered the main dining hall, the two of us were seated along with her mother and an amazing family from New York. I was as nervous as I've ever been and realized I only wanted to propose once in my life, so I had a few drinks to help calm my nerves. As I was attempting to act 'what was normal for me,' two ladies entered the hall and placed the beautiful bouquets on each end of the large table. Everyone seated at our table, as well as hundreds of passengers walking by, were admiring the bouquets and asking who they were for, who ordered them. I looked around while asking who they were for, but when Olivia Rose's mother glanced at me and smiled, I stood up, pulled the ring from my pocket and knelt before my shocked girlfriend.

The hall was on pause as Olivia Rose covered her mouth and I looked into her eyes, "I know I've put you through hell and don't deserve to be here on this ship with you. And I'm aware that I have a lot of growing up to do, but I need a strong woman in my life, in order to accomplish that, and I know you're that woman. So, if you would have me, I would love for you to be my wife. Will you marry?" "Yes! Yes I will marry you, Joel", she replied. Everyone in the dining hall stood up and clapped as the two of us kissed and I held her tight hoping that everything I said about growing up would become a reality because she deserved that to be true.

We spent our last night on the ship gambling in the casino and drinking the night away. My fiancé and her mother were off enjoying one another's company while I played blackjack with a group of men who had witnessed my proposal during the Captain's Dinner. At one point, I was up five-hundred-dollars and when Olivia Rose walked over to check on me, I asked her if she would kindly hold my seat while I went to the restroom.

When I returned, I couldn't help but notice two large stacks of chips were missing. She told me she felt lucky, so she placed half my winnings on one hand, only to lose it all in less than a minute. I was upset to say the least, but the next morning, when I woke up to a debilitating hangover, she dumped all the chips out onto our bed, saying she was smarter than to waste good money.

My fiancé was more intelligent than I was, when it came to many things, and she saw my winnings as an opportunity to have extra money when we made it back to Arizona. I, on the other hand, always lived for the moment because I truly felt I wouldn't make it another day because of the choices I'd been making.

I never worried about overcharging my accounts at bars and clubs while drinking, because I never anticipated waking up and seeing thousands of dollars in overdraft fees on multiple occasions. But somehow—somehow, I always managed to live another day, every single time, and I was grateful for Olivia Rose being wise during the moments where I was trapped inside my foolish ways.

After we returned home to share the news about my proposal on the ocean, I began making payments on an old 1988 Toyota pickup truck, from one of my uncles, and started my own pool route to make an extra income before our wedding. I continued working at the pool company full-time but added clientele through my family and began servicing many of my relative's pools. Life seemed to finally be going in a positive direction.

Early one Saturday morning, the day before Easter, and two weeks before our wedding, I was driving through town to meet Olivia Rose and my grandmother for breakfast. The three of us would eat at the same restaurant frequently and I enjoyed spending Saturday mornings with two of the most important women in my life. Olivia Rose drove ahead to drop her car off at the dealership for an oil change and I followed behind to pick her up. Suddenly, another vehicle attempted a U-turn in my lane. I quickly glanced at the stop light, watching it change from green to yellow, then T-boned the other vehicle at fifty miles an hour.

The impact was so severe, the lone bench seat in my truck unlocked from the frame and my face smashed into the thin steering wheel. I slowly looked up and noticed the other vehicle a hundred feet away in a bus stop and my pool chemicals were scattered all over the intersection. I unlocked my seatbelt as blood was gushing onto the dashboard and windshield. I managed to open my door before falling to my knees, "I can't go out like this Lord. I've gone through too much to die right here in the middle of this intersection. Please, Lord—let me live through this so I may marry this woman and have a family. Please." As I was praying, I was able to remain calm even while the blood continued to squirt out onto the pavement.

A young man approached me and asked if I had drugs or alcohol on me, and at first, I was shocked about why he'd ask me that while I was holding my head, but I quickly realized he was trying to do me a favor and seeking an opportunity to get free drugs and alcohol. I had to think about it for a few seconds and once I gathered my thoughts, I told him I wasn't carrying anything illegal.

As the addict fled the scene, an older gentleman and his young son walked over and assisted me to my feet. They attempted to escort me to the median in the road while suggesting I sit down. I assured them I would be fine and returned to my truck to find my phone. The father shook his head and said, "Young man, that was a bad accident and it looks like Mike Tyson hit you in your eye without gloves on. It would be in your best interest if you sat down and waited for an ambulance." Determined, I said, "I'm alright, sir. This head has taken a beaten. And it seems I'm a hard-headed young man. I'm going to call my fiancé, sir." As the blood poured into my left eye, I took my shirt off and wiped my face and from the expression the young kid gave, when I turned toward him, said it all.

As hard-headed as I'd been my whole life, I listened to the man and sat on the median while I called Olivia Rose. She didn't believe me at first because I was a jokester, but finally caught on when she heard the emergency response vehicles in the background. She arrived at the scene and I was taken to the hospital where they stitched up the gash and told me I had another concussion. My grandmother and one of my uncles showed up to the emergency room as soon as they got word and just as they entered the room, the family of the woman I collided with began shouting at me, blaming me for the accident even though I had the right-away.

I remained calm and respectfully chose to let the family verbally attack me while I assertively expressed my concern for the elderly woman and prayed for her to recover from the brutal wreck.

The next few weeks, before our wedding, I had many doctors' appointments and I was out of work for the better part of those two weeks. My face swelled more than I'd ever seen anyone's face swell before. My nose looked broken and my truck was deemed a total loss. I still owed my uncle thousands of dollars for that truck.

When I went to see the Neurologist, after my CT scan and MRI appointments, he sat down with me and gave me news that changed my life, "Son, while looking over the damage you sustained from this accident, I found that you've had a stroke on the left side of your brain. It's evident that it happened some time ago, but have you been hospitalized in the past for a TBI (Traumatic Brain Injury)?" I said, "Damn, that makes sense." The doctor replied, "What do you mean, son? What makes sense?" "I was hit in the head ten years ago and I haven't been the same ever since," I explained. The doctor replied, "Well…weren't you hospitalized, and didn't the doctors tell you that you had a stroke?" "No," I said, "I was transported to a hospital in Virginia, but they released me an hour or two later because I'm affiliated with a gang that's predominantly African American and many of my brothers were in the lobby. I was discharged without paperwork or any information for that matter on the injury I sustained." The Neurologist didn't know how to respond, and I was stunned at the news explaining my condition.

I knew after stuttering for months and becoming increasingly paranoid after I took the Maglite to the head at the Go-go-go, something significant happened to my brain. The damage I took during the accident gave me what the doctors' called "Post-Concussion Syndrome." I had a migraine for close to one year and dealt with it by drinking which in turn made it worse because my brain swelled, all the more, as I drank.

Though I was embarrassed to have a crooked nose and a scar running through my eyebrow, our wedding took place eighteen days after the accident. Olivia Rose's mother paid for the entire wedding which took place at a hotel in town. The arrangements my mother-in-law made were appreciated and never to be forgotten. Family and friends travelled from all over the country to share the special moment with us and we enjoyed every second of it. The morning after, my new wife and I went on our honeymoon and enjoyed every second of that as well. I made a commitment to myself and to her that I would not drink during that weekend even though my head and face were in pain. And for once in our relationship, I kept that promise.

A few months later, while still fighting the woman's insurance company over whose fault it was during the accident, one of the clients I serviced pools for walked outside during a conversation I was having with his wife. The man overheard me talking about my migraines and how the accident wasn't my fault at that specific intersection. He turned his entire body and said, "Were you driving an older pickup that slammed into someone who did a U-turn?" I perked up, "Yes, sir; that was me." He said, "I saw the entire thing. That was brutal!" Excited, I said, "Wait! You witnessed the accident?" "Damn right I did. I was working that morning and when we opened the shop doors, I saw the car turn while you still had the right-away" he insisted. Up to that point, since the accident, every witness either moved away or declined to answer my insurance company's phone calls.

If I hadn't been at that specific customer's house, at that specific time, I never would've found a witness to assist me in the investigation. I finished servicing their pool then immediately contacted my insurance company and shared his information. Still I understood the accident investigations could take years. Though I wanted to be compensated for the damage I sustained to my already damaged head and to my truck, I needed to be patient and was totally amazed at the turn of events.

The pain in my head was debilitating at times because the impact during the accident was on the same side of my skull where the flashlight hit me. Then add all the other accidents and beatdowns I'd received to the mix, created excruciating moments as I worked long days in the Arizona heat servicing pools. I managed to push forward and a few months after the accident I found a small lump on my testicles. I was stressed out about everything that was going on and kept pouring drinks down in an attempt to mask the fear. I went in for a physical and after the test results were in, the doctor said the lump was benign and that I had nothing to worry about.

Before I left the doctor's office, I shared my concerns of how I wasn't able to impregnate my wife after sleeping with her for over five years. I told her that I'd already fathered a daughter in Virginia and my wife, and I were curious as to what was wrong. So she sent me to a urologist and had me provide a specimen sample.

When the test results were in, Olivia Rose and I went to hear what the urologist had to say. He said my white blood cell count was off the charts and I had a condition called Pyospermia. He then asked if I'd lacked nutrients and my wife immediately took over the conversation and talked about my history of excessive drinking and smoking. As I sat back looking at her, with my eyes wide open, he suggested I slowed down or quit altogether because I was a young man destroying my immune system. He also told us if I lived a healthier lifestyle, I could populate a village with all the sperm that were inside just waiting to swim. He then wrote a prescription for a drug that would help lower white blood cell count if I listened to his instructions.

There were thirty pills in the bottle, and I was instructed to take one pill per day while doing everything I possibly could not to have an erection for those thirty days. That was an atrocious order for a man that had erections multiple times a day, but I did what was necessary because the doctor said it would be painful if I chose the latter. I managed to focus on everything in life but sex, while having blinders on and not looking at women or watching anything on the television that had women on the screen. It was brutal. I had to avoid my wife at all costs because anytime I touched her, I'd get aroused even if she brushed by me and I touched her soft skin.

The day before I was to take the last pill, my wife, parents, grandparents and I drove to the Grand Canyon for the weekend. It was mine and Olivia Rose's first time at one of the Wonders of The World, and it was breathtaking to say the least. We rented a room at a lodge on the 'South Rim' next door to my parents' room and my grandparents had a nice travel trailer that they parked down at the campgrounds.

The next morning, after a torturous long month of self-restraint, I took the last pill. We bundled up for the day and the six of us met up and had a nice breakfast to start our morning. We spent the day walking around the 'South Rim' and it was the most spiritual experience I'd ever had. Like the ocean memory I had as a child, I felt so insignificant compared to what the universe had to offer. I took hundreds of photos to add to my ongoing portfolio and sat in many different areas to relish the spiritual presence I'd felt since we'd arrived. After a long day and witnessing a remarkable sunset, we shut it down and went to bed. I longed to be with my wife the next day.

When the two of us woke up the next morning, I was ready for action, but Olivia Rose immediately informed me that it hadn't been twenty-four hours since I took my last pill. I wasn't playing around and explained to her that the time was up. But because she was the wise one and heard what the doctor said a month prior, I had to wait until after our long day of sightseeing was over.

It was one week from my thirtieth birthday and while we were admiring the Native American art that was designed so intricately, my grandparents bought me a gift to take home and add to my growing Native American collection.

The cold weather became too much for my grandfather, so he went to his trailer and my father and I followed suit, going back to our rooms, while the ladies went on a hike collecting pinecones on the way.

After I showered, I was anxiously waiting to see Olivia Rose, but she hadn't returned yet, leaving me even more anxious and on the verge of exploding. As I eagerly waited for her to walk through the door, I laid on the bed and reached for my new gift. It was a drawing of five native tribesmen in the clouds looking over the Grand Canyon. I pressed mute on the football game and began to read the history of the natives who lived throughout this land for centuries. As I continued to read, I felt the presence of something manifesting in the room and my spirit began to sense that it was another spirit. It was a feeling only those who have felt it would ever believe and my entire body from my toes to my long black hair began to feel the energy as it intensified around me.

I placed the drawing on my lap and reached over to the nightstand and grabbed my camera, "Is there anyone here? Do you wish to show yourself? I feel your presence and feel that you're a peaceful spirit. I respect your sacred grounds and only wish to learn from it. Please show yourself. I welcome you." I turned my camera on and snapped as many photos as possible while continuing to speak to the spirit that I couldn't see with my own vision.

The bone chilling energy was slowly departing, but I was in a spiritual state and was appreciative for what I was experiencing. I began going over each photo anticipating something different than the dark beings I'd seen as a child or when I was incarcerated.

The first three photos showed nothing but my sweatpants, my feet, the television, a small table with a lamp and coffee cups in front of vacant walls. The next two photos showed the same. The sixth photo had a large orb between myself and the wall across from me, but I never accepted that as proof when searching for spirits in my past. As I scrolled to the next photo, there were multiple orbs around the room and a small bright light coming through the wall. As I scrolled to the next photo my spirit connected to something miraculous and I became paralyzed. I was dumbfounded.

It was an image of a spirit, not standing next to me or even in front of me, the spirit was hovering over me. I pressed the button again and the next image was even more defined than the first. The spirit was manifesting over the bed exactly how I'd felt many times in the past and I said, "Thank you. Thank you for showing yourself to me and I will remember this day for the rest of my life." As I sat alone in the room, I began to tear up because I knew I was blessed.

I'd been told on multiple occasions, by many people across the country, that I had a gift, but I was torn in that moment because I knew I wasn't being righteous while being blessed and I just needed a second to understand and cherish the moment for what it was. *What was the spirit here to tell me? Is something going to happen in my life, and was it here to protect me? Or am I about to die?* Those were the questions going through my mind while I was staring into the drawing and shaking my head in awe. As baffled as I was, I stood up and looked in the mirror next to the bed. I took a deep breath and shook my head in amazement because of the situations that I'd experienced while living my life. I walked next door and when my father answered, I explained how the events unfolded and handed him my camera. He too was amazed at what he saw, and it touched his spirit after having his own experiences while on his own personal journey through life.

When the ladies returned, not too long after for dinner, I shared the experience with everyone, breaking down how everything took place and how significant it was for that to happen to me after everything I'd been through. The good and the bad.

Finally, after dinner and after thirty days of obedience and abstinence, my wife and I were able to be with one another. While I was anxiously undressing, she expressed how creepy it was that the spirit was hovering over me in the bed that the two of us were about to lie in. I explained to her how powerful and extraordinary it was and that it was a peaceful presence that came to visit me. I told her there were spirits all around us at all times and that we simply couldn't see them unless they wanted to be seen with the naked human eye.

After our conversation, our bodies pressed against one another's and I took full advantage after not being able to caress her for as long as it had been. As soon as we'd finished, she told me that I knocked her into a menstruation cycle. Olivia Rose suffered from irregular menstrual cycles and they sometimes wouldn't arise for months, but when they did, many times they lasted weeks and it was debilitating for her.

The next morning, before the six of us got into our vehicles and drove away, I walked over to a cliff and took another photo of the place that gave me so much peace. While looking over the photo, I noticed a silhouette of a Native American man wearing a long feather made from a massive shadow that was in the canyon. I just shook my head and said, "thank you, God."

Weeks after the last time we slept together, which was the same day the spirit came to me, Olivia Rose and I found out she was pregnant with our first child. I was shocked and at a loss for words as my mind went places it had never gone before. I understood that the medication was what assisted me in getting her pregnant, but for it to have happened on the same day in the same room the spirit showed its presence was mind-blowing and that made her pregnancy all the more extraordinary.

I'd gone through so many situations in life that made total sense, and many more that did not, but one thing I knew for sure, there were unexplained phenomena out there that were sending me messages and they weren't giving up on me. Even though I believed in God and knew in my heart that He would bless me, if I gave him my all, I always found ways to jump back into self-will while being afraid of responsibilities and searching for answers down in the bottom of a bottle of liquor.

CHAPTER 15

A MONUMENTAL DISASTER

At year's end, I was granted a check with the lump sum of $55,000 for the injury I'd sustained during the accident. Olivia Rose and I decided to purchase our first home, one of my cousins who was a realtor, found for us during the time when thousands of homes were foreclosed due to the housing market crashing.

The 'Obama Administration,' then granted us $8,000 as first-time home buyers to help assist with the struggling economy which put us at $63,000 in our bank accounts. One month later my wife and I received close to $9,000 for our tax returns. I'd never had anything close to $72,000 in my life at one time, and though I'd taken another brutal blow to my head to earn the majority of that amount, I was blessed to have that money in the bank, a beautiful pregnant wife and a beautiful new home that we called ours. The kicker that topped it all off was we didn't even put a dollar into it, they paid us.

We were finally able to pay off the balance toward the child support I owed. We paid my uncle for the pickup truck that was totaled, built a nice backyard with grass and trees to remind us of Virginia and Louisiana, purchased a nice SUV from the same cousin that found us our new home, traded Olivia Rose's car in and got her a new one, put down $4,000 toward braces because I'd always dreamt of having nice teeth and placed the remaining amount into CD's at the bank for it to accrue interest.

It was a reality check when we entered the bank and they acknowledged us by name because we'd put over $60,000 into their financial institution. All the years I'd lived paycheck to paycheck without savings, not one bank acknowledged me by my name before that day. Regardless of my perception and how I felt society's great divide was between the rich and non-rich, I felt confident leaving our house each morning as I headed to work with a financial cushion. Since we had money outside of the two $25,000 CD's we'd opened with the bank, I mulled enrolling into a culinary school due to my desire to cook for others.

I searched every culinary program in the city and after a few weeks, I enrolled at the Art Institute. I was both excited and prepared for the challenge because I was finally going to focus on something I was passionate about and I wanted to show the world I could excel if I put forth the effort without the drugs and alcohol running my life. Plus, I wanted to prove to myself that I was intelligent enough to graduate something after walking away from everything else I ever started.

Months into the school year, I was excelling in every aspect and held a 4.0 GPA entering our second semester. During that same summer, Olivia Rose and I welcomed our first child together. It wasn't an easy delivery like we'd hoped for and it quickly became an emergency situation since our son had complications. The doctors performed an emergency C-Section on my wife because his umbilical cord was choking him to the point of his little heart stopping and I was truly about to lose my mind.

By morning, after pacing the hospital halls, all was well, and Olivia Rose and our son Robert were safe and resting with family gathered around to witness Robert's first day on Earth. It was a bittersweet moment for me, while holding him for the first time, I thought about my daughter Selena constantly and how I hadn't held her in better than a half a decade. I held my baby boy close and wanted nothing more than to be present in his life, not making the same mistake I did with his older sister.

One would've thought that with all the blessings in my life, it would've been an easy deal to accept those remarkable gifts over choosing to pick up a small alcoholic beverage, one that inflicted so much pain to me and those around me. I truly felt like a man for the first time in my life and because of feeling that way, I told myself I would be able to drink in moderation and manage it successfully unlike I had before.

When I drove my family home from the hospital, I hadn't had a drink in three days. When the two of them were settled in bed, I lied to Olivia Rose as always about my whereabouts and went to my Uncle Ray's house to celebrate the birth of my son. To justify my actions, I told myself since Olivia Rose's mother was in town visiting, during the biggest moment of her daughter's life, I knew the two of them were safe at the house while my mother-in-law was looking over them. While I poured back drinks with my uncle and his fiancé, I told myself, *moderation, Joel; you have a newborn son and a tired wife at home.* But once I started, there was no such thing as moderation. Our drinking got out of hand while celebrating, and a quarrel ensued between the three of us.

My uncle Ray's fiancé was being disrespectful toward me about the way I spoke and dressed due to my affiliations and the culture I grew up in. I began to defend myself by telling her, *"to each his own,"* and my uncle being as trashed as he was, walked around the patio furniture, slammed my head against the brick wall and choked me almost crushing my esophagus and larynx.

My uncle Ray was a foot taller than I was and had a hundred pounds on me, so it was impossible for me to escape his grasp without a weapon on me, because he was so big. When he finally released my neck because his lady was pleading for him to stop, I jumped up and immediately began threatening him and his fiancé like I did my father when he choked me with the screen door over two-decades prior.

I walked to Olivia Rose's brand-new car with my newborn son's car seat in the back and told them I was going to return to shoot and kill them both. My younger cousin ran out of the house pleading for me not to drive drunk, but I was on a mission and refused to listen as I closed the door in his face. I revved the engine, turned the Go-Go music up and sped away putting the pedal to metal, only to crash seconds later into a guardrail across the street.

Olivia Rose eventually found me in the desert near one of my other uncle's house's around two O'clock in the morning with cactus stuck in my back. I had also defecated in my pants, probably while my Uncle Ray choked me near unconsciousness. When my wife saw the damage I'd caused to her beautiful car she was distraught and baffled on how I could disrespect her in that way after delivering our first child just days prior.

The next morning our family was spreading the news about what happened and how 'bad' my uncle Ray and I were when he and I were together. I was grateful that I never made it home to get my gun. In the state of mind, I was in, I most certainly would've driven back and shot them both or at least attempted to. I was also extremely grateful that I didn't damage my head any further in the accident. As for my uncle Ray and me, the two of us were back drinking together at a bar by noon the same day.

When shameful situations like that unfolded in my life, I fought tooth and nail not to pick up a drink, but my self-discipline caved in every time. For my loved ones it wasn't if I would drink again, it was always when it was going to happen and what events would take place while I was binging. But with my mother-in-law flying back to Virginia to live her life, I needed to overcome the cravings and step up to the plate and provide for my family without her there picking up the mess I left behind.

Amazingly enough, I was able to hold it together for quite a while and continued to excel at work and at school, but the insanity of my addiction came back around like an old friend when a group of student chefs planned a get together at a restaurant after class one afternoon. The poor souls had no idea of what they'd done when they invited me out with them for *a* drink. *A* drink, for some, literally meant one drink and then they'd go grocery shopping or home to their families. For others, *a* drink meant five or six, but they still left the establishments in a respectable manner. But for me, *a* drink meant vacuuming the bar floors and stacking chairs at two o' clock in the morning while bartenders shook their heads while I continued to ask for drinks. Having *a* drink for me also meant I was pulling chefs knives on other drunks at the bar and flying around town drinking and driving only to end up in strange peoples' houses.

I'd seen it all in the city and I wasn't proud of it. Olivia Rose and Robert were home waiting up for me constantly like Janine and Selena were in Virginia, only to be disappointed over and over again.

The student chefs continued to suggest I'd go home after school, but I insisted continuously that I was well and wouldn't get out of hand like every other time we'd gone to Happy Hour. Not one of them knew me well enough to understand the lifestyle I'd lived or what kind of trauma I dealt with for years, and if I would've shared my past with them, I seriously doubted they would've ever invited me in the first place. I didn't know how to act in a civilized manner, for long periods of time, and from the outside looking in, I was on a destructive path. People began to question if I'd become bored with attempting to achieve success. *Was I bored, longing to be a dependable man, going home to my loved ones where I'd wash dishes and read bedtime stories to my son or daughter that wanted nothing more than to have both their parents in their lives?*

I always pushed the envelope until the envelope fell from the edge, landed in water and disintegrated into mush with nothing left to show from the progress I'd achieved. At night, when Olivia Rose was upset and would lock me out of our home, I'd bar hop until they closed and then I'd go from one relative's house to another until someone answered the door.

Dawson, my aunt's ex-husband, who was addicted to Methamphetamine and to the Meth lifestyle as a whole, stayed up every night and I knew I was always welcome during any hour. I would end up staying at his house and because I'd be intoxicated, and didn't care about anything when I was drunk, I purchased Meth from his dealer. I wanted to get past the drunken stupor all the while hoping to return to work in the morning. Unfortunately, for my family, I ended up going missing for days on end.

After pleading with Olivia Rose to get back into our house and her graciously allowing me back in, I lied to her less than a week later and told her I was servicing my Uncle Ray's pool. My wife was a wise one and she figured it out and showed up while a group of us were hanging out and drinking. As I was turning around to leave his restroom, she punched me square in the face while holding our son Robert before storming out of his house.

It got really bad for a while and our marriage was on shaky ground, so I dusted myself off and was able to get my priorities in order before I lost my family and home. An opportunity presented itself for me to become a chef at a world-renowned luxury hotel in the mountains north of Tucson. The hotel had one-hundred and thirty locations, in thirty countries, and when the executive chef at the school presented the idea to me, I was honored and accepted, after talking it over with Olivia Rose.

Accepting employment at such a prestigious hotel was a dream come true. Many student chefs I'd met only dreamt of having the opportunity to work in such an amazing establishment, so I felt blessed. The morning I went to sign my contract with human resources, the hotel's executive chef walked in and informed me I would need to cut my long hair off before I could begin working in one of his four restaurants. My hair was very important to me and folks often told me to never cut it because it was my strength like in the story of Samson and Delilah from The Bible. Olivia Rose was also one to compliment my hair and said it was the most beautiful hair she'd ever seen. But I had to decide right then and there in front of the boss before signing my name on the dotted line.

My wife complained and wept at the thought of me cutting all my hair off. But she held the large scissors like a warrior, closed her eyes and cut my foot-long ponytail off almost getting sick. We donated it to an organization that advocated for kids with cancer.

I was responsible for opening one of the restaurants after sunrise, I prepped the food for the day and ran the kitchen through to the late afternoon. I also continued to service pools, I held a GPA of 3.5 at the Art Institute and I was present as a husband and a father.

Once again, I felt like a reliable man. I was doing well at home and truly felt successful for the first time in my entire life. To be called chef, by everyone at the hotel, was an amazing accomplishment and I was confident juggling the busy schedule. At the same time, my teeth were finally straightening out and my self-esteem was at an all-time high. I had been embarrassed for so many years about the way my teeth looked. All was going well in my life.

Driving to the hotel took an hour from where our new home was located, but it was well worth the time and gas for such a promising start to my culinary career. The hotel sat in a large cove in the mountains and was a serene site to witness at the start of each day, which gave me an attitude of gratitude and did wonders for my troubled spirit.

A Native American man would stand at the top of a ridge and played his flute while guests enjoyed themselves by a large swimming pool where another restaurant sat by the water. I walked through the locker room where some of the greatest golfers in the world had their own luxury lockers. When they came to play each year, it was a huge deal for the city and especially for the hotel and its staff.

Before my restaurant would open its doors each day, I would look out toward the mountains and pray for strength as cravings would creep in, but I was able to shake them off having remembered how far I had gone and how blessed I was. As the spiritual man serenaded the desert grounds with his flute in the evening, I knew the spirit world was still looking over me. I stood back to appreciate the moment while praying that I would continue to push forward and hoping to accomplish even more.

Being around successful people seemed to relieve me of my negative thoughts and behaviors. I couldn't understand that being around other successful individuals had played a major role in the success I myself had achieved even for those short periods of time. The relationships I had with the executive chef and the other chefs were amazing. We'd sit down in the main restaurant downstairs to review new menu items. They'd ask my opinion on each menu change and that gave me a sense of belonging and importance. But even though I was maintaining, and I felt inspired by my own current success, I would fall again without knowing the fall was coming.

One afternoon after working in the kitchen all day, I felt I deserved *a* drink for having achieved such amazing goals. I knew in my heart it was a horrible idea, but I told myself I would be able to control the drinking and I could be reliable enough to be home before dark. I drove to Dawson's house and picked up a bottle on the way. When the last bit of liquor was gone, the two of us decided to go to a bar for a few more drinks. I did control the drinking enough to function while I fought myself mentally not to be out all night. When Olivia Rose called my cell phone I turned it off and we drove to another bar even after I told myself I wouldn't.

On our way through the city, Dawson vomited all over my dashboard, door and floor. I wasn't happy to say the least because it smelled like a detox facility in my nice SUV. Unlike my life, I kept my vehicles, home, and clothes clean and organized. As I drove through an intersection, rolling all the windows down, lights switched on behind us and sirens began to ring out.

I couldn't believe it. I was able to control my drinking enough not get plastered but didn't go home like I promised Olivia Rose and Robert. I pulled into a parking lot and the officer pulled in behind us, walked up to my truck and said, *"License and registration, please."* I looked over toward Dawson and as drunk as he was, he reached into the glove box covered in vomit, and I handed the officer my identification while I was just shaking my head.

The officer most definitely smelled the nasty stench and stuck his head in my SUV and stepped back, "Wow! It doesn't smell good; what's wrong with him?" "He's not feeling well, officer. I was on my way to take him home. Why'd you pull me over," I asked. "Well, my radar showed you were going fifteen miles over the speed limit. But now that I'm standing here, I smell alcohol coming from your vehicle. Have you been drinking," he asked me. "No officer—he has, and that's why I'm driving him home," I insisted. The officer continued, "Will you step out of the vehicle, please?"

My entire life was about to change if I was intoxicated more than I thought I was.

I stepped out of the vehicle and another patrol car pulled in behind us. "How much did you have to drink," the officer asked. "I didn't drink, sir. I just told you that. I was…" Interrupting me, the officer commanded, "Step over here with us. I need you to walk heel-to-toe in a straight line." Being too clever, I said, "Who walks heel-to-toe officer? I don't walk heel-to-toe, so why would I be good at that now while wearing chef clogs?" He said, "Okay, son, recite the alphabet backwards for me." Sounding insulted, I said, "What? Is that a joke? I'm not trying to be disrespectful, officer, but who recites the alphabet backwards? I'm not going to be tested doing certain things I've never done. That sounds like a set up."

Then he said, "No, actually if you're not intoxicated, you'd be fine taking these tests, but since you're not complying, step over to this officer's vehicle and we're going to draw blood and breathalyze you." And if you don't comply with these two tests, you will be going to jail tonight, and your license will be suspended." I knew I was screwed and was scheduled to work that morning at the hotel and needed my vehicle and license to get there, so I complied to all the tests while praying that I was at the legal limit.

I sat in the back of the patrol car with the door opened and the second officer drew my blood, "Alright, now blow into this." I prayed hard and fast that I was under the state's legal limit of .008 while I blew into their small device. He looked at it, looked at me, and turned the breathalyzer around for me to see the results, ".016. That's double the legal limit. At this time, I'm going to read you your rights as you are now under arrest for an extreme DUI and your license will be going with me and is now suspended. Your vehicle, as bad as it smells, will be going to an impound lot and you'll be able to pick it up after paying some hefty fees." The other officer walked over to my SUV and told Dawson to exit the vehicle before a tow truck loaded it and hauled it away.

I'd driven drunk continuously and did so off and on for seventeen years without being pulled over. At times losing everything in the back of my pickup truck and while heading into town the next day, I would see those items scattered across the road for miles. I snapped out of my blackouts at times and my SUV was just inches from someone's front door. I even drove it up a rock landscape and the front of my truck was kissing an office building elevated twenty feet or so up from the parking lot below me. I drove over medians on multiple occasions in Arizona but managed not to cause any accidents, injure anyone or get pulled over. I justified continuing to do so because I'd gotten away with-it countless times. *It was not the case this time.*

Later that morning, after the sun came up, I sat in my garage while chugging on a bottle of liquor, crying and contemplating if I wanted to go on living. I was tired and ashamed of falling again and I couldn't look my family in the eyes after promising that I would stop this foolishness. My parents drove to our house, after my wife called them, and while they were attempting to talk me into handing the bottle over the phone rang. It was the hotel. "Hey Joel, good morning. How's it going? Are you coming in today?" Very directly, I said, "No chef...I'm not." He responded, "What do you mean? Is everything alright?" I said, "No chef; everything is not alright. I quit." And I ended the call.

I spent countless hours putting in work toward becoming a chef and was well on my way to being part of something extraordinary. I'd only dreamt of achieving something so special, but of course, that was when I was sober, and like when I joined the National Guard years prior, I gave it away to my addiction.

I didn't tell the pool company about the DUI and continued servicing pools, but I worked alone, leaving me with my own thoughts and no one to turn to. As the depression deepened, I began to breeze through my jobs only doing enough to keep my job to support my addiction. When we found out the consequences for the DUI, Olivia Rose and I agreed to get a lawyer and spent $3,000 to help my cause. My wrongdoings were continuing to chip away at our savings.

My poor wife tried so hard to bring me back from the abyss and for micro moments, she had hope. As strong as she was, I wasn't able to find that same strength and wasn't strong enough to get out of the hole I was in. I drank continuously and all the resentments from my past came crashing down at once, creating the precise ingredients for a monumental disaster. I began to stay away for days on end, and at times putting myself in harm's way while my loved ones searched for me.

As I continued to descend, we found out that we were expecting our second child, my third. During such an emotional rollercoaster, I tried so hard to pull it together for our family only to fall back in. Through the turmoil, I walked away from the Art Institute and my dreams of graduating with a culinary degree. Even more disheartening than that, after telling myself over and over again that I was useless and didn't deserve a good life or a loving family, I chose to quit at life all together. I packed a small bag, walked out of our house and I drove away. I abandoned Olivia Rose, Robert and our unborn child as I did Janine and Selena. And though I was serious about giving up on my life, I had no idea what Satan was about to unleash on me while driving toward the gates of Hell.

CHAPTER 16

METHAMPHETAMINE & MACHETES

The day I abandoned my family, Olivia Rose and my parents, along with many other concerned family members, reached out in an attempt to pull me away from Dawson's house, because they all knew about his involvement in the Meth world. They knew if I were to stay too long, the odds of me getting trapped in his house, were so great that I may never return.

Houses where addicts would go to use were called trap houses. The addiction would keep the addict stuck in these places and they would never want to leave. Dawson's house was no different.

Unfortunately, my young cousin, Brooklyn was born into the drug world and raised in this environment. She began learning the ways of the addict world at a very young age. Other homeless meth and heroin addicts sought shelter there as well and though I didn't trust any of them, they always had what I wanted, so I returned there each day after servicing pools.

Methamphetamine quickly became my drug of choice, and for the first time in almost eighteen years, I made the decision to put the alcohol down for good, swapping one substance for the other. Many of the addicts at Dawson's house drank, used heroin and meth. I was done with being a drunk, having thrown up bile thousands of times since I began drinking in my adolescence and just simply grew tired of consuming alcohol, a depressant.

I justified the swap of substances by telling myself, *only using Meth is better than being a sloppy drunkard.* I hated hangovers, I was tired of falling down concrete steps and busting my face open, and then lying to people telling them I was beaten up or in an accident. I was in fact caught off guard and beat down numerous times in the past, because I was too drunk to function. I allowed myself to become vulnerable in too many situations.

As far as heroin, I'd done it before and if there wasn't meth around, I would do it again. I was also becoming more and more paranoid with or without the drugs and knew the heroin would make me strung out and I knew I'd be stuck. I didn't want people to take advantage of me or tie me up and kidnap me while I was nodding out.

A few weeks removed from the family life, I was beginning to stay awake for four, five and six day stretches without eating. The other addicts in the trap house lived this lifestyle for years and could handle the dope, eating, sleeping and functioning with ease. They would bring up the fact that I was a chef and requested that I cook for them, but I lost interest in food altogether.

I stayed away from the pool company's warehouse as much as possible. Each afternoon, when I serviced the pools on my route, I found places in the customer's backyards and used meth until I was high enough. Then I would go to the next house where I did the same thing again until I had no more dope.

One evening while brushing algae off the plaster in a pool at the home of a man who owned multiple car dealerships in the city, I had a heat stroke. I had not slept, eaten, or been drinking fluids for five days. I laid in the company's truck for hours until my body and mind were well enough to drive back to Dawson's house. I was hoping the successful man wouldn't return home to find me in the state I was in.

It happened again soon after that and an amazing couple from New York, welcomed me into their home, laid me down and fed me fruit. They gave me something to drink, offering their aid and assistance for close to an hour. They wanted to phone 911, but I insisted I would be okay to drive home.

The sleep deprivation made me feel like I was losing my mind from early on. I would drive to the wrong addresses and serviced the wrong swimming pools. I began to hallucinate, not being able to control the drug unlike the solidified meth addicts I was around. This drug world was much different than the rest and I'd recognized that very quickly. Though I'd used it in the past, I hadn't used it in this manner or with this amount. I didn't have this many people walking in and out of the door bringing in loads of stolen goods, putting curses on one another and manipulating their way to get what they wanted.

Methamphetamine caused the brain to overflow with dopamine, establishing immense pleasure, but consuming too much of this drug for long periods of time created monsters out of human beings. These types of addicts became obsessive and extremely violent when associating with the same like-minded souls and it made for an intense and stressful environment.

The immense pleasure rang true and I was sex deprived since I'd left Olivia Rose. Instead of sleeping with the girls that walked in and out of the house, I would go into a vacant trailer in the backyard or Dawson's broken-down van and used my credit cards to call phone sex lines in order not to have sex with any of the women. Not all of them wanted to sleep with me, but the ones that would've, drove me to the point of calling the numbers over and over again, fighting each temptation as it was presented.

I couldn't ejaculate for hours on end and it was torturous. I ran up $200.00 phone calls multiple times, and while watching porn on my phone, I would miss an entire day of work just trying to have an orgasm. No voice over the phone and no woman on the internet got me there, so I would scroll over thousands of different videos trying to find the right match for me to get off. By the time I'd climax, the sun went down, and my credit cards were maxed out at over $10.000.

Olivia Rose quickly began moving the money to different banks before I spent it all on phone sex and drugs. When the credit cards were no longer an option, I had to be resourceful and creative in order to survive and support my habits. All of them. My mother-in-law ended up moving out of her home to help my family because my wife wasn't able to take care of everything and she was getting closer to having our second son. Even as disrespectful, careless and selfish as I was, in abandoning her and our children, my wife contacted a

Mental Health Crisis Unit to hunt me down in an attempt to save me, but I dodged their every move. This created stress between the other addicts and me because they didn't want people approaching the house looking for anyone.

Though I loved and missed my family dearly, I was not going to return home to clean up, only to fail again. I wasn't going to destroy the kids' lives like I was destroying my own. The sense of hope I had in previous downfalls, no longer existed. My parents, my sister, aunts, uncles and multiple cousins, reached out or continued to stop by and tried talking me in to returning home, but it was to no avail. Every time they knocked at the door, more addicts were there using drugs and getting trapped in the web of darkness.

As ridiculous as it sounds, I still respected God and His word, even though I was a gang member, a convicted felon and a drug addict that did all the bad things I'd done. Someone who'd abandoned his family, along with a little girl and her mother in Virginia, these people I hung around with spat at the thought of God and would've thrown stones at Jesus if they were to have seen him. I felt every person's spirit as they walked through that door and knew immediately which ones were one of the devil's rejects and which ones were lost just like myself.

The more I witnessed scandalous acts happening in the trap house and felt them conspiring against one another, the more many of them didn't want me around because I knew what they were up to. I had gone through more than any of them could ever imagine and I was extremely intelligent while acting clueless, at times.

"Hey, brother. Why are you here? This world isn't your world. You should go back to your family. This isn't the life for you. Go on now...while you still have a chance." I heard this from different people on many different occasions, usually when they knew I was protecting others from their trickery.

Unfortunately, many addicts, prostitutes and homeless wanderers would vanish without a trace. No one would know because they eventually had no point of contact such as a job, an address, or a home phone. Families and loved ones would lose track and figured they were just out getting high, when in fact, many were taken out to the desert and murdered or lured to some meth addict's home where they were tortured for hours before being killed. I was becoming like one of them.

There were many people I met that vanished and I knew it when they never returned. Most thought they'd gone home, to detox, or a rehab, but I felt the evil manifesting when the evil ones conspired against the weak as they walked out the front door together. Only the ones I felt were evil returned.

One morning before going to service a pool, I gave one of the longtime addicts at the house money to run and grab me a sack of dope. I got to a point where I wouldn't leave the house unless I was freshly high and had more dope on me. Though he told me he'd only be ten minutes, he never returned that day. The rage I had toward the man and my intentions to harm him were at an all-time high. I barely knew this cat and already I wanted to kill him more than I did anyone else I ever resented in my entire life. The methamphetamine magnified my homicidal ideation that had been building up for years and I was furious.

The same addict would walk into Dawson and Brooklyn's house without knocking, take what he wanted and leave. Dawson may have allowed him to do that, but where I was from, respect was everything in the streets and I was going to teach him a lesson. The animosity and drive that was manifesting intensified the longer he was gone with my money. I waited for him to walk through the front door for two whole days with a heavy-duty pipe-wrench in my hand. The energy that went through my body was so vibrant and hateful it burned on while people walked in and out of the house asking me what I was doing.

Finally, after forty-eight hours, almost to the minute, I decided to leave because I needed some things from my house. I attempted to lay the pipe-wrench down, but my hand was cramped from holding it for so long and it took several minutes for my fingers to loosen up.

When I saw Olivia Rose, I wanted to sleep with her so bad it cringed my soul. While I was gathering my belongings to trade for drugs, she began shouting at me and my anger toward her remarks made me furious and I began to rage. I was going to destroy the house in front of Robert, who was so excited to see me. But I couldn't control the hate that was burning in me and the meth was bringing a demon out that she'd never seen before.

As I was pleading for her to leave me alone, I grabbed a video game to give to my cousin Brooklyn, and Olivia Rose demanded that I leave it at home. My wife didn't want any of our belongings at the other house, around other drug addicts, but I didn't see it that way because I was being irrational. No one could speak to me when I was irrational because I was set on 'rage mode' as soon as I felt disrespected. I could've broken that house into pieces inside and out with the evil that was manifesting in me and it carried over from the forty-eight hours I spent waiting on the 'junkie,' who I wanted to obliterate.

Olivia Rose also spoke about the DUI case and she was still worried about me, but I was too paranoid to show my face in the courtroom and I told her to drop the subject. I stopped caring and had no worries about a bench warrant for a 'failure to appear.' I did absolutely nothing the courts requested of me, even with Dawson insisting he'd help me to get my license back, offering to drive me to court. None of it mattered, I was too far gone to care.

I even stopped going to the dentist because I didn't care about my teeth anymore, and Olivia Rose was concerned about that as well. My body became so dehydrated, the ceramic braces sank into my gums, creating small craters that caused excruciating and debilitating pain. I was able to slowly pull them out one brace at a time, by grabbing a set of pliers and pulling them from my meth-soaked teeth. I was flushing $4000.00 down the drain.

My fingertips became so dry, that touching a cotton ball would shoot sharp pains through the injuries in my face and head. When she didn't stop lecturing me about all the concerns she had, I threatened her, and she finally allowed me to leave before something terrible happened.

When I returned to the 'trap house,' I was ashamed of myself after leaving my wife and son the way I did. But I was on a mission for chaos and quickly forgot about the ones who loved me. When I knocked on the door, Brooklyn answered and told me that the man I was waiting for, for those two whole days, walked through the door without knocking ten minutes after I left. He had no clue that I was waiting for him and only God could have saved him from the destruction I was going to inflict on him, because I didn't care if he died. I knew it was God because I didn't believe in coincidences. I believed in God and I believed in timing, and that timing was impeccable because we both lived to get high another day.

Soon after, during another early morning while it was still dark, I purchased electronics at a department store with two drug dealers. During this time, I didn't know about the 'unwritten rule' of 'two for one.' This meant I'd purchase $300.00 worth of electronics in the store and the drug dealers would give me, their customer, $150.00 in meth. This was because I wasn't paying for the drugs in cash.

I thought they'd ripped me off for $150.00 in dope and I chased them through the city with a handgun I had taken from Olivia Rose's closet before I left there days prior. After the drug dealers were able to get away, I returned to the 'trap house' to prepare. I dressed in all black clothing and put my company shirt on over it so I wouldn't look suspicious. I wrapped the Glock 26, 9mm handgun in a plastic bag and I hid it in a 'chlorine tabs' bucket in the back of the pool truck.

While driving from trap house to trap house, searching for the men I thought had ripped me off, a truck began following me and I got super paranoid. I drove down streets with the lights off, turning through allies at full speed and cutting across streets without concern for anyone else's safety. As I sped through another ally, I turned onto a street, lost control and slammed the pick-up truck into a large mailbox at an apartment complex.

I immediately ran from the scene toward a liquor store where I called Dawson to pick me up, but I didn't think he'd show, so I called Olivia Rose knowing she would. The paranoia intensified as the same truck that was following me drove slowly down the busy street. Then I remembered I'd forgotten to grab the gun in the back of the truck.

I jogged toward the accident looking for my SUV, but I couldn't find it anywhere. I was at a loss for words. I thought someone stole my SUV and I continued looking around with my head on a swivel while people that lived on the block began to approach me.

I turned around as I heard a vehicle coming from behind, thinking it was the truck that was following me, but it ended up being multiple police vehicles with their spotlights pointed directly at me. I acted like I was an innocent bystander, searching for the accident, but when I turned the other way, Olivia Rose and Dawson both pulled their vehicles in behind the police.

As the officers approached me, they asked me whose pool truck it was that smashed into the large mailbox. I was so high and been up for so long, I'd totally forgotten that I drove the company truck that night after searching for my SUV the entire time. Once we all figured out who the driver of the pool truck was, I was questioned about my well-being and asked if I suffered from mental illness. I told the officers about my head injuries and how I'd had seizures, but I was still charged with leaving the scene of an accident, which was a misdemeanor Hit and Run charge. I was also charged with criminal damage and driving without a license. Because Olivia Rose advocated on my behalf and confirmed I'd suffered from both head trauma and seizures, I wasn't taken into custody that night, because I hadn't been drinking.

Instead of going with Dawson, the officers' suggested I go home with my wife and seek mental health treatment. As bad as I wanted to go back to Dawson's to use again, I got into Olivia Rose's car as the tow truck drove away with the company truck and the handgun that was hidden in a chemical bucket.

When we got to the house, I was physically, mentally and spiritually exhausted. I took a long shower, walked into my old bedroom and my wife and I became intimate for the first time in months. It was the best sex I'd ever had. I lasted longer than I'd ever had, and I couldn't have fathomed how much the drug intensified those pleasures as I became hyper focused on each part of my wife's body.

She continued to get hurt through my transgressions and still, she continued to do everything possible to please me, while praying daily for me to get out of the dark hole I was trapped in. I was also able to rest my mind and visit with my son I had not held in months.

The next day she drove me to the pool company where we spoke with the general manager about the accident. Though the owner and general manager always respected me and catered to my every need throughout the six years I'd worked with them, they were forced to let me go after seeing all the charges I had building up while behind the wheel.

Before we left the warehouse, I was able to collect my belongings from the truck I'd driven for years. While doing so, I secretly grabbed the handgun, giving it back to my wife before I did something foolish with it.

With everything Olivia Rose did for me, I repaid her by leaving her and Robert that same day. Without a job to support my habit or means to pay for the child support for Selena, I began selling my own personal pool route to legitimate pool companies. After that money had gone to the dope man, I began driving drug dealers and escorts around so I wouldn't be in one place for too long. The paranoia was beginning to get the best of me.

I started meeting different solidified people in the 'Meth World' and when that happened, I began to entangle myself deeper into that web of darkness. I'd once heard how The Bible spoke about witch doctors and sorcerers in the Old Testament and how they created potions to give to the weak minded. Then when the weak minded were under the control of those potions, curses beset them, intentionally putting people under a spell without means to a cure.

I was absolutely under a spell and the demonic actions that were being manufactured around me became more acceptable the deeper I became entangled. It was everything evil about the world and nothing good existed unless people perceived evil to be good. I witnessed bags of stolen goods being dumped onto the floor with rings on fingers and victims' credit cards, social security cards and birth certificates were passed around as gifts. Micro SD cards from the victims' cell phones were also shared, only for the information to be downloaded to everyone else's phones to spread the information throughout the dark web.

People were being buried alive, strippers continued to go missing and the more I saw, the more I became Viking-like in order not to be afraid of the lifestyle that was pulling me down into the Earth. Shadow men, voices conspiring to kill me, thousands of meth addicts on the same battle ground. So many of them succumbed to brutal deaths as other paranoid meth Vikings thought they were the ones who were conspiring to kill them first.

There were bikers, narcs and poor souls being manipulated into killing themselves after not being able to deal with the psychological mind games. Meth addicts, that were part of Satan's plan were very good at tricking the newcomer's mind into doing things, as they too were placed under a spell while others were being attacked with machetes. The females that were solidified and became evil, used sex to manipulate the men and their riders to do savage things when those same females got angry and had resentments.

It was blood-soaked clothing and addicts wearing clown masks. The meth world was an all-day everyday purge. I picked so many addicts up from towns across the desert because they knew when I wasn't too far gone, I was a skilled driver and would get them to where they needed to be without incident. I'd pick my dealer up and load a hundred cartons of cigarettes into the back of my SUV before we drove around town selling them to addicts and successful business owners.

There were millionaires living on the mountains who were manipulated by girls into allowing the dark world to invade their home, only to be tormented psychologically before losing their careers and sometimes their lives. Houses full of addicted and lost girls walking around doing whatever the men wanted them to do, either in those houses or in the streets.

The meth world and underground sex trade went hand-in-hand giving Satan a greater monopoly to fulfil his desires. I witnessed men that were heterosexual having sex with drug dealing men for drugs before being unleashed on the community to commit crimes for their dealers. People's faces and bodies infected with MRSA before those infected areas exploded while injecting themselves with the devil's dope. Syphilis, Hep C, and HIV were being passed around like the needles and pipes the addicts were sharing without care, because nobody believed they'd be saved anyway.

When I felt harm coming my direction, I stayed away from everyone for hours at a time. I drove alone for miles, sometimes parking in do-it-yourself car washes where I'd clean my SUV, but more importantly, staying on the move and not being in one place for too long.

While I drove through each boulevard and avenue, I began to notice how the meth world was structured in the area. I witnessed the same vehicles driving around the streets monitoring the movement of local users, specific neighborhoods were used to house informants. I saw how certain auto shops had contracts with agencies and would service the undercover and DEA agents' vehicles and how those agencies used the girls who were escorts, on the internet, to keep tabs on the dealers and the addicts they slept with. *Or was I just high?*

I observed on a number of occasions, the escorts I made money with, walk into stores, fast food restaurants or gas stations. Then after they entered those locations, certain vehicles would pull into the parking lot and strange people would get out to follow their informants in to have routine meetings. The escorts were in those places for twenty to twenty-five minutes every single time. Then the individuals they met with would walk out of each business and drive away five minutes before the escorts walked out.

I acted as if I was oblivious to their secret meetings, but the more places the girls asked me to drive them, the more I began to realize what was happening in this meth infested town. The more I knew, the more restless I became. I began wearing masks, carrying firearms, machetes, axes and even carried flammable liquids and muriatic acid in gallon jugs.

While I was piecing the structured chaos together, the weirdest situations occurred, and the addicts, I associated myself with, began to irritate me to my core. Someone I knew planted a GPS monitor on my SUV and other addicts began hacking my cell phones. It happened often enough that I was throwing every new cell phone I purchased out the window of my SUV because I was paranoid.

I got into an on-road conflict with two males in another vehicle and attempted to run them off the road while I was pointing a firearm at them. The police cars that were following me turned their sirens off and turned around as if nothing ever happened. The same addict I wanted to kill months prior for ripping me off and walking through Dawson's door without knocking, got under my skin once again. I chased him down while he was riding a bike one night and followed him for a few minutes until my hate for him returned. I almost crushed him between my SUV and someone else's house.

Another time I found him at one of my dealers' houses; I ran toward him with a baseball bat and swung at his head. Luckily, my dealer's girlfriend jumped in front of him and I was able to stop the bat just centimeters before crushing her skull. People, including my drug addicted relatives, were spreading lies about me to hide their own truths. But when I insisted we have meetings to confront the facts, they declined to speak about the matters in front of other addicts.

I continued to warn people who were involved in deceiving others, that when they spoke lies and attempted to set people up on false claims, their worlds would eventually be turned upside down, crushing them without warning. I was ready and willing to lose it all and because of the stressful and deceitful lifestyle I chose, I began to manipulate my own mind into forgetting about my loved ones. I did so because I didn't want to fall weak to the experienced meth addicts who were causing me to lose my patience.

One morning, a few hours before sunrise, one of the online prostitutes asked me to pull into a popular supermarket. When I glanced over to see where she pointed, I noticed the supermarket was closed, but I recognized the same vehicles that monitored these call-girls, and their 'Johns,' were sitting in the parking lot at three o' clock in the morning. I continued to drive past the supermarket, stopped at a red light and asked the girl why she was doing what she was doing.

She said I was paranoid, and I most certainly was. I had every right to be. I'd done a lot of disturbing things in front of these girls, including violent acts toward other meth addicts in the months leading up to that morning. With all of the experiences I had with law enforcement and being told on by the people in my life, I heard a spirit and respected what it was telling me.

The spirit was telling me to stop transporting these people around before I ended up gutted like a fish or spending the rest of my adult life in prison. But I was driving around in order to dodge certain places and specific people, so I wouldn't be stranded somewhere and murdered. The only way I felt I could cut these people out of my life would be to sell my nice SUV, that I'd purchased with Olivia Rose, when I was still a chef.

Later that morning, after I'd woken up in a rundown motel with the escort, I made the decision to sell my SUV for $380.00 and a bag of dope. I was tired of being around other mentally unstable people and felt the best solution for me was to park the SUV at someone else's house and walking away like the spirit was telling me to do. I'd been so stressed for so long that my head was beginning to cause more pain and the nerves in my body began to go haywire. Trading my SUV was the best thing I could've done. Too many people knew my SUV and knew who I was driving around in it, so a target was put on my vehicle. I was a paranoid maniac and would've done something horrible to any person who irritated me, or someone else would've definitely done the same to me because of the vibe I was giving off.

There were too many signs that something brutal was going to happen to someone, and after I sold my SUV, everyone I chauffeured became bitter towards me, but I did not care. My dealer, my cousin Brooklyn, the escorts and my relatives were all shocked I'd sold such a nice vehicle for pennies and a bag of meth that was gone by the end of the day. For the first time in many years, I had no vehicle and no means to escape if necessary. When I returned to Dawson's house, I phoned an old friend who was a respected chef and asked if he would give me a ride because I was paranoid. I didn't want to get trapped in that house all over again. My old cooking partner had no clue about what I'd been up to in the year since I'd disappeared from the culinary world, so I expected a 'shock and awe' moment if he took me up on my request.

To my surprise he agreed to pick me up that night and when I approached his vehicle, his face showed signs of someone who'd seen a ghost. I opened the door and tossed machetes, axes and a few other weapons in the backseat. He was in fact as shocked as I thought he'd be. His face was pale, and I felt he was worried for his safety. I assured him he was safe and then he asked how I lost so much weight. I told him the truth and the more detail I spoke, the more he became sad and questioned why and how someone, who was living such a blessed life with a loving family, could fall so hard and so fast.

I'd spoken to Olivia Rose earlier that evening and it was all bad, so I didn't know what to expect by showing up unannounced. When my old friend dropped me off, I stashed the weapons around the yard and rang the doorbell. When my wife answered the door, she closed it in my face. I sat by the front door and searched through my bag, but I'd forgotten my phone chargers, so I had no way to call anyone to pick me up. I didn't want anyone using methamphetamine to know where my family lived. They did home invasions daily on the homes of anyone they knew, and it happened to their families and their families' family's homes too. I was paranoid that this could happen to my family.

Instead of continuing to ring the doorbell, I strapped two machetes on my back and headed for a gas station down the street. I was in constant paranoia about other meth addicts finding me and I never wanted to be caught off guard, thus the reason I carried machetes and or guns everywhere I went.

While I was grabbing two pieces of pizza and a soft drink, I noticed two females looking at me from across the store. I immediately felt a vibe and knew something was up, so I purchased what I had, bought a pack of smokes and headed out the doors. "At it again aren't you, son? You'll learn." I turned around and the older gentleman who'd spoken walked into the store without ever looking at me.

I continued walking down the road near the desert towards Olivia Rose's house and was on high alert. When I arrived in the neighborhood, I was expecting off-road desert trucks with meth addicts to come flying up on me because of what the man said and how he said it. On top of that, the two females who were looking at me in the gas station, gave me a reason to think they were after me for something I'd done.

As I walked closer toward my estranged wife's house, I noticed multiple police vehicles patrolling both sides of a playground with their spotlights on. I glanced down toward her house and there were multiple vehicles that looked familiar from the city because I'd seen them following me before. At times, I would turn around and follow those same unmarked vehicles when I was really showing my ass and felt like a super-human. I'd shut my lights off, put a mask on and pull up behind them, trying to provoke them into doing something so I could have reason to attack.

The more experienced I became at driving on meth, the more I was able to hydroplane and cut corners like a professional racecar driver. This allowed me to escape whoever it was chasing me that day. But I had no clue as to who these folks were that were watching me and why they'd been sitting in front of the house I'd purchased two years prior.

I crept in the dark, pulling the machetes from my back, slid them under the dirt in the desert, then continued on toward the house. While approaching, I walked past a friendly neighbor and his son. I'd serviced their swimming pool and became close to him and his family throughout the time I lived there. When he saw me, it took him a while to recognize who I was before he became tearful. I was so tired by then that when reality hit me, seeing him and his son, I didn't care to lie anymore, and I was ready to tap out. We spoke for a brief moment, he gave me a big hug and wished me well, all the while shaking his head. He grabbed his young boy's hand and the two of them walked away.

When I approached the house, the front door was wide opened and the two females from the gas station were sitting on the couch I'd purchased along with multiple police officers who were speaking with Olivia Rose and her mother. It was the Mental Health Crisis Unit that had been searching for me for over six months and here they had finally caught up to me. I turned around, walked toward the street and sat on the curb where I ate my pizza, drank my soft drink and smoked a cigarette waiting for law-enforcement to take me away.

I was shocked when the officers told me they weren't taking me to jail. I thought I was going for sure; I had the 'failure to appear' for the DUI plus multiple charges that had accumulated since then. But the officers handcuffed me and took me to a Psychiatric Emergency

Hospital called the CRC (Crisis Response Center) for 'Homicidal Ideation.'

I'd never been in a psych hospital before and I wasn't looking forward to it. I was frail after going at life so hard under extreme measures and I knew this was meant to happen at this exact moment in time. When we arrived, I was paranoid that every worker at the hospital was related to either a meth addict, or any one of the major organizations who were involved in that lifestyle or on the distribution side of it. There was a whole lot of scary stuff going on in the desert and when the doctor spoke to me about having sleep deprivation, which was true, I agreed with him, but he had no clue about the reality of what really happened to those who lived in it.

How having so many paranoid individuals in one area, who were putting their hands in places they had no business putting them, was causing chaos and violence. Only people living such a barbaric lifestyle would have understood this.

I was asked if I'd seen things or heard things and I laughed softly. I told the doctor I'd seen things he couldn't have imagined and heard things that may or may not have been there. He asked if I suffered from schizophrenia, and I told him no. He asked if I was paranoid, and I told him yes. I then told him that under the conditions of the life I had been living, I was considered a 'paranoid methaphranic' and the things I'd seen were real, regardless of what they said about me not sleeping for days on end.

After a twenty-four hour hold at the CRC, I was transferred to a different psych hospital where they kept me long-term. When I was there long enough for the meth to get out of my system, I was diagnosed as having, Bi-Polar Disorder, Generalized Anxiety Disorder, PTSD (Post Traumatic Stress Disorder), Intermittent Explosive Disorder, Impulse Control Disorder and Polysubstance Abuse Disorder (meaning I did every drug I could get my hands on), on top of suffering a traumatic brain injury in addition to multiple concussions.

A woman representing a mental health agency came to visit me, once my mind was somewhat clear, and I was enrolled with services that allowed me to seek help from a psych doctor and therapist in the community along with many support groups if I was able to stay clean and advocate for myself.

I was placed on multiple psych medications that turned me into a zombie and though I'd loved getting high, I hated taking their medications. When I was released, my family was hopeful and skeptical at the same time. When Olivia Rose met with both hospitals and the mental health agency, the case managers encouraged my wife and parents to persuade me to enter a long-term treatment facility.

The thought of being away from the meth maniacs, I had surrounded myself with, gave a sense of peace to my spirit, but the fact that I was considered 'mentally ill' gave me more anxiety than I ever had before. I didn't know how to deal with life after everything I'd done to myself, my children, both women I'd abandoned who'd birthed my amazing children and the family who never gave up on me. The shame I felt seemed too much to tolerate and I didn't think any place would be able to aid and assist me with what I was dealing with. I'd been stressed for decades, taking brutal physical punishment, stuffing my emotions with chemicals and acting out toward society while other humans acted out toward me. The paranoia wasn't just going away. I'd seen too much. I didn't feel that I was strong enough to get past everyone's judgement toward me, let alone the judgement I felt toward myself.

I didn't feel the medications would work either, but if they did, I'd feel that I was a crazy person like I'd been called thousands of times. All the reasons I told myself about why I didn't want to enter a rehab facility and I should just run back out to the streets to use drugs, were the exact reasons why I knew I needed to go into long-term treatment.

So, in November, three months before Olivia Rose's due date to give birth to our second son and my third child, I walked into the Salvation Army Rehabilitation Center six-month program for men in an attempt to turn my life around. I hoped that by some miracle this would help me become a reliable husband, father, son, brother and friend and prove to myself and any other doubters that I could become more than just another lost soul.

CHAPTER 17

SUICIDAL IDEATION

W*hen I walked through the doors of the Salvation Army, I was terrified and I thought about walking out immediately, but the look in my father's eyes is what gave me the courage to stay and fill out the intake forms.*

The facility housed up to eighty-six men, from all walks of life, and when I was first approached by the large group on their way to lunch, I noticed they were all dressed in collared shirts that were tucked in. It was mind blowing when I saw men tattooed from head to toe laughing and enjoying themselves on the way to the cafeteria.

Every single one of the men were clean cut and had a presence about them—a glow per say. I couldn't understand how they came to be like that. At first, I thought it was a cult and they were somehow brain washed. *What kind of place could've transformed violent gang-members, convicted felons, thieves, raging alcoholics and twisted and disturbed drug addicts into confident well-mannered men with smiles?*

After the paperwork was complete, a gentleman approached me and introduced himself as a beneficiary of the program. He went on to tell me, the men (or beneficiaries) were the ones who worked in the facility. They worked at the front desk, in the kitchen, in the laundry room, did the janitorial duties and one beneficiary was assigned to work in a canteen area where coffee and snacks were sold after WTAs (Work Therapy Assignments). Also, a majority of the men worked in a large warehouse where the Salvation Army trucks, I'd seen in the

226

city for years, would be unloaded on their docks before the donations were sorted through and sold in stores.

He continued on about how the donated items were cleaned and refurbished and that the proceeds were what the program used to pay for the entire operation. He also explained how each Salvation Army program transferred colonels, majors or captains, to each location, where they oversaw the operation every few years. They were spreading the word of God to our homeless, drug addicted and alcoholic population before transferring to different locations around the world, where they continued to spread the word of God.

I'd thought the Salvation Army was about feeding the homeless during the holidays and they did just that, but I was intrigued to learn the organization used donations to pay for expenses. The recovering addicts were put to work in order to build their character, strength and confidence for six months before returning to society to search for jobs.

I got settled into my five-bed dorm room and quickly went to work the next morning in the large warehouse where I sorted through donated clothing. I was resentful when they told me my WTA was in the warehouse and not in the kitchen since I'd worked in kitchens for years. But I was just grateful to be in a safe environment away from the streets where misery was waiting for me just on the other side of the front doors.

I befriended three older gentlemen, from different cities, and the four of us grew closer as the days passed. We held each other up when the others were down. We attended service in the chapel on Wednesdays and Sundays, and when we were done with our WTA's, we attended the same twelve step meetings throughout each week.

The program was strict and created men out of boys. We had to make our beds with a forty-five-degree crease at the ends, shave every time a single hair grew on our face and we were provided with donated clothing, so every man looked respectable. Every class, meeting and work assignment was mandatory.

There wasn't enough time in the day to become lazy. We were given thirty days to find a sponsor in any one of the twelve-step fellowships that were available throughout the city. We had one-on-one counseling sessions, group therapy sessions, twelve-step meetings, chapel twice a week, eight-hour work assignments and of course, many of us were hitting the weights which helped us to become more self-confident after all we'd put our bodies through.

I was exhausted to say the least, but I became stronger spiritually by the minute. During the holidays, we were free from our WTA's and they allowed us to enter into tournaments such as cards, ping pong, billiards, bingo and my favorite, two on two basketball. I was skilled at playing ping pong from being incarcerated in the past and I was pretty good at shooting pool, but I failed to place in both of those contests. The last contest I entered was the basketball tournament and I partnered up with a young Hispanic brother from Phoenix that had size and strength. We ended up winning that tournament and after beating every team we faced, my confidence was beginning to surface, when before, it was all but gone.

Every day I was there, I respected every single one of the men that I came in contact with. Yes, there were small beefs that manifested throughout the week, but none of the arguments became physical which showed there was something special happening in the safe haven that was called the Salvation Army.

Even though things were going well, my anxiety and depression was creeping in on me. One night, a few days before Christmas, during our in-house twelve step meeting, I began shaking slowly as the meeting's chairperson began to read the literature. "Don't do it, brother." I looked over to the Native American brother that was sitting next me, and he must've felt my spirit as the cravings began to take over. "Don't...we have to wait until the miracle happens. Are you hearing me? Don't do it," he said. I was listening to the chairperson read, and as he continued on about methamphetamine, my body reacted giving me an erection, I needed to defecate, and my hands began to sweat profusely.

I got up from my chair, walked out of the meeting and quietly gathered my belongings from my locker in the dorm room. As I was shamefully saying goodbye to the three men, I'd become close to, each man I passed in the halls told me to *wait until the miracle happens*. It was what the alumni and commanding officers would say during graduations on Wednesday nights before service. But the enemy within kidnapped the lovable me and walked me out of the six-month program back into the dark streets in the worst neighborhood in the city.

Of course, I made my way back to Dawson's house and stopped taking my psych medications all together. Brooklyn and Dawson attempted to keep the drug dealers away when I returned because I was a disturbing individual on meth and couldn't handle the dope. That was saying a lot coming from other disturbed individuals.

The drug dealer I'd become closest to was arrested and sent to prison while I was in rehab, so I began calling different dealers that Dawson didn't care for. But I wanted meth and since he wasn't supporting my downfall or looking forward to seeing our family while being interrogated about my whereabouts, I went against his wishes and met up with one of the dealers I knew from a while back.

When my family found out I was getting high instead of being in rehab, they were terrified and attempted to pick me up from the house, but I became enraged with everyone who knocked on the door. I just wanted to hide and get as high as possible forgetting about everything that was good. I used so much dope that I quickly became a lunatic and began collecting weapons preparing myself for a massacre. The time I'd spent working on myself at the Salvation Army, fueled my depression even more because I'd thrown away an amazing opportunity. I continued to manipulate my mind into becoming a savage rather than being depressed and by Christmas morning, I was in the greatest state of paranoia I'd ever experienced.

As everyone in the house was scattered in different rooms, I began hearing bikers riding around the neighborhood. My mind was telling me that Dawson was resentful toward me for returning to his home and going against his wishes by getting high. All the while, I was reaching out to the drug dealing biker, who I got along with, and my mind was telling me that Dawson wanted me dead.

I quickly began booby trapping their house, tying clothes together, dowsing them in paint thinner and spreading them out like a twenty-foot spider. I had two gallons of muriatic acid in the storage room from when I cleaned pools and I poured them into multiple buckets, making it easier to toss on whomever it was I thought was walking through the doors.

I found a double-sided ax that I'd sharpened and polished for hours and I placed it in the dark bathroom. I looked for a spiked bat that a disturbed man gifted me with one day, but remembered I wasn't allowed to enter the house with it, so I found a box of razor blades and stuck them in a tennis ball that was attached to a bungee cord hanging above the front door.

As the bikers rode closer to the house, I grabbed a large torch that we used to smoke the devil's dope, set the buckets of muriatic acid in the hallway and bathroom and pulled one of the flammable ropes of clothing toward me. I left the lights off and prepared the torch by lighting it and setting it on the sink. As I heard someone entering the house, I grabbed the torch and pointed it directly at the dowsed fabric. I heard chains and sounds of someone being tortured on an electronic device. Tricksters used that tactic to scare their prey before finding and torturing them.

I went to light the clothing, but something told me not to. I set the torch on the ground next to the toilet, grabbed the ax and charged down the hall with the ax above my head. I was anticipating slamming the ax down on someone else's head but there wasn't anyone on that side of the house. Adrenaline forced me through my cousin Brooklyn's bedroom door and as I attempted to jump through her window, I tripped over hundreds of stolen items she hoarded after stealing them from other addicts who decided to use drugs in her house.

As she screamed at me with the devil's tongue, I ran into the backyard, ripped my shirt off and began hollering at whoever was in the house looking for me. I paced back and forth swinging the ax and when I heard a door open, I dug my feet into the ground, clinched my jaws and held the ax tightly like a baseball bat. I saw two silhouettes moving through the closed in porch area. I was prepared to die and ready to fight to the end. When the last door opened to the backyard, two men walked out, and I tightened my grip. I noticed it was Dawson and one of the men who was staying there.

I walked through the house holding the ax and no one else was there besides the people that had been there. I was baffled, so

I walked out the front door looking for motorcycles, but there were none. I walked back into the house and everyone was shaking their heads while telling me that I needed to get help.

I sat down, lit a cigarette and remembered that it was Christmas morning. Many of my relatives were at my parents' house celebrating the good Lord's birthday and I almost burnt down Dawson's house because of my mental instability.

Olivia Rose drove over with my son to pick me up before dinner was to be served at my parents' house, but I needed more dope. The addicts in the house encouraged me to go with my wife, but I needed more dope, so I stayed, leaving my son Robert crying and my pregnant wife distraught and at a loss for words.

I entered the Salvation Army Program a second time hoping to clean up before our son was born, but I walked out soon after. Without taking the medications as prescribed, my mental illness was too much to bear and no one knew what to expect from me even when I was clean and sober. Shockingly enough, after I went AWOL from the program, I was able to sleep in my son's room at our house in another attempt from the family to try and save me. We started attending church services at Pantano Community Christian Church, and on August 12th of 2012, I was baptized in front of hundreds of churchgoers and felt like everything was going to be alright.

I began detailing cars at the church and my parents helped pay for the detailing equipment. The big shocker to the family was they gave me the car my mother owned since the nineties. They were praying to God that it would become a motivation and make it easier for me to get work. They wanted to steer me in a positive direction before the baby was born.

My older sister despised the way my parents treated me. I could've admitted to murder and they would still love me. She frowned upon the fact that they continued to enable me by paying for work I'd done in their yard or on their pool, knowing I was working for dope money. They continued answering my phone calls regardless of what time it was, they picked me up from psych hospitals and from jail over and over again. They bought groceries for me when I was close to starving to death and purchased landscaping equipment for me to use on jobs.

I attended the substance abuse counseling that was part of the terms and conditions of me staying at home. When the medications became the primary focus for everyone in my family, the daily question would arise, "are you taking your medications?" Of course, I told them yes, but I hated the feeling the medications gave me, so I lied and tossed them in the trash until they caught on. Then I had to take them in front of someone every morning, afternoon and night.

Things were far from great and everyone around me was walking on eggshells, but I was looking like a human being again. It seemed that everyone and their ancestors were doing whatever they could to save me from myself. But as always, as soon as I made enough money and had the urge to use, I escaped back into the darkness using methamphetamine and my family was hurt beyond imagining.

I disappeared with the car and I was out using meth with complete strangers again until the morning our son Jaymes was born. When I received the phone call from my family telling me Olivia Rose was in the delivery room, I headed to TMC hospital but arrived late because I needed to find more dope first. I'd only been present for one of my children being delivered and my addictions were to blame in the two deliveries I'd missed.

My family was in tears when I showed up and it wasn't because they were happy about my son being born. My parents, mother in-law, aunts, uncles, cousins, and grandparents were all present to support my wife and when I walked in, unfortunately, the focus turned to me because I was so skinny. I looked like death was knocking at my door. During that binge, I weighed one hundred and seven pounds, an all-time low for me as an adult.

That night, after our supportive family members left, I drove to meet one of my drug dealers across the street from the hospital to pick up a sack. After he and I talked a while, I ordered some food for Olivia Rose and returned to her room where I immediately hid in the restroom and got high for over an hour.

I knew my wife was unable to reach the restroom because I saw how brutal her first C-Section was, so I took advantage of being in a safe place where I could get high and enjoy a long shower that was much needed. When I opened the restroom door, the cold air hit me like I was standing naked in the Arctic. It was so sudden that it gave me a jolt of energy like no other, but I felt out of place as I glanced over toward my wife and new baby son while they were lying there peacefully. Bug eyed and attempting to act as normal—as normal was for me, I walked over and kissed them both on the head, told them I loved them and walked out of their lives again.

I met different addicts to use with, in an attempt to stay away from Dawson's house, but the same evil was in every meth addict. There was a time when a group of people attempted to put fear in me by wearing clown masks outside of a trailer in the middle of the desert. I jumped into "Omen" mode and showed them I wasn't afraid by putting my mask on and pulling a sword on them.

Times were always disturbing, and it was because I became disturbing. I woke up on a stranger's floor after overdosing on heroin, ecstasy and meth. I thought these strangers were going to kill me because they thought I was dead, and they only knew me for about an hour before I overdosed.

I woke up another time at Dawson's house, after going close to a week without sleep, and I was strapped into a strait jacket. When I woke up, there were bikers walking in and out and I thought I was done for. They strapped it around me because I was too wild and did disturbing things when my brain was soaked in drugs. There were so many strange people walking in and out that I would pull guns on them to protect Brooklyn and her father's house. In turn, Brooklyn would steal my belongings along with everyone else's and talked ill about me behind my back. When I would leave, because I wanted to kill everyone for being deceitful, she would call me and ask me to return to the house so I would protect the house and all the stolen property that was scattered through it.

It was an endless psychological mind game on meth. Dawson got involved with a new woman and one night, I noticed her eyes turned black when she attempted to burn the house down while watching a stand-up comic on TV raving about a house burning to the ground.

Another morning, the same woman became angry with Dawson and after he left for work, I heard her speaking to the devil in a demonic voice. It was pure evil, and I was close to putting a bullet in her head because she was into witchcraft and I thought she'd put a curse on me and the family. New faces meant new demons. I sat on the couch while addicts who'd just got arrested for large quantities of dope, walked in the door an hour later with better dope and no one in the house thought that was odd. I couldn't fathom how these scenarios were playing out just like they couldn't fathom how and why I would walk away from an amazing life and loving children.

Brooklyn and two strippers stole my dope one morning and then acted like they were trying to help me find it. I became so enraged that I jumped in one of the girls faces and was going to chop her head off with the two machetes that were strapped to my back. This became my everyday life—being hateful and ready to go to war because I believed everyone on dope was out to get me.

I got into an altercation with Dawson one afternoon and I picked up a large motorcycle muffler I found on the living room floor. I began to swing it at his head, but Brooklyn jumped in the way, so I dropped it and walked out of the house before I was sent to prison for smashing in his skull. It began to make me sick physically—the more I knew what was happening around me and I thought, many times, I was having a heart attack.

I knew at that point I needed to leave again, so I began detailing motorized bicycles called 'spooky tooth's', for a drug dealer who would give me dope for working on his bikes. Soon after, he introduced me to a woman who lived by herself. She asked if I could do some work on her house, so I immediately removed my belongings from Dawson's house and moved them into her home.

I worked on her yard, her pool and whatever she needed. She paid me with drugs, fed me and allowed me to rest my head there. I never slept with the woman, but she and I became good friends until I witnessed the evil nesting inside her after she accused me of stealing something that was in the house the entire time.

I fought a battle within to make sure I stopped stealing from others after I'd been in the Salvation Army Program. I was an addict, but I was becoming stronger the further I walked through the storm. I worked on landscapes, pools, detailed vehicles, painted houses and began doing things besides sneaking around and robbing people. I felt more at peace, not stealing, after being a klepto for twenty-eight years. So, when the woman accused me, I barked back, and it shook her enough that she sent other addicts to find me while I was looking for somewhere to take my belongings.

As the woman's drug dealer and his entourage pulled into her driveway, Dawson arrived, and he walked over and stood next me. After a few words were exchanged, the men agreed to let me remove my belongings in peace before Dawson and I moved them back to his house that night.

The next morning I drove toward the mountains where I'd serviced swimming pools for dozens of clients, and while I was praying for guidance and a moment of serenity, something told me to drive to one of my old pool customer's houses. I walked to the front door and knocked softly as the sun had just risen.

The woman in her seventies walked toward the front door as she was tying her robe, and as soon as our eyes connected, tears fell from her eyes. The door unlocked and when she opened it, she hugged me and invited me in offering me a cup of coffee. As I sat on the kind couple's couch, awaiting my cup of coffee and some conversation, their large dog began barking. He wasn't barking at me; he was barking as if there were someone behind me. I slowly turned my head but there was no one there and I felt something spiritual happening. The kind lady entered the room and I turned back around as I felt cold chills running through my spine. She began talking saying, "My husband and I have missed seeing you ever since you left the pool company. It hasn't been the same. You're such a hard worker, young man. And your hair…oh my goodness you cut all that beautiful hair off and you've lost at least fifty pounds. What happened, Joel? I can feel something has happened to you. Your spirit is broken, and I can feel it. Are your wife and children okay? What about that baby? Has your third child been born yet?" Before I was able to sip my hot beverage, I began weeping as the woman I'd spoken to about life, for many hours throughout the years, questioned me, concerned that I'd become broken as she implied.

I spoke to her for over an hour and half, and during that conversation, she told me I had many spirits who were looking over me. She said I was being looked after by many angels and that's why their dog would always bark around me, but not directly at me. She also felt that I was a 'good omen' and that I had a purpose in life. And though I was blind to it day-to-day, those angels were there protecting me, fighting off evil as it would attack and attempt to pull me into the darkness, creating a monster out of me.

That morning something told me to drive to her house. No one else's house in or around the city, but that specific house with that specific human being. It was one of those moments in life that was precisely meant to happen when it did because I needed to hear some spiritual guidance from a wise person. And the exact words, names, times, and troubles I was dealing with, were accurate in every account without her seeing me or having followed me along my journey.

Soon after I'd spoken with the spiritual woman, I found the serenity I prayed for that morning, but the internal war continued while I was trying to find my way to the light. I went to jail for the DUI and got arrested numerous times on misdemeanor charges. After cleaning up again, while being incarcerated, I quickly caught another charge after turning my headlights off and driving away from police when they pulled in behind me.

Before they stopped me, I hid the drugs in small areas of the car like always but forgot where I hid them. I hid so many things from myself on meth and never found them again because I was too high to remember where I put them. It must have been fate that the police didn't find the dope or the crossbow I had hidden under the back seat with a dozen arrows with razor blade points doused in paint thinner. Those were charges that would've put me away for a while.

After I was arrested again, the car my parents gifted me was impounded. My parents' were at a loss, but still never gave up on me. Olivia Rose and her mother had other ideas. While I was getting high at Dawson's house, the two women dumped all my belongings in Dawson's front yard. The 'tweakers' that were staying there were salivating from the mouth because they knew they were going to steal most of it whenever I would finally pass out after a week or so of not sleeping.

After months of insanity and continuously going at it with wackos and witches, I had someone drop me off at my old neighborhood to grab some things that Olivia Rose intentionally kept but I wanted to trade for dope. When she opened the door, I was surprised she allowed me in, but my mother in-law quickly took the boys in the bathroom and hid them from me.

As I gathered a suitcase with different items of mine to barter with, she pleaded with me to stay there, take a long shower and enter the Salvation Army Program again. I couldn't explain to a mentally healthy person how hard it was when drug addicts needed a fix. I couldn't explain how I didn't want to steal anymore and without a car or way to earn cash, I needed to trade for the drugs in order not to do anything else even more foolish. Anything I thought to say, I knew she wouldn't understand, and I was trying to compose myself while fighting off my need for a fix.

I was coming down hard and I needed the drugs fast. While I was shooting her ideas down, she began to push my buttons and I didn't want to get to the point where I'd go mad. "Please, just let me go. I need to go. I just needed to grab a few things and I'll be out of your hair. Please, just let me go," I pleaded. I was trying to leave in a peaceful manner, but she knew exactly what to say and how to say it. "Daddy! Daddy," my son said." Hey little man! Come here" I replied. "No! Don't touch him. You stay away from them! What?" She instructed my mother-in-law, "Mom, get the babies." "What? What are you...," she asked and continued to provoke me as I was attempting to walk out through the garage? Then she jumped in front of me and I threw her out of my way.

As she blocked me from going out, I grabbed my belt and began swinging it with so much force, it went through the drywall. She continued to provoke me, and I simply grabbed my suitcase and started to leave again saying, "Just let me go. I just came to get my things. Please. Let me go." Then I heard her voice saying, "Yes...ma'am. My husband is trying to attack me. Will you please send officers out? He's threatening to kill me, and my sons are here." *I was baffled beyond words.* I wheeled the suitcase into the garage and just lost it.

I walked over to a shelf and grabbed one of my masks, put my hoodie on and grabbed a machete that I'd hidden the last time I was there. As I was walking out to the driveway, my mother-in-law walked out and tried to grab me and I screamed, "Don't touch me! Don't you dare touch me!" She pleaded, "Just stay, Joel. Irate I replied, "I can't believe she called the police on me. I just came because I don't want to steal anymore." She continued, "What? What are you…?" I interrupted her and yelled, "Fuck! Just let me be. Just. Let. Me. Be." I wheeled the suitcase down the wet driveway and into the rain.

I quickly began calling for a ride as I pulled the luggage down the street, but the person I was reaching out to didn't answer. Every step I took, I began to play out the scene in my mind when the police were going to confront me and the closer I got to the end of the neighborhood toward the desert, the more I envisioned myself being shot and killed after I attacked them with the machete in a 'suicide by cop' situation.

I could hear sirens from all directions, and I knew they were blocking all exits. So my three options were to run through the desert, which I knew wasn't going to happen since I'd been up for days and lacked the energy. Give up and go back to jail, which wasn't going to help me to get more dope, or fulfil my vision of running at the officers so they'd shoot me dead and end the misery that seemed inevitable for the rest of my life.

I glanced through the desert and saw the lights moving quickly from the main roads. I lit a cigarette, puffed on it for a few seconds, tossed it in a rain puddle, tied my boots, put my batting gloves on tightly, strapped my paintball mask over my face and pulled the machete out preparing for a depressing send off into the spiritual world.

As I was talking to God and preparing for the afterlife, an SUV drove up on the curb startling me. "Joel! What are you doing? Go get help sweetie. You don't have to do this. Go back to the Salvation Army. Please, Joel!" It was my mother in-law making a last-ditch plea for my safety. "Put your hands in the air where I can see them! I will shoot you where you stand." It was the police and I looked over to my mother in-law as she slowly moved the SUV out of harm's way.

I thought about a young man that was killed by law-enforcement the night before in the city. The way he went out, he probably suffered from mental illness as well, and like him, I didn't see another way out of the darkness. I was tired. I'd been going down this stressful journey for decades and with all the head injuries, trauma and pounds of chemicals I'd put into my body, I didn't see a future with my wife, sons, or my daughter that I'd abandoned. "This is your last warning! Hands up," the officer warned. I managed to muster up, "Oh, Lord... Forgive me for who I am." I looked up, took a step forward, and out of nowhere, my legs gave out from under me and I dropped to the ground as if someone forced me onto the wet asphalt.

I felt miserable as they handcuffed me and sat me in the back of the patrol car. I wanted to die. I just wanted the misery to be over. I was exhausted, but I wasn't ready to fall to the asphalt and I wondered what had happened and how I fell to the ground.

Before I was released from jail again and stood in front of the judge, he looked at me and stated, "Son, you've had an Extreme DUI, NO Mandatory Insurance, Leaving the Scene of an Accident, Criminal Damage, Speed Greater than Reasonable and Prudent, Failure to Appear in the 2nd Degree, Expired Registration, Stop Sign Violation while you attempted to evade our city's police officers putting innocent people in danger, a Suspended License, Disorderly Conduct, another Criminal Damage, Paraphernalia, another Failure to Appear, and Threatening and Intimidation against your family. God knows everything else you've done and haven't been arrested for. At this time, you will no longer be able to see your children or your wife, in whom you've caused so much stress against. I am placing you on a restraining order; you will also undergo domestic violence courses where I hope you will learn to control your anger. And if you ever wish to drive again, you will be given a list of courses and classes that will hopefully teach you the dangers of using drugs and or alcohol before getting behind the wheel. And after that is all completed, if we're all so lucky, you will have an interlock device installed in your vehicle for one whole year." When I was released later that day, my father took time from work and picked me up like he'd done time and time again.

Even though the restraining order had already been served, he drove me to my wife's house where he was going to grab some belongings for me before dropping me off to the only place that would take me, Dawson's house,' but Olivia Rose wasn't home.

Before we pulled away from my old neighborhood, we noticed the neighbors lowering their garage doors and closing the blinds in their windows. My father said, "Well, they know Billy the Kid is back." That was a shameful feeling knowing my old neighbors were afraid and that I was the talk of the neighborhood. I wasn't welcomed there anymore.

In the months since I'd been out of jail, I'd lost my mind all over again. I knew it when I began digging holes in Dawson's yard looking for Hell. The trap house was alive and had multiple evil spirits tormenting the addicts that resided there. I had an evil spirit hold me down on the couch, yell as loud as a freight train and the energy it drove through me seemed to have struck the nerves in my body leaving me almost paralyzed.

I hated my life. I hated myself. I hated everything about everything. I thought about my family constantly, but it was too late. I'd done things that I wouldn't be able to take back. My estranged wife drove to Dawson's house one morning after I was so high that I was trying to enter the wrong house. I was as lost as ever, and she'd seen it for herself and was only there to have me sign divorce papers before driving away.

I began contemplating suicide every week after that morning. Then it was every day. Then it became the only thought I had every second. I did heroin just to die and I wouldn't die. I sat with the lone drug dealer I had left, who was about to go to prison, and we talked about our suicidal thoughts and how we both planned on finishing it. Unfortunately, he succumbed to a self-inflicted gunshot wound to his head soon after our last conversation and I was left without any means to get dope which made me even more eager to kill myself.

I was in the darkest place I'd ever been, *and I'd been in plenty.* Spiritually, physically and mentally I was ill beyond any sane person's imagination. I began meeting some new people through the people I was using with and they were placed around me for the sole reason of helping to save my life, which I didn't understand in reality. One of Dawson's close friends, who was misunderstood but also a wise and intriguing man, offered me a place to stay in his home. He was trying to help me decide not to end it all. A woman, who was the mother of an addict I used drugs with, also entered my life in the most precise time.

The two of them without knowing one another, fed me, provided me with side jobs to keep me busy and spoke at great lengths to me about not giving up and about changing my life. And though it was difficult for me to stay in these kind folks homes while fighting the ongoing cravings, I dug deeper than ever to stay away from the people, places and things that I fought so hard to escape.

I did everything I could think of to sway my mind and not be miserable and depressed but there didn't seem to be a light at the end of the tunnel for me. So, early one morning, while the woman and her grandchildren were eating breakfast, I requested that she take me back to one of the psych hospitals I'd been committed to before; in a monumental attempt to seek help before committing suicide.

After the kind woman dropped me off at the hospital, I walked around for two hours contemplating whether or not I should jump in front of traffic or walk through the doors to get assistance from doctors and get back on the medications they prescribed for me over one year earlier. As I circled the hospital, in my black hoodie, I came across an older Native American man and I asked him to light my last cigarette. I then took a long walk along the sidewalk where vehicles were driving passed at fifty miles an hour.

I looked up to the sky, took a deep breath, reached into my pocket and pulled out my wallet to look at pictures of my children. I quickly closed the wallet and began to pump myself up because I hated what I'd done to my daughter and her two brothers.

I walked up and down the side of the busy street trying to shake the images of my children out of my head, but it wasn't working. I remembered asking my mother as a child why people were walking down the street shaking their heads and she replied, "Aww, baby; they're sick. It's very sad, but a lot of people in the world are lost." Now it was me that was shaking my head in an attempt to make the images of my family disappear.

The longer I paced back and forth, the more I contemplated lunging in front of traffic. I became so anxious that I was sick to my stomach when I envisioned my body being scattered across the road. I shook my head, shook my head, shook my head, until I began crying and I fell to my knees.

As people drove past staring at me, I began to take control of my breathing. The tears continued to drop, but I was beginning to calm down and my head was shaking at a slower pace. I glanced up from under my hoodie and noticed a young child staring directly at me while she and her family were stopped at the intersection. I looked at the child in her eyes and she tilted her head attempting to see my face.

I wiped the tears and pulled the hoodie back just enough for her to see me. When I did so, she sent me a huge smile that miraculously ignited something in me. The innocence of her little heart gave me a speck of hope that I hadn't felt it quite some time. I sent a faint smile back her way before the car drove away and I stood up from my knees, taking the deepest of breaths. That sweet smile reminded me of my daughter's from over a decade prior and came to me at the exact moment I needed it to. Both of my sons who were in the same city, where I was contemplating jumping into the ongoing traffic, were only sixteen miles from the hospital. That moment gave me just enough clarity to keep me from acting on those suicidal thoughts.

I decided to walk away from the street and toward the building where I built up enough courage to walk through the doors in an attempt to save myself from myself. As I sat in the lobby waiting to be admitted, I clenched my hands tight and prayed to God that he would give me another chance at serenity. I was aware of the realities of what I'd manufactured over the nineteen-year span of being an addict and an alcoholic, but I sought peace and walking through those doors was the first step I needed to advocate for myself for the first time in my entire life.

CHAPTER 18

SALVATION ARMY OF TUCSON

Though I wanted to seek help, I didn't anticipate staying at the hospital as long as I did. I did benefit by staying longer, because I needed to adjust to all the medications, but the paranoia continued to haunt me. I continued to think there were undercovers acting as patients and I still believed the staff were involved in some way and that they all knew what I'd done while on methamphetamine.

As the medications continued to bewilder my mind, I began seeing triple for the first time in my life and it freaked me out because it didn't dissipate throughout the morning. My behavioral health home, which was the agency that worked with me in society over the past years, had an employee pick me up to drive me to a 'Project Home.' The Project Home was where clients from that agency were given a bed, food and other services before being transferred to either a rehab or another facility.

When the male employee arrived at the hospital to transport me, I immediately asked to see his credentials because I believed wholeheartedly he was going to drive me into the desert to kill me. I even attempted to jump from his car on the highway, but he locked the doors on me, making it even more believable that I was being kidnapped. When we pulled into the parking space at the home, it was difficult for me to focus on anything because I continued having triple vision. I apologized to the man when he unlocked the doors, for the way I interrogated him throughout the entire transport. He told me he was used to it and it went with the territory working in the behavioral health field.

When we entered the home, there were at least twenty people who suffered from mental illness walking around and going about their business. I was given a bed with one roommate and because I was unable to shake off the triple vision, I made my way into the backyard to shake the anxiety and I felt better once I saw they had a basketball hoop.

One of the clients kindly handed me a ball and I began shooting in hopes my vision would go back to normal. I stayed outside shooting free throws for close to an hour, focusing on the hoop, but it was to no avail; the triple vision remained, and I began to think I was going to be left like that forever.

When I walked in the large house, people began to ask me all types of questions, but I was still paranoid and wanted no part in any of the conversations. I entered my small bedroom to be by myself and a young man came out of the restroom and began asking me all kinds of questions as well. The whole ordeal was strange to me and I was fully aware that I was a strange one myself. The more the kid spoke about situations I'd personally been involved in and brought up names of people I'd known on meth, the more I knew my time at the home would be short lived.

As soon as the talkative youngster walked out of the room, I removed the pillowcase from the pillow, loaded my belongings and walked out of the door never to return. It was extremely difficult and dangerous walking through the streets seeing triple, but I managed to find my way four and a half miles east toward a female's apartment who I'd used with at Dawson's house. I finally found her apartment, but it took me hours because I was delusional from the medications. When she opened the door she seemed to be annoyed at my presence and questioned me about why I looked lost and scared. For me, it was a blessing because as soon as she opened the door, my vision went back to normal. It may have subsided because I was comfortable for the first time in weeks seeing someone I knew, even though I didn't trust her for one second.

The girl was connected in many ways and always had access to dope. I'd been clean for weeks, since I'd entered the hospital and she wasn't showing any signs of offering me drugs, so I asked her to get me high anyway. I knew in my heart that I was on my way out of the drug life and felt it in my spirit, but I was uncomfortable and wanted to shake off the way the medications were making me feel.

I told her I was trying to make my way through the city to get to my parents' house and asked for help in that regard because I had no transportation or money. She quickly made a phone call for someone to pick me up and reiterated that I needed to quit using dope because I was always causing chaos. She spared me looking like a lost child and got some drugs so I could get high before she sent me away even as she encouraged me to change my life and never return.

With the girl's connections, I knew in my heart the older woman who was driving me across town was a 'shot caller,'—a well-connected and respected individual with a high status that called shots to have others do things for them. Before I opened the door, to head through the desert to surprise my parents in the middle of the night, the woman looked at me and touched my shoulder, "Alright, darlin'; you take care of yourself. I don't want you ever going back to your uncle's house…you hear me? It's not a good place for you to be at. Go and live your life sweetheart…and don't ever look back." After the man who allowed me to stay in his house for months and who tried to assist me in removing myself from that lifestyle, had warned me by saying, "Go and make it right by your wife and your kids," and then this lady basically saying the same, I knew I wasn't welcome in their world anymore.

When her car drove away, I tossed the pillowcase over my shoulder and walked through the desert which was dimly lit only by the moonlight. When I approached my parents' house, I looked through the window and noticed the two of them sitting in their living room. After all the years of going through everything I'd gone through and everything I put my loved ones through, *I tapped out* after a nineteen-year long battle at the age of thirty-four. I was simply exhausted and beat down. I was extremely fortunate and grateful to have made it out with only the psychological and physical trauma I had already experienced, along with many twisted memories of everything I'd seen and done.

I knew, at that moment, while standing outside alone, that I was retired from all the nonsense and ready to return to my family. I missed eating great meals during gatherings, sleeping in a comfortable bed, watching sports the way I enjoyed when I was a child and I wanted to learn how to live life in the simplest of ways.

When I nervously knocked on their door my mother answered and wasn't shocked or upset. In fact, I was shocked that she wasn't upset. She said to me, "I felt you coming. I knew in my heart that you were on your way here. Come in, son." When I closed the door behind me, I walked in and noticed a Shaman painting of a Native warrior called 'Autumn Shield.' My parents' neighbors were selling Native American artwork close to a year prior. I'd stopped by to see them and though I'd purchased a few pieces at the garage sale, the one sitting on the floor looking directly at me was the only one they wouldn't budge on when it came to lowering the price.

The warrior in the painting represented a man that had fought many battles in his own life. Though I had no wall in a home to hang the painting on there was a spiritual connection and I imagined him looking over my living room if one day I could miraculously escape the battlefield myself. I wanted the painting badly enough to negotiate with the nice lady who worked at the city's Christian radio station called K-LOVE. I returned soon after and worked on her family's swimming pool as a bartering chip for the painting but forgot all about that when I returned to the darkness.

As I picked the large painting up and admired the warrior, he stared into my soul and my mother told me that the neighbor dropped it off that day. I just shook my head because once again the timing was impeccable. The same night I decided to walk through their door to tell them that I was done running and tired of fighting, out of nowhere and many months later, the painting was finally mine.

After I put the painting down, my mother immediately asked me to step on their scale and it showed that I was one hundred and seventeen pounds. It was unfortunate they had to see me like that for years. I knew they had grown tired of my mischiefs, but they still allowed me to stay. They fed me, provided a warm shower, spoke to me like a human and opened their spare bedroom for me to rest while I figured out a plan for my future.

Later that morning when I woke up, I poured a cup of coffee, grabbed my smokes and walked outside. I sat on a chair next to their swimming pool where I read The Bible. I did this every morning, reading one Proverb each day and everything that was written was everything I had dealt with on methamphetamine. It spoke about thieves, stolen riches, liars, tricksters, boasters and provokers. It spoke about women that looked beautiful on the outside but had evil intentions and manipulated a man's mind, tricking him into entering her home while her husband was away. Verse after verse, every word sent chills through my body and it was as if they were writing scriptures about drug addicts and that disturbing lifestyle as a whole.

After reading every morning, I would work in my parents' yard and eat a good meal. I was gaining at least two pounds a day and within the first week, I weighed one hundred and twenty-eight pounds.

The second week, my father drove me to a rehab that was linked to the behavioral health agency I was enrolled with. When we pulled in, I knew that it wasn't the rehab for me, but since we were there, I wanted to hear what the place had to offer because I was serious about proving to myself that I would make it.

When we got out of the truck, a young man called my name out and when I turned to look on the balcony to see who it was, I noticed there were men and women walking around. A woman walked past the two of us with short shorts on, a cigarette in her mouth, curlers in her hair and was talking on a cellphone. I was used to rehabs that were closed in and only housed males. Integrating men and women in one rehab didn't sound like a smart idea because an addict was an addict and for the majority of addicts, drugs and sex went hand and hand.

I didn't believe most could focus on themselves while the opposite sex was attending the same meetings throughout each day. Many addict men had huge egos and wouldn't be honest or vulnerable about their trauma or be willing to share specific things around females. It just felt like a set up for the poor souls to fail who hadn't yet gained enough spiritual tools to avoid those intimate situations so early on in their recovery.

I also witnessed many of the clients walking around using their cellphones. That wasn't a smart idea either. Giving addicts access to the internet or a means to call their dope dealers while they were hoping to focus on their recovery is never a good idea. After observing my surroundings I was becoming anxious, but I still agreed to sit down with my father and a young woman because I knew how important it was to my father that I enter rehab as soon as possible. When I asked if there was any paperwork for me to go over, the young woman replied, "Nope! You don't need to fill anything out. Just let us know when you're ready to admit." *But I needed structure.* I was an extremist in every aspect of my life and if there wasn't any structure during enrollment, I wasn't going to succeed or survive there, and I knew it.

I thanked the nice young lady, looked at my father and asked him to drive me back to the Salvation Army. Though I'd AWOL'd twice, neither of us cared. I had to get back in that place because I had to be in a hardcore structured environment without females or cellphones.

When my father and I arrived, I knocked on the doors and a beneficiary that worked the front desk walked out. I said, with a greeting, "Good morning, brother. I'm trying to get back into the Sally... Can I come in to speak to the intake coordinator? I know him well." The beneficiary said, "Well, he's really busy this morning, but if you call back later, we'll get you on the list. We have twenty men on the waiting list right now, so just give us a call, brother." I said, "List? There is no list. Even if there were, three men would be walking out together today to get high, that's three beds right there and a handful will be kicked out because they're not complying with the rules. I've been here twice, brother; I know the drill. Please, just let me speak to the intake coordinator." He replied, "I can't, brother; just call us for availability. Have a blessed day." I was becoming impatient with the man, but I was composing myself and it wasn't easy. It was my life on the line, but I also knew I needed to humble myself before ruining the most important opportunity of my life.

As soon as we got back to my parents' house, I called. I called again that evening. I called so many times, they must've thought about changing the phone number. Every morning after I read Proverbs and prayed for guidance and strength, I called. Unfortunately for the man I met that morning, he was the one answering the phone damn near every time I called. I'd asked, "Is there a bed yet." Swiftly, he replied, "No, sir," and the phone would *click*. Persistently, I'd call again, "Hey, it's Joel again. Is there a bed yet?" He'd respond, "No, Joel; you just called an hour ago." I was on a mission and when I was on a mission, no one on Earth could stop me, but me.

Twenty days after I walked through the desert to my parents' house, the Salvation Army called back and told me I had a third and final opportunity to attend their program. As soon as I hung the phone up, I began crying because I knew I'd been spared rejection and was blessed to have gotten another chance at finishing something I'd started.

Tough people needed tough programming, and I was so grateful that my prayers had been answered. I waited while sweating it out nearly two weeks to hear back from them and it was nothing short of brutal not knowing if they were going to allow me back in after I'd walked out twice. I knew in my heart it was God testing my will, observing my every thought and action while I was being denied an answer for those three weeks.

My family and I celebrated that weekend and I was able to visit with Olivia Rose and my sons for my youngest son Jaymes's first birthday. I was ready and prepared to walk through those doors and though my family was once again anxious and skeptical about my intentions, I knew this time was going to be different because *I'd retired.*

On March 1st of 2013, I walked through the doors of the Salvation Army of Tucson's Rehabilitation Center for men and I was finally home. I quickly went to work in the large warehouse sorting through and hanging donated clothes and though they didn't place me in the kitchen again, I was ecstatic just to be given another opportunity. There were many men in the program who'd returned after they'd graduated and came back to run twelve step meetings. It was inspiring to see how they grew and changed their lives while turning back to aid and assist the brothers who were struggling with the same kind of problems.

I found a sponsor, in one of the twelve step programs, and I thought that because he was diagnosed with the same mental illnesses and lived the same lifestyle I had; he would be a perfect fit to sponsor me. It didn't work out as I'd anticipated though and within a few weeks I asked a younger gentleman to sponsor me. The young man knew the 'Big Book' inside and out and he knew how to break each page down verbatim. He helped me to understand what each step meant and what the fellowship was trying to accomplish by passing the message of recovery to the newcomer.

I was also finally adjusting to my medications and that was a game changer for me. Once in my system, they helped me to get through the paranoia, night terrors, anxiety, PTSD and my intense mood swings. I learned throughout my struggles with the medications that if I stayed open minded and stopped fighting the thought of *'I'm crazy and need meds,'* the medications worked better because I was allowing them to work better.

Changing my environment was the key component. I was never able to stay on my medications because I was arguing with my estranged wife about my wrong doings, incarcerated somewhere or in psych hospitals where the medications were forced upon me. When I was on the streets trying to survive, I didn't want to be vulnerable on the medications while being in those chaotic and disturbing environments.

Having implemented the twelve steps into my daily routine and working one-on-one with a sponsor also helped me to gain a sense of responsibility I'd been lacking for years. My sponsor and I were able to slowly dissect my past, focus on all of my character defects and pinpoint the issues that kept me from reaching out for help. Those issues, in turn, were the reasons why I ran from everything that was good in my life. They were why I continuously used substances to mask the pain and self-medicated when trying to deal with my resentments and undiagnosed mental illnesses.

Soul searching was one of the scariest places I'd decided to go while alive on this Earth and that's why millions of addicts, and alcoholics were afraid to look at themselves under the microscope. We were afraid to go back into our memory bank to see the things we'd done or look at the things that had happened to us. It was terrifying and made me sick at times, but it was the only way I could get past it, to move through the past and not get stuck there. It was okay that I became vulnerable as a man after stuffing my emotions my entire life. I learned it was okay to be afraid because it was the only way I could become brave when facing my transgressions.

I believed wholeheartedly, while working on my step work, that mentally healthy people who weren't addicts would benefit from doing the twelve steps as well. It gave us a way to soul search with a stranger who knew how to guide us, one step at a time, without judgment, unlike most family members would if they heard about all of the situations we share with our sponsors. A sponsor was a guide who assisted us in climbing a treacherous and monumental mountain to a spiritual awakening. It was much safer and easier, taking one step at a time, with someone who knew the path up that mountain. Without a guide, we would've gotten lost somewhere on the mountain finding it too difficult to climb through the terrain which would give us more reason to doubt ourselves and send us tumbling down the mountain where destruction was happily waiting for us.

The steps were about giving everything up to a higher power, cleaning up all of our resentments and character defects, making up with our friends, families, co-workers and anyone else we desired to reconnect with by making our amends. They were about keeping up on the daily inventories of what, if any, wrongdoings transpired throughout each day. It was a one day at a time conscience cleanser.

It was acknowledging any resentment we may have gained and immediately smashing them on the spot. It was about not allowing those situations to take us down like before. Resentments were the number one offender to a relapse and when I learned that, it rang true in almost every scenario in my life. I knew I was going to need to work vigorously on getting past them, because I had many.

Recovery was about mindfulness, learning to live in the moment, looking back through the day and reflecting on our acts of kindness shared with others. Recovery was also about making sure we weren't doing everyone else's inventory or trying to change them. Mindfulness helped me to understand that I could only change my moment, my mind, my happiness and myself.

Recovery was about self-sacrificing and giving up everything negative in my life in order to find peace and serenity before I moved on from this world. Having gained knowledge, wisdom and understanding, the vices I was using to fill a thousand voids were not making me stronger but in fact killing my spirit.

When it came to working steps four and five, which were about making a searching and fearless moral inventory of ourselves and admitting to God, to ourselves and another human being the exact natures of our wrongs, I had to walk away at times. My sponsor and I began digging deeply into my resentments and wrongdoings before releasing them to God in step six.

I resented myself first and foremost for abandoning Selena and Janine, then doing the same to Olivia Rose, Robert and Jaymes. I never focused on how sad it was to choose to take off and vanish, because when I did think of the pain I'd caused, I would quickly drink and or use dope to forget.

I also resented myself for hurting my parents, breaking my girl-friend Nora's thumb in high school, slamming the teacher's head into the brick wall at school when she touched me, kicking the young man in the head with my boot, drowning the Guinea pigs, throwing my dog Prince in a rage, destroying property when I was angry, almost killing a number of boys as a kid, hitting the man on the bike while I was drinking and driving, bringing men into my drama only to watch them all die, living in or staying in over four dozen different people's houses across the country because I was too lazy to man up, shooting at rival gang members, being a liar, being a thief, and being an alcoholic and an addict.

I resented myself for giving up in school and sports, getting discharged from the National Guard, giving away an amazing career as a chef, walking away from the Art Institute, physically, mentally and or spiritually assaulting hundreds maybe thousands of people I'd come in contact with along my journey.

I resented the demons, evil and the shadows when I was a child. I resented God for my best friend Matthew dying at seven years old. The boys who bullied me when I was young, the boys that told on me when I got into the fight in Arizona and the neighborhood kids who blamed me when they were the ones who actually attempted to break into the school in Virginia.

I resented coaches for not picking me in sports, girlfriends for walking away, Marley for being in Nora's house while we were still dating in high school, Janine for not wanting me to call anymore, the number of men that put guns to my head and the ones that shot at me, the different gangs that beat me to a pulp, Dre, after I learned he was physically violent with my sister, the men that kidnapped me, my brother Joker who ran while I got beat down in DC, our brothers that told on brothers to get lighter sentences, the shadows that dragged me through the facility when I was locked up, the evil spirit that held me down at the trap house, hundreds of drug addicts for a thousand different reasons, Olivia Rose for not wanting me to drink in our home while she was pregnant and afraid, Dayton and Diego who sat on the stand and testified against me in court, plus stacks of pages listing all of the resentments that I was able to pull out by working the steps with my sponsor.

It was a spiritual test and it was ruthless. I witnessed countless men walking out of the Salvation Army of Tucson when they were faced with the fourth and fifth steps. It was too much for them to bear. It was vital that I gave everything to God immediately, because I was determined not to fail. Not again. I looked back at the pain I'd caused so many, plus pictured the people that did me wrong and it was a feeling that only those who soul searched would understand.

After hours of going through my list resentments, my sponsor asked me, "What, if anything, did you do wrong to create those resentments?" I didn't understand what he meant at first, but he wanted me to focus on my part—my wrong doings because they were what began each avalanche that ended with me being bitter toward others. Besides the spirits that tormented me, Matthew passing away at the age of seven and the boys blaming me when they broke into the school, I had a crucial role in damn near all of the resentments I wrote down.

If I were a good person, not high and drunk, I would've been a better boyfriend to my girlfriends and maybe they wouldn't have walked away. If I wouldn't have become gang affiliated, a thousand resentments wouldn't have existed, because I wouldn't have been in certain places with certain people.

If I hadn't been addicted to crack cocaine, I wouldn't have been kidnapped and almost buried in the forest. If I wasn't a runner, a liar and an unreliable young man, Janine would've let me into Selena's life. And again, if I was a good husband and a reliable man, I would've been present for Olivia Rose, Robert and Jaymes.

If I would've, if I would've, if I would've...

I got the point, finally, and that point was paramount to becoming more in tune with what happened to me growing up. I made horrible decisions and became bitter toward everyone who grew tired of me and if I hadn't made those poor choices the majority of all the people I despised wouldn't have been a part of my life to begin with.

The time for making excuses was over. Blaming others for my downfalls, because I resented them, was over. As I was getting closer to finishing my steps, I worked on physical, mental, spiritual, materialistic and every other boundary I could think of that I'd crossed over the span of my life.

I was learning how to hold myself accountable for my own personal actions and how to become a reliable man in society. Ego and pride had gotten in the way and I understood wholly that the streets didn't respect one human. Every human was less than life itself and I needed to humble myself before life and the streets took me out.

Recovery was about spiritual principles and not hyper-focusing on the personalities I didn't connect with. This was something that caused resentments and sent millions back into their addictions. Not agreeing with other people's opinions caused much strife and I learned that being assertive and respecting our differences was a step to gain more understanding about why trying to force people into changing their belief system was flat out wrong.

"Dire circumstances require desperate measures", is what I was told that a thousand times along with, "the truth will set you free." I was all about becoming a wise man and a child of Almighty God, so I stopped talking and listened instead of automatically saying, "I know," every time someone shared their wisdom with me. If I'd known everything, I'd have been the wisest man alive and I wouldn't have acted out on my impulses for years.

I learned how to focus on solutions rather than hyper-focusing on the problems. That in itself helped me with my anxiety. Looking at my past and gaining understanding about what I feared helped me with my PTSD. Learning what triggers me, like the situations that set me off, gave me knowledge about what to avoid and allowed me to tame the rage. Gaining positive ways to cope when those situations manifest, helped the pains in my face and head to subside when I was able to handle situations that used to baffle me.

I also gained more understanding about why I was so insecure and why I had a low-self-esteem which related to not being good enough to make the teams in high school. It's not that I wasn't good enough, it was that I quit every time I felt rejected. That depression is what opened the floodgates as to why I began drinking, became gang affiliated and eventually became a drug fiend.

I was becoming a master of my own mind the further I walked with God at the Sally. I acknowledged that lies travelled faster than the truth while being around eighty plus men. Being aware of my surroundings, I observed men that were wise—becoming students of God's word and also men who continued to act out of ego and pride.

I changed as a person when I learned to be honest with myself instead of the lying and stealing I did for twenty-eight years. I also understood that the truth was undefeated. And how the truth would create more opportunities for me to become a wiser and more understanding man while giving me a safer and more productive life with my family.

I did not, for one moment, discount the courage and fight I still had in me. I'd been through hell and high water and that spoke volumes because there were many who wouldn't have continued to fight the way I did. But I chose to create my own rules instead of following the rules of society and I learned in the hardest of ways. I learned how to survive and what not to do. I learned through my struggles, there truly was a God and he loved me regardless of what I'd done. He was giving me another chance to live life as his humble servant.

There was an immense spiritual awakening that took place and I'd gained an attitude of gratitude for where I was and who I was becoming. "To Thine Own Self Be True," was on many of the walls in the meetings I attended and I wrote that quote down quickly to instill it into my spirit along with the scripture I wrote down thirteen years earlier when I was incarcerated in Virginia: Matthew 6:33-"But seek ye first the Kingdom of God and his righteousness and all things shall be added unto you." It didn't say some things or most things, it said *All* things would be added unto my life if I sought him in everything I did. That scripture came to me for a reason and I remembered it during the thirteen years since I'd written it down on my folder.

I also remembered vividly the dark entities dragging me through the facility before I sat down with the corrections officer who took his time to share the wisdom God had passed onto him. I was beginning to discover many things about my journey I'd stuffed away throughout the years. The more I searched, the more I could remember.

I was now more focused than I'd ever been, and it showed. Still I felt bad when I couldn't explain the Holy Spirit that was in me and around me. There weren't words to describe God's agape love for humankind. When men would ask how or questioned if God was even real, I was unable to explain the overwhelming love I felt or what I'd gone through in order to get to where I was. I just encouraged them to have faith, pray until they learned how to pray, read the scripture, and work their steps, honestly, with an open mind and willingly until the feeling came.

When men resented God for their troubled past and the disturbing, unfortunate situations that happened to them or their loved ones, I shared my thoughts on how humans were to blame and not God. Humans were the ones that were destroying everything and leading us down a path of destruction. I knew from my own experience that I needed someone to blame, so it was easiest to blame God when life was taking its course.

Many of us who didn't follow God, were in a state of denial, not even comprehending we were in fact lying to ourselves in order to protect ourselves from feeling certain types of ways during tragic times. I acted like I was fine for years, but my insides were torn to pieces. I didn't get out of my own way, so God was unable to work through me. He played spiritual chess on countless occasions, sparing me a brutal death and I truly believed He had a plan for me. But for that prophecy to be fulfilled, it was necessary for me to get out of my own way, giving Him the opportunity to work His miracles in my life.

Without allowing God to work through me, I was troubled for decades. I caught a case of the handcuffs a dozen times, I was locked in mental institutions, kidnapped, beaten brutally, rejected, starved, cursed by witches on meth and the list goes on. I knew in my heart I didn't stand a chance against the evil forces and I would continue to suffer without God's mercy, grace, love, strength and armor.

I was defeated when I tried to do things on my own and that's what created the sickly, lost and lethargic young man I had become. So, stepping aside and allowing God to fight my battles for me opened the gates for the medications to work, gave me the peace of mind I desperately needed, allowed me to have the courage to re-enter the same rehab and not worry about being ashamed to show my face again.

I was blessed to have a sponsor who God could use as a voice to assist me in my struggles. God also placed a counselor, the majors and the Chaplin (who was a saint) on my spiritual team. She sat me down in her room and prayed over me. Then after we spoke for a while about my struggles and how God was working through me, she got up slowly, walked over to her library and handed me a book about a gang member named Nicky Cruz who ruled a gang in New York in the fifties, then turned his life around and gave his life to Christ.

I opened the book and it was signed by the man himself. She said, "You remind me of this special man, everything about you—from the destruction to the glow. Take this book and read it, Joel… it's a gift from me to you. It'll help you get closer to Jesus." I had a spiritual moment with the Chaplin that day and I wouldn't soon forget it. Sadly though, she passed away soon after we prayed together and went to be with the Lord.

God also granted me the physical strength to work eight hours a day after years of using drugs and going so long without employment. Though I didn't know it in real time, God placing me in the donation trucks and travelling through the city's streets instead of cooking in the kitchen like I'd wished, gave me the strength and comfort I so badly needed. It was helping me to transition back into society after having so much anxiety and PTSD from the things that happened in those city streets.

One way to keep troubled thoughts out of my head, when I had down time at the Sally, was to stay busy. I won another two-on-two basketball tournament played ping pong, billiards, foosball and I worked out daily which gave me a structured routine while helping me to feel good about myself. I gained thirty-three pounds since I walked through my parent's door and weighed one hundred and fifty pounds.

A month and a half before I were to stand on the stage and share my testimony in front of nearly one hundred people, Olivia Rose came to visit me. She was glowing when she noticed the miraculous change that had transpired in me. We sat down in an office and she pulled out a stack of paperwork I previously thought to have been divorce papers, but it was actually bankruptcy documents because I'd ruined our credit due to my negligent behavior.

We once had seventy-two thousand dollars and there we sat together almost two and a half years later, filing for bankruptcy. I was pleased to find out that it wasn't divorce papers I was signing that morning. Though it was an unfortunate situation, I knew God would bless us if we in fact stayed together and worked out our differences while seeking his guidance throughout.

On August 28th of 2013, the day had come for me to graduate and I was extremely anxious knowing I was walking into society after one hundred and eighty days in the place I had considered my home.

It wasn't an easy program to complete. Though the first three months were long, the last ninety days flew by quickly and put my faith in God to the test. While I stood on the stage in front of my brothers in the chapel, I noticed my sponsor, grandmother, parents, mother-in-law, wife and my two sons sitting in the front row looking up at me on the stage.

When my name was called and I stood at the podium, I was as nervous as anyone could be. My fear of public speaking was real and all the times I'd witnessed a brother graduating, I never thought it looked that nerve-racking when I was sitting in the crowd. The call and response commenced, "God is good!" "All the time!" "All the time!" "God is good!" The chapel was acoustic and when my brothers and I shouted, we felt the Holy Spirit because we sounded like Christ's Army.

As soon as I opened my mouth to make amends to my family, I broke down not being able to speak a full word. "We love you, Joel! You got this, brother," my brothers encouraged me and a moment of fighting the tears back and praying softly for courage, my words were able to flow like milk and honey. "Through God, I've been resilient in the face of adversity, became sanctified here in my third attempt at the Salvation Army, and went from useless to useful. I am a new creation under Almighty God. True to myself, without worrying about what others think of me. Not focusing on the currency of the flesh but directing my focus on God's currency: faith and spiritual principles. Life pushed me around and I was wounded, but I pushed back even harder, and now allow God to conquer my battles for me.

I've cut everyone off that is negative, or that I consider dead weight, and through God's strength, have been able to delete every single one of them from my life. I know if we keep one percent of the negative people that we know, those individuals will have the power to knock the walls down for every other negative person to ransack our lives all over again. *I am walking away. I am retired.* Retired from the lifestyle as a whole. And will be staying away from the people, places and things that are negative in my life. It's our only option if we are to survive, brothers. We know what that life offers us: nothing but pain. I rarely lost anything in life but the people that died around me. Everything else I gave away. My girlfriends, my daughter and her mother, a family that cared for me, friendships, a high school education, the opportunity in the military, a career as a chef, my wife and two sons, and most importantly, the love for myself."

"Someone once told me, 'used to bee's didn't make no honey,' and I am not what I used to be. If I do what I've always done, then I'll be what I've always been—and that was a runaway, self-destructive lost soul that lost his self will to live. Removing myself from the temptations of the flesh, is the beginning of me turning my life around. I used to fill voids by chasing women, chasing my next fix, robbing people, committing acts of violence, drinking myself comatose, and living like a Viking, but today, I choose to fill those voids with God's word. Being able to lift my head high and becoming a self-disciplined man, I know God is working His miracles in me today. Brothers…don't leave until the miracle happens. Thank you for being part of my recovery, my name is Joel, and I'm a recovering addict-alcoholic, and child of Almighty God."

I was handed a certificate of completion, a gift card to the Salvation Army's thrift shops, a recovery coin, a pin that went on my tie that my father pinned on me on stage and most importantly, I was granted a relationship with God, the Salvation Army as a whole, which gave me another opportunity to be the man my family so desperately needed.

CHAPTER 19

ALL EYES ON HIM

Before walking out of the Salvation Army with my family, I gathered phone numbers from the men that inspired me in the program—the ones I chose to accept into my new family. I'd learned that it was up to me to decide and choose who I called my family. Just because we had relatives who shared the same last name or carried the same blood through our veins, didn't mean we had to keep them in our circle per say. I learned that having seven plus billion people on Earth, it was up to us to empower ourselves and choose who we associated with and considered family.

I chose the individuals who had been to the darkest places on Earth, who had been incarcerated for years, seen death, battled addiction and mental illness and were strong enough to pull it together miraculously turning their lives around and dedicating their time to serving others.

When the day finally arrived and I returned home to my wife and sons, the true test presented itself. As I entered our home, the past hit me like a freight train. The holes in the walls were present and patiently waiting for me to patch them up. Because I was absent for over two and a half years, the house and yard needed a lot of attention. Olivia Rose and her mother fought hard to keep our home and raising our sons in a safe environment was my wife's number one priority. But I had my work cut out for me and I was prepared to step up and face the challenge.

It was a must that I gave everything to God because I was anxious walking out of the program that served as a safe haven for me.

I'd been an extremely clean and organized person, since I was a child, and even without being diagnosed as suffering from CDO (which for me was Compulsive Disorder Obsessive or OCD in alphabetical order), it was difficult walking into a home that had my sons' toys everywhere. The house had rules that were already implemented well before I returned, but they weren't my rules and I needed to let go of that power struggle.

I'd gone from the streets, trap houses, psych hospitals, jails and rehab to becoming a husband and father in a home that hadn't had a husband or father present in years. It was tough. When I would try and discipline my boys, Olivia Rose wasn't having it. When I became frustrated about their toys being everywhere, she would say, "It's a house...with a family. Leave their toys out until they go to bed." I became so uncomfortable when there were a few dishes in the sink, pee on the toilet seats from my little boys' or when our garage would turn into a storage room, I would utilize the spiritual tools I'd learned so I could avoid going into rage mode.

It was a battle and I prayed constantly for patience and continued taking my medications, which helped with the mood swings. I allowed God to fight my battles and though it wasn't always easy, the more I saw His miracles working through me, the more I surrendered unto Him.

During my struggles and time at the Salvation Army, Olivia Rose lost her car and subsequently had to downgrade to a car she wasn't pleased with. Every penny we had in the bank was gone and though she worked full time, it was a struggle for her and her mother to try and make ends meet.

So, before graduating the program, I prepared by creating a large network with the people in recovery who had multiple years of sobriety. I knew I had to hit the ground running when I finally went back home to provide for my loved ones. I'd chosen a 'home group' which was a twelve-step meeting I would attend weekly, because those specific men inspired me and had multiple years in recovery.

They had the wisdom I sought and because I dealt with anxiety, when in large rooms around a lot of people, I chose an outside meeting because I felt comfortable while we shared our words under the stars. The fire we surrounded represented a spiritual significance and Wednesday nights, after attending chapel at the Sally, the Fire Pit meeting was where I'd go to feel at peace.

The chairman of the meeting was a man named Alfonso who I went through the Sally with my first and second times around. We knew each other well. After Alfonso graduated, he worked his way up to become general manager at a carwash franchise that was taking over the southwest region. When he and I initially reunited at the twelve-step meeting, I spoke to him and asked if he would hire me under the condition I graduated from the program. When that time came and I received my certificate of completion, he shook my hand and gave me a job at the carwash early that September.

Minimum wage in Arizona was $7.90 an hour in 2013, and for me, that was a step up. I'd gone from homeless and asking for food at churches, to working eight hours a day at the Sally for $3 to $14 a week depending on how long I was in the program.

I was grateful for having a new opportunity and understood that not being employed for as long as I was, plus having a record as a felon would make finding a job much harder. I was prepared to do whatever it took to put food on the table, with the exception of going back to my old ways.

My first week at the carwash was another test of will because the General Manager, Alfonso, was on vacation in Las Vegas and it turned out I wasn't needed at the carwash that entire week. It was Monsoon season and it rained off and on throughout each day, so the company only worked the men and women who already knew how to work each area. This saved the company money by not putting everyone on the clock when business was slow.

Olivia Rose, her mother or my mother would kindly drop me off, every morning at 10:30am, and I sat on the side of the building waiting for an opportunity to prove my worth, but it was to no avail. There were many employees who left after fifteen minutes of waiting on the sidelines and the ones who stayed to wait it out, complained all throughout the day because they weren't given an opportunity to work.

As they continued to be upset, I continued to pray in silence, for guidance and for patience. My grandfather once told me, "Grandson, when you're in a hurry, the world is not." That wisdom stayed at the forefront as I continued to humble myself while waiting eight and a half hours a day, until Olivia Rose finished working and picked me up.

My wife was concerned because I was sitting on the side of a building all day and not staying busy and she thought it may have irritated me to the point of walking off and using again. I assured her my time would come and I would be given an opportunity to prove myself. I had a plan in place for when that day came.

The morning before my boss and brother in Christ Alfonso returned to work, I reached out to him and explained my situation and how I waited for forty hours that week without one penny to show for. I asked to open the auto detailing department at 6:30 the next morning and he must've felt bad for me because he approved my request without a fuss.

I was aware there were no shortcuts in life, and I was going to start from the bottom regardless of where I was employed. But I knew with God's strength, I was going to climb quickly keeping all eyes on Him, and I was excited to prove to Alfonso and myself that I was the man for the job.

The next few months, I worked hard proving myself, my work ethic and most importantly how reliable and honest I was while working with the crew there. It gave me a sense of purpose having a job around individuals that dealt with addiction and mental health issues. I knew I had a job to do, but while I did it I became the person who people would confide in when they were struggling in their own personal lives.

While home life was becoming better than ever, I continued to attend my twelve-step meetings and chapel services every Wednesday evening. Because I was doing so well at the car wash, Alfonso approved my request to have Wednesdays off. I wanted to consume the soul food I desperately needed from the church service in the middle of the week at the Sally.

Through all these changes, I was being mindful of the number of things I needed to accomplish to get the courts to get off my back. So, I began writing everything down to keep from becoming over-whelmed, which used to be a huge trigger for me when I drank and used. I was told by the courts that it was paramount I complete close to one half year of domestic violence classes. I also had thousands of dollars in restitution to pay off for my DUI and multiple other charges. By writing each task down on paper, I was able to focus on each goal and understand which ones were attainable for each day.

Olivia Rose had lifted the restraining order against me months prior and with the bankruptcy being finalized, the two of us were becoming stronger as a married couple and our faith in God was increasing. Within a few months of my returning home, we found out she was pregnant with my fourth child. It was amazing how different our relationship was after I found my true self. It was as if I was a stranger to everyone because I was an addict before any of them ever met me.

Soon after sharing the news that Olivia Rose was pregnant again, my older sister in California reached out and told me she had news about my daughter Selena. Janine reached out to my sister via social media and the message was for me to contact Janine in Virginia as soon as possible.

At this time I personally hadn't utilized social media, after being a chef, due to my addictive personality and my lack of poor choices in life. I wanted to give my family my undivided attention. There were people searching for my family members for years hoping to get in touch with me, but I didn't need anything getting in the way of my faith, my family and the fellowship in recovery.

Later that evening, while sitting around the fire at the meeting, I got up and walked away from the meeting to call Janine. I'd been praying to be near Selena for over a decade and now maybe I had a chance. I was questioned about why I hadn't called in years, but instead of getting resentful, since Janine was the one who requested I never call them again, I accepted it for what it was. I explained to her what I'd been going through, where I was and where I was going in life.

My ex-girlfriend was shocked, but the reason she wanted to hear from me was because my now teenage daughter wanted to come visit me during a trip they planned to Las Vegas. I couldn't believe it. I prayed every single day that I would have a relationship with my daughter. Though it was a process to arrange, my prayers to see my baby girl had been answered.

I was so excited and nervous at just the thought of being close to Selena. *What would she think of me? How would she feel?* The fact that she, along with her mother and grandmother were on a plane, flying west to visit with us and the family, was without a doubt the greatest gift since giving my life to God.

After they landed and were settled in their hotel, my family and I drove to the casino hotel west of the city where they were staying. The moment we entered the casino lobby, I was able to hold my daughter in my arms for the first time in over a decade. It was a moment I'd only dreamt of and when I held her, I took it all in and didn't want to let go.

Selena was finally able to meet her little brothers Robert and Jaymes and it was an amazing feeling to have all my children in the same place together. I knew in my heart it was uncomfortable for my daughter, but I was an open book and God and recovery were the foundations of every conversation. I held nothing back in sharing my struggles, but the triumph was what I desired to share the most.

I shared how I struggled with mental illness and that I was an addict since before Selena was born. I told her how I'd become a chef at one of the most prestigious hotels on Earth and how I was looking to advocate for others who dealt with mental illness and drug addiction.

One of the last times I'd seen Selena, I bought her a princess bicycle and then I vanished again. Yes I was ashamed of my actions, but God's love for me allowed me to share my love for them and express my excitement about their visit. I knew their time in Arizona was limited and I wanted my daughter to know everything about me.

We went to dinner at a Mexican restaurant and my parents were able to see their granddaughter for the first time since they'd moved from Virginia. *I was finally whole.* I had God, recovery and my family all at once. As everyone was eating, sharing a good meal and talking, I sat back and thanked the good Lord for that moment, and I cherished every second of it.

When time was up and they were ready to leave for Las Vegas, I held my little girl, who wasn't so little anymore, and told her how sorry I was for who I'd been. I also expressed how much I loved her, and I told her there wasn't a day that went by that I didn't think of her.

After they were gone, it felt like her visit was only an amazing dream. It was hard for the two of us after her departure and unfortunately, our relationship turned into Selena resenting me because I wasn't there for her, yet I was raising her brothers.

It was a struggle for me, as time passed and she didn't respond to my calls. At that time I was still battling anxiety and PTSD, especially when I walked into crowded environments such as a grocery store or even meeting my son's teachers at the elementary school. I was paranoid that people knew what I'd done. I thought they were judging me, but when I spoke about those concerns in my twelve step meetings, someone told me I was the one judging myself and everyone else was just trying to survive while dealing with their own personal issues.

That's why I continued going to the twelve-step meeting and attending chapel weekly at the Salvation Army. It helped me to gain understanding and perspective from another person's point of view. I was growing as a child of God and becoming a true man who was doing what real men did: working, telling the truth and being present for their families.

As I continued to pray for a closer relationship with Selena, I proved to management at the car wash that my work ethic was vital to their operation. They quickly promoted me to 'Detail Specialist.' I was a supervisor, working with a dozen employees, and many of them held a grudge against me because I was a 'new guy.' Some of them had been there years without getting a promotion of their own. Then a few months after my first promotion, I was promoted a second time to 'Detail Manager.'

By then, those who resented me learned what I was about and what I represented. They knew I was a man of God and when they were sent to me by other employees, they knew I spoke the truth about life. They also knew I was aware of all the drug usage and drug dealing going on at the car wash. But instead of judging my people, I shared my experience, strength and hope with them. I was hoping they would see how someone who'd struggled for years, could surrender his life to God and stay true, even in the most tempting of work environments.

The further I walked with God, the further I went in life. I began sharing my testimony around the city and after two of my brothers from the Salvation Army got hired on as RSS's (Recovery Support Specialists) in the behavioral health field, people began to encourage me to get certified as an RSS myself. When I was a patient at the CRC (Crisis Response Center), battling my demons, I learned the CRC was different from any of the other psych hospitals where I'd been committed. They had something the other hospitals didn't have and that was a team of men and women who were called 'Recovery Support Specialists.'

The RSS's were people who were in recovery from addiction and or mental illness and found ways to manage their own lives. They were willing to help others by sharing their experience, strength and hope with the patients. While I was battling my meth addiction, paranoia, homicidal, and in the end suicidal ideation, a man dressed in green scrubs sat with me and shared his personal experiences about his life in the meth world. It was a day that changed my life as well as my views about that facility.

As the RSS went on about how he'd changed his life, I began to understand there were people out there who not only understood what we'd gone through, but remarkably, those individuals were able to change their lives. They were getting employed in this field and paid to share their experiences with others. They were hired to prove that recovery was one hundred percent possible if we just advocated for ourselves and found the courage to ask for help during those dark times. The moment I heard my brothers were helping others and receiving a paycheck to do so, I thought of the RSS at the CRC and I had a vision that I would one day shake his hand and thank him for sharing his story and hearing mine.

When I attended the court mandated classes for domestic violence, I ended up inspiring the woman who facilitated the domestic violence groups. She also encouraged me to look into working in the field. Week after week, I began speaking in front of small crowds and inspiring men and women with a powerful message. A message of hope, unity, being of service to others and about how all things were possible with the power of God.

At the same time, I began mulling at taking the eight-day course to become certified as a Recovery Support Specialist, and was able to pay off my DUI fines which was one step closer to getting my driver's license. I also completed my domestic violence classes and that opened up more time to be with my family.

I was steadily chipping away at the enormous list of 'what to do's' that needed to be done. With the support of my growing family, I put in a four-month notice at the car wash telling them I had faith I would get approved for the RSS course. Then I planned to graduate, get a driver's license, somehow purchase a vehicle, have an interlock device (breathalyzer) installed because of the DUI, and then find a job, in the field, within those four months.

Many people looked at me like I was insane, like I'd totally lost my mind, but if they'd known me before, they would've known I was a journeyman who'd lived a lifetime of insanity in the past. They would know the God I spoke of daily, was in fact real, and I had faith for things that had yet to be seen.

I applied for the RSS course through my behavioral health agency and I graduated from the academy without an issue. As God was opening doors for me and I was doing His will, my grandmother fell on her side in her restroom. Because she laid on her side for so long before being discovered, blood clots grew on her lungs and she needed medical attention. While she was in hospice, my relatives agreed to place my grandmother in an assisted living facility, because my grandmother had fallen in her apartment on a number of occasions and her children were concerned for her safety.

During this time, my parents confiscated the car they'd bought for her and gifted it to me. And like I'd prophesized earlier, I enrolled in the RSS course, received a certificate of completion, owned a vehicle, had an interlock device installed at $100.00 per month, obtained a driver's license for the first time in years, and just needed to submit resumés around the city and then I'd be working with others in behavioral health field.

I learned that being honest, open minded and willing to work hard for what I want in life, that people were always around to assist me with whatever it was I needed. I learned that just because I wanted something, I wasn't necessarily going to get what I wanted when I wanted it. God made me wait in order for me to gain patience and when He deemed it necessary for me to have what I needed and if I worked hard to get it, He would grant me the blessing.

One of my brothers in Christ, Duke, who worked as an RSS and lived where the Fire Pit Meeting was held, drove me to the meeting for two years then drove me all the way out of city limits where my family and I lived. That was one of his many ways of giving back to the community after living on the other side of the law for decades. It was inspiring to witness the transformation taking place in certain individuals God placed in my life at the exact time.

Anytime I needed anything, I had people there to assist me. It wasn't always on my clock, but I could hear my grandfather and his saying again, "When you're in a hurry grandson, the world is not." And because I was continuously getting fed knowledge, wisdom and understanding, I was able to maintain an "I am blessed" attitude.

One evening, a little over one month before my fourth child was to be born, I drove to the Salvation Army to visit with some men in the program. I'd been asked on multiple occasions, by different men, to sponsor them. I was an extremely busy man balancing time between family, work, my meeting and chapel. I always expressed my appreciation for being asked to be a sponsor, as it was humbling, but I told them I wasn't sponsoring men until I knew it was the right time for me to do so.

I wanted to give these men my undivided attention, if I was going to be sponsoring them, and I didn't have that to offer at this time. This wasn't a bad thing because I was setting boundaries for myself and that was growth on my part. I just wanted them to succeed with someone who had time for them. I didn't want to jump into something that might have hurt them in their recovery, and I was once told that if I committed to something, it was necessary to see that commitment through.

That night at the Sally, while speaking to one of my brothers who'd relapsed and re-entered the program, I looked through the large crowd and saw Jax, the man I used meth with in 1997. This was after I'd been sent away from Virginia and dropped out of high school. I asked another one of the beneficiaries his name and when I'd verified it was in fact Jax, I sent one of my brothers to grab him for me. He walked over and I asked him if he could recognize me. Of course after almost twenty years he had no clue as to who I was. I said, "DC...Drama City." He opened his eyes wide and I thought he was going to fall over. Jax was in just as much of shock as I was because the odds of seeing someone from almost two decades earlier, in a different state from where I'd grown up, was slim to none.

The two of us sat down and shared our stories of what happened after we parted ways years prior. Giving him my phone number before I left that night, it was up to him to decide if he used my number or not, and I knew, from experience, how difficult it was to reach out to people when we were struggling in rehab.

For weeks Jax rode the Sally bus to the Fire Pit Meeting, and it was one of those scenarios in life where God placed someone next to someone else in an attempt to save one of His lost sheep. I knew I was the instrument being used between God and my former associate, so I did everything in my power to assist him while he was in the program.

After the meeting ended on Wednesday nights, I would give Jax a few dollars for hygiene products and a pack of cigarettes to get him through each week without him having to worry about his tobacco habit. Unfortunately, Jax left the program, relapsed and they found him dead after he'd overdosed. I didn't know if Jax used the money I gave him to save up for his relapse, but I learned a valuable lesson and never gave any of the other beneficiaries money again. I remembered how my family wouldn't send money to me for that reason alone. When I asked for something, they would purchase what I asked for instead of giving me the money.

I was praying for guidance after his death and hoping to hear from my Selena, when Olivia Rose began having complications during her pregnancy. On the day of Jax's funeral, and fourteen years to the day my friend Alden was executed in his bathtub in Virginia, Olivia Rose went into an emergency C-Section protocol.

I thought I'd had difficult trials since being in recovery and giving my life to Christ, but this situation took the feeling of being powerless to a whole new level for me. I was in the delivery room when the doctors pulled our son Joe from Olivia Rose's stomach and our baby boy wasn't crying.

I was color blind but knew the color of our son's skin wasn't normal for a healthy baby. When the doctor slapped his little bottom, he didn't make a sound. Olivia Rose was out of it from the drugs they'd given her, but I was fully alert and aware of what was transpiring in that room. When the doctor carried Baby Joe to another room, I saw the young nurse's face and knew something was terribly wrong with my son. My mother walked in and immediately began worrying; she too could see her grandson was struggling for air.

I never questioned God, because I knew in my heart that life happened on life's terms and as powerless as the situation was for everyone in the family, I did what I knew I needed to do. I prayed. I prayed for Baby Joe to get the medical treatment he deserved and for air to enter his tiny lungs.

When a young male nurse entered the room and wrapped Baby Joe in a small blanket like a burrito, I asked to be allowed to follow him to the NICU, but the nurse declined my request. *I was a mess.* The family was in a state of worry, saying their own prayers and Olivia Rose was now asking questions. I walked out of the hospital and phoned Duke who was attending Jax's funeral.

Within thirty minutes Duke and another brother I'd known through the Sally pulled into the parking lot and were there to support me during the greatest test since I'd walked away from my addiction. I did what the Salvation Army of Tucson taught me to do in trying times. I prayed and I picked up the phone before picking up a drink and the drugs.

Miraculously, the staff at TMC hospital were able to aid and assist Baby Joe. He was what they call a preemie and weighed only four pounds. They finally allowed me to visit with him in the Intensive Care Unit and I sat with him as long as they allowed me too. When I saw the young male nurse who'd taken my son away earlier that day, I shook his hand and thanked him for providing such invaluable service for our baby boy.

As I walked back toward my son, I noticed newborns that were only one or two pounds. As tiny as Baby Joe was, the other babies were only half his size. I sat and prayed for all of them and their families. Baby Joe was the first of my children born while I was clean and sober. It meant the world to all of us that I was present to support Olivia Rose and our newborn as they were being monitored by medical staff. My behavior was a testament to what the Salvation Army had done for me and I pulled every ounce of strength I could from God while they were in the hospital.

I found out that even in my darkest and most powerless moments, I wasn't powerless at all. I was able to pray for my son and that was extremely powerful. I was someone who used to pray only when law-enforcement was looking for me or when I was lost somewhere, in an unknown state, wandering the streets drunk and high. That moment, while praying over Baby Joe, was a monumental moment in my life. That strength gave me the insight I needed for me to become the spiritual man I wished to be along my journey down this recovery road.

CHAPTER 20

RECOVERY SUPPORT SPECIALIST

After my family was home from the hospital, I went to chapel and thanked God for getting me through the ordeal without ever craving dope or alcohol. I submitted three resumes at three different behavioral health facilities in the following months. All three interviews went extremely well, but when two of the agencies called me, their Human Resource departments said I needed to be three years clean and sober before they would hire me.

I was two and half years clean at the time and though I felt discouraged, I accepted it for what it was and knew that it was their loss in the end. I had faith that God would open up a door where He wanted me to work and I waited on Him to do His will.

Less than eighteen hours later, the CRC facility where I'd been a patient during the most disturbing times in my life, called me and offered me a position as a Recovery Support Specialist.

Now, I'd completed every task I'd written down on the notice to the carwash like I told everyone there that I would. The carwash had a special place in my heart. I'd spent two years with that crew, but unfortunately, over time, everyone we'd hired from the Salvation Army, along with the man who hired me and had multiple years in recovery, relapsed and returned to the dark hole of addiction.

As many of our brothers and sisters were losing to the war on drugs, another drug was beginning to get national recognition for the number of fatal overdoses that were taking place. The drug was called Fentanyl, a narcotic that was being laced with heroin. I knew from experience that once the dope was in your system, it didn't matter if you knew it could kill you; your body would fiend for more.

With the drug problem in the city, I was told I would have my hands full working in the behavioral health field. I would become an advocate for homeless people and those with mental illness; the core groups, and I was about to embark on the greatest journey of my life. I would be doing what God called me to do after personally enduring so much with mental illness and addiction.

My sponsor congratulated me, but let it be known very quickly that getting paid to help others wasn't service work. And in order for me to stay clean and sober, he suggested I continue to serve others outside of my new career without accepting a paycheck or expecting something back in return for those services.

So with my general manager Alfonso relapsing and walking away from his commitment as chairman of our twelve-step meeting, I stepped up and became a Co-Chairman. It was as real as it got in the drug community. And while I sat back and observed the group weekly, many of the men in the fellowship were disappearing from their chairs, only to be buried by their loved ones.

The first day I entered the doors of the CRC, I used the elevator, walked to the unit where I met the RSS who would change my perspective on life. I approached him, while he was on a computer, "Excuse me, brother." He asked, "Yes, how can I help you?" I continued, "Well, I just want to say that I appreciate you and thank you for taking the time to share your wisdom. You helped to change the way I looked at life when I didn't want to live anymore." "Wow," the man responded with his eyes wide, "I don't recognize you brother. But it's an honor." "You wouldn't recognize me; I'm a different man today" I said. I walked away just like I foresaw in my vision the day I knew I would shake the man's hand again.

As a Recovery Support Specialist, I worked side by side with some of the most inspiring people I'd ever met. One individual at a time, we sat with people who were lost and showed them how they could be found. We were there when no one else understood exactly what they were going through. Because I used to be a patient at that hospital, I was well respected and sought after when I entered the doors each day.

We were their voices when people had lost their own. We were their ears when they couldn't hear. As an RSS, we were looked upon as the "strange ones and troublemakers," by some staff, not all, but we were the ones who'd faced our past and then chose to move on.

The stigma was very real while working side-by-side with some of the people who went to college for years and earned a degree, yet we were the ones the patients loved and respected. It was because we were survivors who wanted to share a powerful message. The longer I worked there, the more I noticed things beginning to change about that stigma.

I wasn't only a voice for the individuals getting psychological treatment, I was a voice for everyone who needed my support. I spoke to everyone I encountered just as I did at the Salvation Army and the carwash. I didn't want anyone to feel left out. *It was my time to shine.* It was as if God had lit a spark within me. It was God's plan for me to become a voice for his people even if they didn't believe in God.

When I met individuals, who were paranoid and scared because of the things they'd seen or gone through in the meth world, I spent time with them like another RSS had done for me. When the doctors would tell them it was the drugs making them paranoid and they needed to sleep, I would advocate for them, telling the doctors they had every right to be paranoid. I told them they'd endured an extreme kind of stress from being stuck in a web of evil that mentally healthy humans couldn't possibly understand.

I continued to spread the message to every addict and alcoholic who wanted to listen. To every human that crossed my path, who'd suffered from mental illness and felt like an outcast. Not only did I work with men and women at the CRC, I worked with children who were troubled as well. Youth from the ages of five to seventeen who had gone through trials I wouldn't wish on my worst enemies.

It helped me to gain an understanding of how to treat my sons. Also, I could now see how badly it affected my daughter when I left her and her mother. The teenage girls would explain their hardships of not having a positive male influence in their lives since their own fathers had abandoned them for street life and drugs.

While working with teenage boys, who were drug addicts and or gang members, I remembered vividly how I'd perceived the gang member who spoke to us in high school and how I felt he was weak for changing his life and walking away.

Listening became my greatest asset. I heard the young men out and when I learned their story first, I used my relatable testimony to provide them with a mental picture of what both sides of the fence would look like, depending on what their next move was when walking out of the hospital. I shared wisdom that an amazing woman shared with all the fathers at the Salvation Army with the mentally ill parents, or the drug addicted parents who I worked with and who had broken relationships with their children.

The wise woman asked us as beneficiaries how we spelled love. All of us thought we'd nailed it by spelling it *"l-o-v-e,"* but she shut us down. She spelled it *"t-i-m-e."* She said it's through time, we showed our love. By spending time working on our mind, body and spirit, we learned to love ourselves. She said spending time with our children and our families showed them how much we loved them. By giving people our time, that was time well spent.

I used every experience I'd had, depending on what each individual specifically needed to hear in that moment, while they were locked in the hospital. From seeing shadows and demons, losing countless brothers and sisters, being kidnapped, locked in the same building, abusing drugs and alcohol, being homicidal and suicidal, suffering from mental illness, becoming a chef, a reliable and trustworthy husband and father, then most importantly, working with others to inspire hope, I found ways listen and then be relatable.

One evening while driving home from the CRC, I received a phone call from one of the Gomez brothers in Virginia. He told me that Otto, the brother I'd committed my most heinous crimes with was murdered by his cousin. I hadn't spoken to anyone in Virginia in quite a while, but the reality was that people were dying everywhere and I wanted to make a difference in the world before it was my time to meet the Lord.

A short time later, my parents shared the news that my father was diagnosed with prostate cancer. It hit us all hard and became another test of will—not only for me and my strength, but for my parents who drank together for decades.

The amazing thing about recovery was we were able to come together as a family while he went through his treatments. When everyone in the family saw the transformation in my life, many of my relatives decided to become sober. They attended church services, joined twelve step meetings and one of my aunts, who drank for decades, became the chairman of one of the most popular meeting sites in the city.

While my father continued his cancer treatments, I was constantly on my knees praying for him to beat the disease and I shared my family's hardships with the recovery community. I did everything, with God's power supporting me, to focus on my father's recovery just as I did when baby Joe was in the intensive care unit.

I also spent valuable time with my grandmother while she struggled with being placed in a care facility. She was hurt by this and at times became extremely depressed—to the point that she felt like she didn't want to live anymore.

I would drive to see her, and I took her hard candies to help her throat. I'd sit with her and go over family photos and we spoke about God at great lengths. I was being of service to someone who felt alone—even though she had many family members going to visit with her. As time passed, her outlook on life and her situation began to change. My grandmother began to have an attitude of gratitude once again. Her relationship with God was restored and God used me, once again, along with other family members, to spark a light in her spirit.

Being at peace with the accomplishments I was achieving through Almighty God, Olivia Rose found out she was expecting my fifth child. Her and I laughed about it because we remembered the doctor who told us I could "populate a village" if I got my white blood count under control. It seemed he was correct. With adding another member to our growing family, Olivia Rose and I began looking at other homes with more square footage and more bed-

rooms. I reached out to one of my cousin's for help and he introduced us to a realtor he worked with. We found a house closer to
our boys' school and the realtor met us at the house to give us a tour.

As soon as we walked through the front door of the vacant
home, everyone in our family fell in love with the house. The yard
was five times bigger than our other yard and it had four bedrooms
with a large loft. There was a balcony in the master bedroom that
faced the mountains and our boys' school was less than a mile down
the road.

When we told the realtor we wanted it, he looked at us and
said, "I know you guys want this house; it's a nice house. I live in
this neighborhood myself, but there is a long list here of people that
are possibly looking to buy this house as well. And if…if…there's a
chance that you have an opportunity to move forward, you still need
to sell your house before anything can happen. So, I'm not saying it's
impossible, but we need to be realistic. I don't want your family to
get their hopes up." I looked at the man and said, "Hey, brother—
God is in control of this. God knows." "Well, I guess you can look
at it that way" the man said as we went our separate ways. I shared
my faith with everyone, and I let it be known every time someone
doubted a situation. *I was on fire spiritually.*

As soon as I returned to the CRC, after walking through the
home we fell in love with, I received an email from the realtor about
the house. He was surprised to learn his wife's good friend for years
was the agent who was selling the house we'd just left. The owner of
the home gave us a specific deadline to sell our house and asked us to
provide earnest money to put a hold on the sale of the house, showing the seller we were serious about buying their property.

I was anxious because we didn't have that kind of money in our
savings, but when I called my mother to wish her a happy Mother's
Day, she suggested I call my grandparents to ask for help. I didn't feel
right by doing so, especially after betraying them years prior, because
I stole from them when they opened their home to me.

I walked into the RSS office in the hospital and made the phone
call. As difficult as it was calling that number, I prayed about it and
thanked the Lord, because I knew somehow, it would work out. My

grandparents asked when I would pay them back and after I gave them my word and told them it would take me five days, they agreed to assist us.

I was overcome with joy and wept before walking back onto the psych unit to inspire others. That experience of my faith in a real-life situation and a bit of hard work, gave me inspiration. I told the clients about that day and said if we advocated for ourselves, put forth the effort without ever giving up, regardless of our circumstances, the blessings would come, and others would see the change in us.

Olivia Rose and I paid my grandparents back as I'd promised, proving I was trustworthy because I kept my word. When the deadline to sell our house came to an end, the homeowner of the house we wanted to buy blessed us with more time and within a few days, after over twenty-five families walked through our current home, we finally had a buyer.

Not only were we not homeless for a week, like our realtor said we may have been, as soon as we signed the documents selling our current house and handing over the keys, an agent from the title loan agency walked through the door with another stack of documents. They were the documents for our new home. After telling my realtor that God was in control of this, one month prior, Olivia Rose and I signed the contract for our new house and received the keys at the same time. *God was good!*

I continued sharing my testimony around the city, speaking about the blessings in my life, after entering recovery, and giving my life to God. Though Olivia Rose and I had just purchased a nice SUV, with our fourth child on the way, we were looking at trading it in after only one year to upgrade to a minivan. The dealership authorized the trade-in, under the conditions that our monthly payments would jump up $320.00 more a month and that was on top of the original payment of the SUV we were trading in. It just wasn't possible at that moment, but I had faith.

One night, while sharing my testimony in the city, an older gentleman approached me after my speech and handed me his business card. When I looked at the card, I felt the Holy Spirit running through me. The man worked for the same dealership where we were trying to trade our SUV in for a van. I was in awe. It was a God moment for sure.

Two days later, while I was working, Olivia Rose walked into the dealership and drove away in a brand-new minivan at an employee discount. When I reached out to meet the kind man again, he no longer worked there. When I reached out to him via phone, he never answered. It was one of those moments where God placed someone in front of me to hand me another blessing.

On September 11th, 2016, one month before Olivia Rose's due date, and on the anniversary of when my father was in the Pentagon during the attacks on 9/11, we welcomed Josiah into the world. God blessed us with our fourth son. And while people seemed sad he was born on September 11th, I was grateful he was born on a day of significance and that both my father and my mother-in-law who also worked in the pentagon were alive to welcome their grandchild into the world.

Now I was providing for a family of six and still paying child support for Selena. But I was focused, more than ever, on trying to make ends meet. Olivia Rose and I did what we could to support our family.

When Josiah was born, I tapered off my medications and began doing more meditation. I was working out and I continued seeking God's wisdom while driving men from the Salvation Army to twelve step meetings. It was the service work my sponsor suggested when I began working at the CRC. When in doubt and times were tough, I allowed God to work His miracles. When I got in the way, even for one moment, I saw how my stress levels grew out of whack and I quickly gave it to God again.

A month or so, after I was off my medications, our five-year-old son Jaymes began having abnormal reactions on his skin. After sending him to an allergist and not seeing positive results, we took him to a dermatologist. Jaymes was diagnosed with Pityriasis Lichenoides or Pleva, a rare skin disease that caused the development of small, scaling, raised spots (papules) on his skin.

While patiently waiting to see if the treatments that the doctors suggested were helping our boy, Olivia Rose and I decided to plan a trip back to Virginia. I reached out to Janine and Selena and told them we were flying out after one of my brothers asked me to be his best man in his wedding outside of Washington DC.

The emotional roller coaster of knowing I was going back to see Selena was definitely one I prayed about. She and I still weren't on the best of terms and I was fully aware it was my fault for abandoning her. I continued to pray for guidance and hoped that she would work on the resentments she had toward me, because I wanted her to see her four little brothers.

The resentments I had toward certain individuals around the metropolitan area, I gave them to God while at the Salvation Army. It wasn't their problem that I continued to make poor choices. I needed to learn from my past and move on; it was my problem. I had the power to take control of my life and the best way to manage it was to be clean and sober and having the courage to carry that out.

After landing in the nation's capital, Olivia Rose and I traveled through our old neighborhoods and saw our old schools, and our old homes. I then reached out to my brother Malcom, someone I had a lot of respect for, the same brother I sat with at the bar before I moved to Louisiana. When Malcom saw me with my wife and four sons, he was proud. He and I talked a while and I told him I'd given my life to Christ and how I worked with the community in our city, advocating for people who had struggles in life. The expressions on his face showed he was both proud and amazed about how much I'd grown as a man.

After spending well needed time with my brother, I drove my family to one of the Gomez brothers' houses across town. I still loved listening to Go-go music and while visiting my brother who played in a band, he played the congas for my sons and they were amazed at how fast he was making the beats with his hands.

Olivia Rose and I were able to visit with people we hadn't seen in years and when I was finally face to face with Selena again, I felt like the most blessed man on the face of the Earth. We had dinner with Janine, Selena and the rest of their family at the home where I reached out and pushed the doorbell before I was kidnapped later that same evening in 2003. This trip to Virginia was an experience to say the least.

I made amends with Selena's family after years of having the desire to do so. The feeling of uselessness and self-pity slipped away. I'd become a true man and as uncomfortable as it may have been for some of her family members, I felt I was doing the right thing by showing up—even if it were thirteen years later.

Selena was about to graduate from high school, and she had become a beautiful young woman who was working at a shopping mall. She played soccer for years and she ran track for the high school that sat next to the Virginia, West Virginia border. I knew in my heart she was hurt, but the only thing I could do was to pray and keep doing the next righteous thing.

Taking care of my family was what I represented and though Selena would continue to resent me, I appreciated her for spending time with her brothers the week we were in Virginia. She also spent the night with us, in the hotel, the night before she witnessed her father standing as a best man, in a wedding, in the place I used to call home.

Before we flew back west, my family and I were invited to a barbeque my brother Marlon threw and it felt good to be back around those I hadn't seen in what felt like a lifetime. Though I'd held onto resentments for so long, I wasn't about living that kind of life anymore and I was humbled to be around my brothers again. I sat and talked with my brother Branch who served over fifteen years in prison after another brother told on him. Branch inspired me by the way he carried himself after what he'd gone through. I spent so many years trying to gain respect from my peers by committing violent acts and showing loyalty, but when I arrived with my family and told everyone I was a child of God, I gained more respect by simply being myself.

As we flew off into the sky, I prayed Selena would open up to me about her feelings toward me, but only God knew the outcome of our relationship and what would transpire in the future. Just like the first time I'd seen her in 2014, this visit was like an amazing dream when we were together. Though I felt her pain from thirty thousand feet in the sky when we left, I wouldn't give up on my only daughter and the relationship I desired so deeply.

CHAPTER 21

WALKING THE PATH

When Robert and Jaymes started school after summer break, and while we were still monitoring Jaymes's skin condition, he came back from his first day of kindergarten and told us that he was bullied by another little boy.

Three days later the same little boy threw Jaymes's lunch box and water bottle across the classroom floor. While Olivia Rose was making phone calls to the school, I prayed for strength. I thought *to thine own self be true*. I knew if I reacted from impulse, as I'd done for decades, it would've been a huge mistake, because I was still learning to manage my emotions while working my program. But this was my son being bullied and I knew what that felt like since I'd been bullied before as a child. I didn't want him to have to go through what I went through.

After a week had gone by and things seemed to have calmed down with the bully, I decided to surprise Jaymes in the school's cafeteria during lunch. I was at peace when I saw how he was laughing and enjoying himself with his classmates, but when I returned later that afternoon to pick my boys up, I noticed Jaymes was crying while walking toward our van. "What happened baby boy," I asked with concern. In tears, he said, "That boy punched me in the head and took my scissors in class."

I was pissed.

It was another vital moment where I had to give another situation up to God immediately. Though I wanted to confront his teachers, while my son was wiping his tears away in the backseat, I knew myself too well and I did the right thing by driving my boys home before I embarrassed my family.

Olivia Rose may stand at only four-foot-eleven, but she's been dealing with me for over seventeen years and she's not the woman you want to mess with—especially when it comes to her boys. She went to the school for a parent teacher conference, but I chose to assist my cousin Haley who was battling drug addiction. Olivia Rose was upset with me that I chose to help Haley over advocating for Jaymes, but I didn't want to lose my cool at school, so I felt I did the righteous thing.

I wasn't cured by any means, after getting clean and sober, but I was learning and making wiser decisions. I had a lot of people ready to go to the school and show support for our son if things didn't get handled in a timely manner, but Olivia Rose did what she did best and that was protecting her family.

After the school investigated, it was determined Jaymes wasn't the only child in kindergarten who was being bullied. It wasn't by just one little boy either; he had two little friends who were simply being followers. It reminded me again of when I was ten years old and the three boys who pushed my buttons until I lost control.

Jaymes was enrolled in the Chinese Immersion Program, at the school, and the so called 'ringleader' of the bullies was as well. They expelled the boy from the program after learning how many children were being affected.

I'd worked with many kids at the hospital who were bullies or predators. I also worked with many kids who were getting bullied or the prey. There are many reasons why someone becomes a bully. Many of them have to do with abandonment issues, being in an abusive household, having no guidance, a traumatic brain injury or undiagnosed mental illness. When I heard their stories, I felt their pain even though my son was a victim. I chose to focus on the potential of each child rather than taking it personally.

I spoke about Jaymes' situation to many of the kids I worked with and it gave me more understanding about bullying. I was able to gain wisdom about why kids think and act out the way they do while also helping me understand my own negative behaviors when I was young. It also helped me to get this off my chest instead of allowing it to fester inside which gave me the ability to work through it and grow as a father and as an advocate to other kids.

Jaymes's skin condition didn't get better after the treatments that were provided and instead, seemed to be getting worse. So, Olivia Rose set up another appointment to see his doctor while I was working, and a biopsy was taken and tested. The results identified an additional skin condition known as Mycosis Fungoides, also known as Alibert-Bazin Syndrome or Granuloma Fungoides. It is the most common form of Cutaneous T-Cell Lymphoma. It's affecting his skin as the Pleva does but has the potential to progress internally. The cancerous cells began leaving lesions on top of the Pityriasis Lichenoides that was already affecting him.

As difficult as it was to grasp what was happening, I continued to pray and work on my recovery. Without God and the twelve-step fellowship, I would've broken spiritually during that time and a relapse would certainly have followed. I continued taking the suggestions that were freely given to me while the days ahead brought more battles. I prayed for more strength as situations continued to present themselves.

Olivia Rose suffers from Multiple Hereditary Exostosis, also known as Osteochondroma, which is an overgrowth of cartilage on the bone that happens at the end of the bone near the growth plate. Because this is hereditary, it was passed down to our son Robert. The two of them continue to see specialists while being monitored for the growth of each bone tumor.

While our family is dealing with a number of unfortunate issues, I decided to focus on the solutions rather than the problems. Olivia Rose is a saint when it comes to setting up doctors' appointments, speaking to specialists and taking care of our children while I focused on my recovery and worked at the hospital advocating for others.

The hospitals know Olivia Rose and boys well and unlike me, she is always able to comprehend all the information provided to her in regard to each specific condition and the treatment options. I'm just grateful to comprehend the information on my own personal mental conditions and how to manage my own life on a daily basis.

I continued working to provide for my loved ones, and when a new rehabilitation center opened on the eastside, a friend of mine from the CRC recruited me for a Behavioral Health Technician (BHT) position. She'd left the CRC for the newly opened rehab.

Five days before I began my new job, while eagerly waiting to face the challenge, my mother shared news that she needed open heart surgery to repair a leaky heart valve, replace a second valve and to close a small hole in her heart. Life just kept testing us as a family, but we continued to fight back. As I sat in the waiting room during her surgery, I couldn't help but worry for the woman who loved me unconditionally, regardless of what I'd done throughout the years. I caused her so much stress and I began to think I may have been the reason why her heart was so bad. I began to blame myself while I was anxiously waiting to hear from the surgeons about her status.

I talked about it with my brothers and sisters in recovery and it always helps to talk about things that are weighing us down. My perception had changed, and I was proud of myself for being clean and sober, while being present for my family, when they continue to deal with their own personal sufferings.

After her surgery, many of our family members went to visit my mother in the ICU. It was brutal seeing her there in the shape she was in, but I was at peace. I saw how the doctors and nurses assisted her at TMC and how well they took care of my mother before she was discharged a few days later.

On September 11th, 2017, Josiah's first birthday, I began my new job at the rehab. I continued to work at the Crisis Response Center and because there weren't any part-time RSS positions available, I had to leave my crew to become a BHT at the hospital as well.

People were congratulating me on my promotion to BHT, but I didn't look at it as a promotion. Yes, I made one dollar more an hour to check vitals, draw glucose levels on patients and monitor fifteen-minute safety checks while protecting my people, but being a Recovery Support Specialist was an amazing gift for those of us in recovery who wanted to share our life experiences with others.

As a BHT at the hospital, I wasn't looked at like a hero to our patients anymore. We were looked at as the bad guys because BHT's were the security on the floor and we had to physically restrain people when they lost their minds and became violent. If individuals became too violent, they would be restrained and that is something that triggered my PTSD many times. I prayed to God about my decision to become a BHT at both places. I learned quickly that I was able to inspire our clients regardless of the color of my scrubs or my job description. I was still the same compassionate man.

Every morning before entering the doors, I pray to inspire everyone, not just the clients in the two facilities but every person I came in contact with. While the war on drugs was a major focus across the planet, I began meeting folks who had used heroin for decades without dying, only to hear later about them overdosing and dying as soon as they injected fentanyl.

I sat down and listened to a family member who was crying while sharing a tragic story about how their child who used drugs for the first time at a high school party, and tragically passed away from an overdose after swallowing their very first fentanyl pill.

When working with the parents of addicted children, I encourage the parents to work on themselves before they too fall apart. I share how we weren't created or built to carry everyone else's burdens and how Jesus carried those burdens for us. I shared that praying is powerful even when situations seem powerless. I suggest they may need to pray from a far and not to give in every time their child comes crawling back, only for their child to vanish again, after they'd got what they wanted, leaving the parent lost and depressed all over again.

My parents grew tired of trying. The unfortunate part of loving someone in their addiction is that the family carries the burden while the addict is unwilling to put forth the effort to seek treatment when they are stuck in the curse. At some point, it was vital the parents empowered themselves, allowing them to have a life before they died stressing out about their addicted children.

There are support groups all throughout the city for whatever it is you may be dealing with: twelve step addiction meetings, mental health support groups, sexual assault support groups, emotional support groups, combat veterans support groups, anger management groups and the list goes on.

Parents empowering themselves to support other parents and having somewhere to go and share their pain, is a huge asset to the community. When I began working both jobs, I wanted to connect with more parents, because I witnessed for decades what I did to mine as they were watching me fade away in my addiction.

I share community resources with anyone who is open to attending the groups. I encourage everyone to fight past the social anxieties of entering through doors where there are groups of other humans who fought through the same anxiety when they entered those rooms themselves. It isn't an easy task to seek help, but the answer is not isolating yourself from the world and waiting for a miracle to happen.

I read a study about how the opioid crisis swept across the U.S. from 2000 to 2017. There was a 147-percent increase in foster care entries due to parents' drug use. Many of the addicted parents were waiting for their government checks at the beginning of each month as I did, along with a food stamp card, then trading them both off for a fix. The drugs are an absolute curse.

The process between the beginning and end is a butterfly effect. The drugs are manufactured in other countries, traveled through extreme conditions, handed over to America's drug dealers, broken down and sold to each individual addict, who then opens a small baggie and uses the drug, killing them and leaving their families to bury them.

Without seeking treatment and medical assistance, alcoholics are dying during their detox on their own couches just as prescription narcotic abusers are. IV heroin and fentanyl addicts are dying while using the drug and methamphetamine addicts are dying brutal deaths by the hands of other paranoid and enraged meth addicts. The overdose deaths from methamphetamine users is quietly on the rise and no one is really talking about it due to the opioid epidemic being as bad as it.

Working at the rehab has given me a map of the battleground for aiding and assisting those who need services. For many, it began in a detox unit for men and women and depending on their symptoms, they would detox anywhere from three to eleven days with medication adjustments.

There's also a twenty-eight-day residential program and I was promoted to a Lead Behavioral Health Technician in both areas. I supervised an amazing group of human beings who were the 'go-to' people who assisted the doctors, nurse practitioners, nursing staff, therapists, case managers, receptionists, lab technicians, maintenance crew, housekeeping, the kitchen staff and, most importantly, our clients.

Stepping into my new position at work, I was more successful than I've ever been at multitasking and though it's been brutal at times, when people in my circle are being killed, overdosing or committing suicide, I'm somehow able to push right on through while being a family man and child of God. I continue to work on my personal inventory of issues daily and when I become frustrated, I meditate while listening to sacred Native American healing music. I inspire others to do whatever helps them when they are baffled and while seeking immediate results for peace of mind and to do it without using or drinking.

The day before Thanksgiving 2017, three weeks after Olivia and I took Jaymes to get a double biopsy, he was diagnosed with Lymphomatoid Papulosis, another rare skin disorder characterized by crops of erupting self-healing lesions that looked cancerous under the microscope but were benign. The news of one of our children having a rare skin cancer plus two other rare conditions was devastating. The doctors were doing everything they could to provide answers for something they'd never seen before and they were doing everything in their power to research treatments for all three conditions in one tiny human being.

While Jayme's doctors were battling the insurance companies because we couldn't afford an Ultraviolet Phototherapy Cabinet for one of his treatments at home, I continued to do the next righteous thing, by spreading the word of God and sharing my testimony around the city. Two months after our boy's double biopsy and a thousand prayers later, the insurance companies would agree to help. A large truck pulled up to our house and the three hundred twenty-seven-pound unit was dropped off in our driveway. Every other day Jaymes steps into the machine wearing goggles and his favorite superhero undies. On top of that treatment, he was put on Methotrexate and other medications. Olivia Rose and I began looking into smoothies and other beneficial foods for kids with cancer.

For me, I keep going over the serenity prayer, understanding that accepting what I cannot change is a wise move and allows me to be a better person which creates a better environment at home for my family. I learned that having the courage to change my own personal idealisms and becoming more spiritually in tune with reality will help me to love my family even more during these tough times.

On November 9th, 2018, months after my grandmother's health started to decline, I went to visit her while she rested peacefully. Her bed was in front of a large window that was facing the Arizona mountains. I rested my head on hers and told her how much I loved her. I thanked her for never speaking negatively about me. She didn't say anything back to me; she didn't speak at all. My grandmother always opened her doors to her family even when she knew we were up to no good and I will forever love her for that.

Two days later on November 11th my grandmother passed away at the age of eighty-three. I spoke at her celebration of life in front of family and friends. I was grateful to have been a part of her life while I'd been clean and sober. It was another sad day, one of many, I'd gone through in my recovery. Every time I kneel and pray to God, I become stronger without picking up a drink or a drug.

I was afraid and depressed while grieving or thinking about loss or my family's well-being, but I didn't dwell on it. Instead, I began teaching my sons to play basketball—the one sport that always helped me to get out of my head when I was anxious and or depressed while growing up.

Our now ten-year-old son Robert decided he wants to play the saxophone instead of sports. Also, because he's a handsome boy and was accepted by a modeling agency and invited to New York and Los Angeles. Unfortunately, we're trying to make ends meet and had to decline the agency's offer.

Robert's bone condition hasn't slowed him down one bit and though tough times may be ahead, knowing what Olivia Rose goes through while battling the same thing, we are not powerless with the power of Almighty God leading the way. We are grateful for what we do have and continue to count our blessings.

Though our now eight-year-old Jaymes has gone through three biopsies, bone marrow testing, therapy and has doctors' visits scheduled from here to the unseen future, we still don't know what tomorrow will bring for him. We were told that there are no foundations in the state to help our son because he's dealing with three different conditions at the same time. So instead of sitting back and waiting for a miracle to happen, Olivia Rose plans to create a foundation in Jaymes's name while we continue to monitor him daily.

While we continue to pray and hope for the best, Jaymes stepped on the basketball court, this fall, at St. Paul's church in Tucson, putting up 28 points, 12 rebounds, 5 steals and 1 assist emulating his favorite NBA player from the Phoenix Suns, Devin Booker.

Our five-year-old son Joe, who was in the NICU in 2015, is a bright and polite young boy that loves cooking, swimming and just joined his first baseball team before the Covid-19 pandemic took over the world. He's excited to enter pre-school where I know he will be a great leader just as his older siblings are.

Our three-year-old son Josiah is of course a typical three-year-old. Destroying everything in his path and leaving it to us to clean up the messes he leaves behind. But he knows he's as handsome as one could be and loves dinosaurs, dancing, singing and sports. He too has been diagnosed with having Osteochondroma.

Olivia Rose and I continue to work as an amazing team and I still don't understand how she does what she does, all the while battling her own lifelong condition. It also hasn't been easy for her to be married to a man with PTSD, anxiety, mood disorders, a traumatic brain injury and nineteen years of battling substance abuse disorders. How and why she opened the doors for me after leaving her and my sons for over two and half years is a mystery to me. But there is one thing I do understand, God has a plan for all of us in this family, and

I am forever grateful to my wife for being a strong woman, because without her, there would be no me.

My amazing and beautiful daughter Selena is still battling her resentment toward me for abandoning her and her mother twenty years ago. I pray for their entire family every morning before I set off to inspire the world. I will never stop praying that she and I will have an amazing relationship before it's too late. I've since joined social media and now she can see how I'm doing, and her four younger brothers, two-thousand miles away, anticipate seeing her again because she is loved more than she may ever know.

My parents have been married for forty-five years and my father continues to work for the government at Fort Huachuca. I pray he will be able to retire in less than two years and enjoy his life. He's worked with the United States government for over four decades.

Without my mother-in-Law, our family wouldn't be where it is today. She stepped in to aid and assist my wife and sons when I was afraid to man up and do it myself. To this day, my mother and mother-in-law help with our children. Because of those two special women, our family is blessed, and my boys are lucky to have them in their lives.

Though I have a busy work schedule, I finally agreed to sponsor three men in the twelve-step program. These men have come a long way since I met them while they were detoxing from the poisons they'd put into their bodies. It's been an honor and a privilege to work with such amazing men who have moved mountains.

The Salvation Army saved my life and gave me a foundation as a true man of God. The Sally sadly closed its doors on September 27th after nearly sixty years of serving the Tucson community. "Saddened," is the only word I can use to describe the sudden shut down, but extremely grateful I was able to attend the last Alumni dinner before witnessing the remaining thirteen beneficiaries graduate. God is good!

I spend every birthday and holiday with my family. When my sons ask, "Daddy, why aren't you dressed up for Halloween?" I tell them, "I am Awesomous Prime. Your daddy has transformed more than you could ever imagine." Watching them go from door to door or watching them open their presents is better than any high I ever had. I just wish I would've been there for Selena as well, but I am not perfect. I will not allow outside noise to interrupt what I am going to accomplish, and I understand that no human has the power to grant me happiness. One of my favorite quotes is from Buddha: "A man who conquers himself, is greater than a man who conquers one thousand in battle." *The battle and the battle ground are in my mind.*

For the past seven years, I've studied mindfulness, read scripture, read morning devotionals and inspirational quotes and listen to motivational speeches; this helps keep me grounded. I chose to do the twelve steps over again with another brother who knows "the solution" as the young man did for me at the Salvation Army of Tucson. But I want more. I'm going to gain as much knowledge as I can, because I desire to pass that on to my children.

Today I am an advocate for Cannabidiol, also known as CBD. It has been a game changer for my PTSD, anxiety, mood instability and the pains in my head which have continued for the last twenty-two years. I don't encourage others to stop taking medications, but I let it be known that CBD has changed my life and why I will continue to be a huge advocate.

I continue to meditate, attend twelve step meetings because "it works if you work it," and I enjoy sharing my experience, strength and hope with others to prove that recovery is 100% possible. I'm intrigued by the universe and I truly believe in extraterrestrial existence and I love playing sports and teaching my children everything I know. I faithfully watch the Arizona Cardinals, Phoenix Suns and Arizona Diamondbacks knowing that one day I'll be able to take my family to cheer on our favorite teams—live and in action.

Kevin Johnson, Allen Iverson and Steve Nash are my favorite NBA point guards of all time; Jerry Rice and Larry Fitzgerald are my favorite NFL players of all time, and Ken Griffey Jr is my favorite MLB player of all time. I love photography and watch boxing and mixed martial arts with my father and teach my boys obedience and discipline. I encourage them to make their classrooms better each day.

There were many situations on my journey that kept me away from things that made me who I am. Things that caused me to use drugs, to drink and behave foolishly. Other situations like Olivia Rose, Robert and Josiah having Multiple Hereditary Exostoses, watching Baby Joe lying in ICU at birth, my father battling Cancer, my mother lying in ICU after open heart surgery, Jaymes having cancer, Selena struggling to forgive me for abandoning her and Janine while struggles with Celiac disease and my grandmother passing away, will not be enough for me to walk away from my current life and go back into the darkness.

I am no longer going to stand by and be a dead weight for my family while they battle through this life without a strong man protecting them. I have become a reliable man who they can all count on. I went from a liar to an honest man, a thief to a giving man and a dually diagnosed drug addict and alcoholic to a man that spends his time advocating for those who seek wisdom and guidance.

Today I am authentic, trustworthy and passionate about serving others and because of that, I have been promoted once again in the behavioral health field. It does feel strange to sit behind a desk, in an office, after only being sent to offices when I was in trouble, but I am learning as I go. I'm making the decision to turn my will and life over to the care of God and he has made a man out of me. I am forever grateful to everyone who has had a part in my recovery. I've found that the adrenaline rush that came from the lifestyle I lived for so long now cannot compare to the satisfaction of being of service to others. But I also know that without the path I'd chosen, I wouldn't be the person I am today.

Recently, I drove a young man to get baptized at the church where I'd been baptized. On the way to the rehab that morning, I had a vision about our conversation as I passed the church and God gave me an answer without knowing the young man was going to ask the question three hours later. Everything that happened in my vision, as we passed the church, became true as he and I talked on the way to his baptism at the Pantano Community Christian Church. He asked what a relationship with Christ was like and when he sinned, what he should do. I told the recovering addict how I had the exact conversation in my vision and when the young man asked that question, my body was filled with the Holy Spirit. I couldn't explain the feeling any clearer than that.

I answered his question like this, "I had a vision this morning, brother, that I was a young boy, following Jesus along a path through a long row of trees. The sun was shining, and though I didn't see Jesus' face, He knew I was following Him. As we strolled through the path, I was tempted by something down the steep hill.

When the temptation was too much for me to bear, instead of calling out Jesus' name for guidance, I stopped following Jesus and slid down the hill to fill a void for whatever that temptation was. I knew it was wrong, but I did it anyway. When I was satisfied, I climbed back up the steep hill, but it was much more difficult climbing up than it was sliding down. When I finally reached the path and wiped the dirt off, I saw Jesus waiting for me, and I continued to follow Him because he loved me no matter what I was doing down that hill." Today, because of Jesus and His love for me, I am able to share this true story with you.

ACKNOWLEDGMENTS

To Grandma Carla. Though it was painful for
you, you aided and assisted me in proofreading
this entire story. I will be forever grateful.

This entire book was written while listening to Max Richter's
"Nature of Daylight & War Anthem." Thank you, Mr. Richter,
for conducting such transcendent masterpieces that opened up
my mind and allowed me to affectionately dissect my past.

Joel faced many adversities while struggling to find himself through a brutal nineteen-year war with drug and alcohol addiction. Joel had visual hallucinations as a young boy in Europe, lost his best friend at the age of seven years old, and attacked and injured 2 boys who bullied him when I was ten years old in Phoenix, Arizona. When his father (who was in the Air Force) was stationed to the Pentagon, Joel found himself addicted not only to drugs and alcohol, but to and violent lifestyle because he yearned for acceptance by his peers. Joel's behaviors spiraled out of control while at war with his addiction as well as rival gangs, during the attacks on 9/11, where is father was working at the Pentagon on that horrific day. The DC/ Beltway Sniper killed a Vietnam Veteran across the street from Joel's apartment in Manassas, Virginia, while he battled resentments toward his peers who testified against him in court. Joel was then kidnapped in a wooded area in Virginia and seconds away from being brutally murdered by drug dealers, and suffered a stroke after being hit in the head during a gang war, outside Washington DC in a Virginia suburb. Joel's paranoia and distrust from his closest peers, Joel was on the move again. This time to Louisiana during Hurricanes Katrina and Rita. Joel quickly lost his self-will in the foreign place and after multiple near death experiences and rotating between jails and mental institutions, Joel was faced with the biggest decision of his life. Committing, or not committing suicide while living his most disturbing lifestyle while addicted to Methamphetamine in Tucson, Arizona. Today, Joel is clean and sober, an advocate in behavioral heath system, a sponsor in one of the many 12-step programs in the desert southwest, an alumni of the Salvation Army Rehabilitation Program, a faithful husband and a father of five talented and amazing children.